Event Tourism and Cultural Tourism

Event and cultural tourism as a social practice is a widespread phenomenon of global socio-economic importance. The purpose of the book is to bring together current thinking on contemporary issues relating to the management and marketing of cultural events and attractions. The contributions to the book provide interesting perspectives on a number of topics including innovation in festivals, destination and event image, cultural events and national identity, religious festival experiences, effective management and marketing of events.

The book is divided into two broad themes: event tourism and cultural tourism. The cultural tourism theme covers issues such as: socio-cultural and environmental impacts of tourism development; tourist experiences, motivations and behaviour; development of cultural tourism; hosts and guests; community participation; living heritage; and destination image and branding. The event tourism theme covers issues such as economic, socio-cultural and environmental impacts; tourist experiences, motivations and behaviour; development of event tourism; event management and sponsorship; destination image and branding; and planning and marketing hallmark events.

The book is in response to the increasing demand for empirically-based case studies on event and cultural tourism and will appeal to both academics and practitioners. Case studies are also ideal as teaching material for both undergraduate and post-graduate programmes internationally.

This book is a special double issue of the *Journal of Hospitality Marketing & Management*.

Larry Dwyer, PhD, is in the School of Marketing, University of New South Wales, Australia. He is President of the International Academy for the Study and Tourism, and President of the International Association for Tourism Economics.

Eugenia Wickens, PhD, is a Reader in Tourism, Faculty of Design, Media & Management, Bucks New University, England, UK.

Event Tourism and Cultural Tourism

Issues and Debates

Edited
Larry

 Routledge
Taylor & Francis Group

LONDON AND NEW YORK

First published 2013
by Routledge
2 Park Square, Milton Park, Abingdon, Oxfordshire OX14 4RN

Simultaneously published in the USA and Canada
by Routledge
711 Third Avenue, New York, NY 10017

First issued in paperback 2014

Routledge is an imprint of the Taylor and Francis Group, an informa business

British Library Cataloguing in Publication Data
A catalogue record for this book is available from the British Library

ISBN13: 978-0-415-62368-1 (hbk)
ISBN13: 978-0-415-75478-1 (pbk)

Typeset in Times New Roman
by Taylor & Francis Books

Publisher's Note
The publisher would like to make readers aware that the chapters in this book may be referred to as articles as they are identical to the articles published in the special issue. The publisher accepts responsibility for any inconsistencies that may have arisen in the course of preparing this volume for print.

Contents

CONTENTS

Event Tourism and Cultural Tourism: Issues & Debates: An Introduction

LARRY DWYER

*School of Marketing, Australian School of Business, University of New South Wales,
Sydney, Australia*

EUGENIA WICKENS

*Department of Travel and Aviation, Bucks New University, High Wycombe Campus,
Buckinghamshire, England*

This special issue of *Journal of Hospitality Marketing & Management* contains 13 articles selected from those presented at the 2008 International Conference, "Cultural and Event Tourism: Issues & Debates," held November 5–9 in Alanya, Turkey. The conference was jointly hosted by the Faculty of Business at Akdeniz University and the School of Sport, Leisure, and Travel at Buckinghamshire New University, England. The conference venue was the Belediye Kültür Merkezi in Alanya, Turkey.

The aim of the conference was to provide hospitality and tourism scholars, practitioners, and other stakeholders with an opportunity to explore and debate contemporary and future issues relating to the planning and management of event and cultural tourism. The conference offered a unique networking opportunity for scholars, industry experts, practitioners, government officials, and policymakers to exchange ideas and information.

CONFERENCE THEMES

The "Cultural Tourism" theme covered: Economic, socio-cultural, and environmental impacts of tourism development; tourist experiences; tourist motivations and behavior; development of cultural tourism; hosts and guests; community participation; living heritage; and destination image and branding.

The "Event Tourism" theme covered: Economic, socio-cultural, and environmental impacts; tourist experiences; tourist motivations and behavior; development of event tourism; event management and sponsorship; destination image and branding; and planning and marketing hallmark events.

Event Tourism

Articles in the event tourism section of this issue were selected for their interest and relevance to researchers and other stakeholders in the area of event tourism. A total of eight articles were selected in the area of event tourism.

In their article "Building a Preliminary Model of Event Management for Rural Communities," Capriello and Rotherham explore a network-based stakeholder approach for marketing and managing community-run events and festivals with a focus on the implications for regional development. They adopt a qualitative case study method in order to explore selected social networks and stakeholders' power relationships. Their case study is based on a series of local events in rural communities between the Orta and Maggiore Lakes in Italy. The empirical findings emphasize the importance of event organizers' skills and abilities in working with stakeholders. The commitment and trust of key players in the local hospitality and leisure industry are found to be critical for success and dependent upon shared goals. From the research, a model for the event industry is proposed in which networking processes with stakeholders help explain organisers' problem-solving activities. The theoretical framework applied facilitates the analysis of key aspects related to event management such as strategic marketing planning, product innovation, and socio-economic impact.

Florek and Insch, in their article "When Fit Matters: Leveraging Destination and Event Image Congruence," develop a framework for conceptualizing and managing destination and event image congruence. Building on the foundations of Roth and Romeo's product-country image fit matrix, a framework for categorizing the interactions between destination and event image is presented that can be applied to leverage positive, relevant associations and rebalance less positive associations of both types of images. The usefulness of the matrix is shown through an in-depth case study of the image rebalancing program of the FIFA 2006 host country Germany. This case and others demonstrate the suitability of the framework for managing, and more importantly leveraging image congruence in this context. Implications for managers and researchers derived from applying the framework are also discussed.

In her article titled "Innovation and Creativity in Festival Organizations," Larson contributes to our understanding processes of innovation and creativity in festival organizations. Her focus is on the internal work of renewing the festival. Three case studies of Swedish festival organizations demonstrate how festival workers attempt to renew the festival product. Processes of renewal include various ways of encouraging new ideas and creative solutions, such as brain-storming, imitation of similar products, and influences from the external environment. Three main processes of renewal were identified: institutionalized, incremental, and emergent. The study further elaborates on the emergent process of renewal, thus identifying incremental and improvised renewal. Different factors contributing to or hindering innovations are distinguished; the demands of potential visitors, the management's view on renewal, the team's view on renewal, the organisational culture, and change of managers and staff.

Cultural festivals can assist local communities in showcasing cultural attributes and can offer the chance to strengthen a sense of identity, according to Buch, Milne, and Dickson in their contribution, "Multiple Stakeholder Perspectives on Cultural Events: Auckland's Pasifika Festival." The Pasifika Festival, held annually in Auckland, New Zealand, is a celebration of the city's Pacific Island communities. Drawing on audience and stallholder surveys, and interviews and meetings with festival organizers, the authors provide a multiple stakeholder perspective on the festival experience and what it means to those who are part of it. The article also addresses the important question of how to conduct robust, cost-effective research in large festival settings, focusing on the use of online survey tools.

Soteriades and Dimou in an article titled "Special Events: A Framework for Efficient Management," begin by noting that the academic literature suggests that events have a positive contribution to the host area, including both tangible and intangible outcomes. This study reviews the related literature, identifies key issues in events tourism management and highlights the need for a systematic framework for managing events. The aim is to propose a conceptual framework that enhances efficient events management, in order to optimize their contribution to wider development objectives. From a destination perspective, it is suggested that a value-chain approach and a network analysis could provide an appropriate basis for this exploration model and would contribute to efficient events management, in order to optimize beneficial outcomes.

In their article "Utilizing the VICE Model for the Sustainable Development of the Innibos Arts Festival," van Niekerk and Coetzee focuses on a need to ensure the continuous and sustainable growth of the Innibos Arts Festival in South Africa, while balancing the needs and demands of the visitors to the festival, the tourism industry as a whole, and the surrounding community with a focus on the environment. Continuous growth of festivals in South Africa is ensured as government supports and promotes this as part of its strategy for economic development. However, the sustainability of the festivals has come under scrutiny as many of these festivals compete for similar tourism markets. Destination managers and developers all over the world, but specifically in New Zealand and the United Kingdom, have identified the VICE model as a critical success factor in the sustainable development of any tourism destination. Equitable interaction among the visitors, industry, community, and environment (VICE) must occur before the tourism destination will be sustainable. The VICE model is used to identify the profiles, demands, and needs of the visitors to the festival, the role and impact of the event on the industry and businesses, the impact on the Nelspruit community and environment and how these elements should synergise in order to ensure sustainability. Self-completion questionnaires were used to determine the sustainability of the festival. The results of the study indicated that the VICE model has been successfully utilized in the study of the Innibos Arts Festival. It highlights critical areas in the different categories of the VICE model that require attention and development. The successful management and development of these critical aspects will ensure the sustainability of the festival. The authors conclude that the VICE model can be utilized to ensure the sustainability of festivals generally.

Events can affect a destination image. Mendes, Oom Do Valle, and Guerreiro, in their article "Destination Image and Events: A Structural Model for the Algarve Case," consider this issue for Portugal's top tourism destination. In looking to develop the traditional sun and beach tourism, the Portuguese government launched the Allgarve program in 2007 with the aim of positioning the region as a premier tourism destination, promoting the cultural industry as a modern and competitive component of the regional economy. Using partial least squares modeling, the authors explore the relationship between the image projected by Allgarve and the image of Algarve as a tourism destination. Results show that the programme has had a positive and reasonably strong influence on the destination image. In terms of affective elements, findings show that these were not easily perceived by tourists, as anticipated by the Allgarve programme. An important outcome of this study is to contribute towards better management of future editions of the Allgarve program.

The final event tourism article in this issue is "Cultural Event as a Territorial Marketing Tool: The Case of the Ravello Festival on the Italian Amafi Coast," by Simeon and Buonincontri. The authors begin by emphasizing that destination managers creating cultural events employ *territorial marketing* policies to make a destination attractive. These cultural initiatives are able to strengthen the local identity and to enhance the distinctive resources, both tangible and intangible, of an area. This article analyzes the event Ravello Festival as a tool of territorial marketing to increase the competitiveness of the Amalfi Coast and Ravello, becoming a distinctive symbol of the territory. The authors first focus on the Ravello Festival, examining its history, management and supply system. Ravello as tourist destination product (TDP) in which the Ravello Festival and the local resources are considered the fundamental elements is subsequently examined. The authors also consider the Ravello Festival strengths highlighting their coherence with the development strategy of Ravello. The strategic role of Ravello Festival is emphasized, as a quality event able to promote Ravello as a "city of music" in the world.

These articles provide interesting perspectives on a number of topics in the area of event tourism, some of which have been unduly neglected by researchers. The articles make a genuine contribution to our knowledge of tourism and events. They also call forth areas for further research. It is hoped that other researchers will take up some of the research challenges that are highlighted.

Cultural Tourism

Articles in the cultural tourism section of this issue were selected for their interest and relevance to researchers and other stakeholders in the area of cultural tourism. A total of five articles were selected in the area of cultural tourism.

Issues pertinent to the theme of tourist motivation and behavior are explored by Bakir and Baxter in their article, "Touristic Fun: Motivational Factors for Visiting Legoland Windsor Theme Park." The authors argue that whilst there is rich literature on motivation, little has been written on what motivates families to visit family theme parks. Contributing to our knowledge on visitors' motivation, the article addresses the shortcomings in the literature by discussing the motivation constructs of families for visiting Legoland Windsor. The case study made use of semistructured interviews and nonparticipant observations. Adopting Strauss' version of grounded theory the article discusses the construct of "fun" that emerged as the main motive for the study's participants. Fun is deconstructed into its "push–pull" parts using traditional and revised push–pull frameworks. The methodology employed in their study will be of interest to academics undertaking similar investigations in other tourist attractions and in other parts of the world. Furthermore, the discussion of the motivation constructs of families visiting Legoland Windsor will be of interest to the marketing managers of such cultural attractions.

In their article "Turkey as a Heritage Tourism Destination: The Role of Knowledge," Alvarez and Korzay discuss the perceptions of Spanish nationals regarding Turkey as a tourism destination. The key aim of their empirical study was to determine whether respondents' knowledge and awareness related to the culture and ancient civilization of Turkey is instrumental in creating a more positive image for the country. As the authors explain, Turkey has been affected in the past by its image as a cheap mass tourism destination and is currently attempting to reposition itself as a heritage destination. Drawing upon empirical data collected through a Web questionnaire, the authors also discuss the sources of information used by respondents, and which sources were related to respondents' greater knowledge and more positive perceptions of Turkey as a tourism destination. Implications for the marketing and promotion of Turkey as a heritage destination are also considered in the final parts of the article. The article concludes that the promotion of destinations such as Turkey with its rich history and culture should be based not only on directly promoting the attractions and monuments, but also on increasing the knowledge regarding this historical and cultural legacy. The article represents the growing interest in the relationship between knowledge regarding the history and culture of a place and perceptions of a place as a heritage tourism destination. It will be of particular interest to academics undertaking similar investigations in other Mediterranean countries.

In her article "Balancing Tourism and Religious Experience: Understanding Devotees' Perspectives on Thaipusam in Batu Caves, Selangor, Malaysia," Kasim argues that the excitement of making profit from religious tourism should not be allowed to overshadow its traditional role of promoting spiritual healing and piety. Using Malaysia as a study context, the article presents and discusses qualitative findings from an open-ended questions survey on Hindu parents of University Utara Malaysia students. The discussion reveals the meaning and importance of Thaipusam amongst the devotees, the balance of tourism and religious activities while at the sacred site as well as issues, concerns, and improvements required to increase their quality of experience in Batu Caves. The analysis shows that understanding the significance of a religious event amongst its followers will preserve the real purpose of religious travel and provide insights of a balanced management approach of a religious tourism destination. The article concludes with a discussion on the implications of the empirical findings on the management of a religious tourism destination. This contribution furthers our understanding of religious or faith-based tourism experiences and is good example of pro-poor tourism.

Although the theme of religious tourism is also addressed in Simone-Charteris and Boyd's article, their main focus is on issues concerning the development and promotion of politico-religious tourism. In "The Potential for Northern Ireland to Promote Politico-Religious Tourism: An Industry Perspective," the authors argue that tourists who have interest in political and religious attractions share similar motivations and often visit similar sites. This connection between religious and political tourism is evident in Northern Ireland where political attractions tend to reflect a religious perspective and religious attractions tend to echo a political view. The article discusses the views of public and private tourism sector organizations on the development and promotion of "politico-religious" tourism in the Province, and explores the different players' willingness to collaborate. One of the key findings of Simone-Charteris and Boyd's study is that the relationship between public and private sector organizations is an uneasy one, and that there are some barriers that need to be overcome before trust is instilled and cooperation can take place. Although this is case study of tourism in the Province, the study will be of interest to destination managers and researchers involved in similar work on political and religious tourism in other parts of the world.

The final article in this issue focuses on the Shangana Cultural Village project in South Africa. Briedenhann's article, which is based on qualitative research, considers "The Potential of Small Tourism Operators in the Promotion of Pro-Poor Tourism." The article begins by noting that work undertaken in the field of pro-poor tourism focuses predominantly on the large tourism actors and their potential role in the alleviation of poverty through the development of sustainable supply chains and joint venture arrangements. Employing qualitative methods such as semistructured interviews and participant observation, Briedenhann's study explores the role that could be played by the small operators who collectively comprise the bulk of the South African tourism industry. The article argues that the Shangana project, which was built upon the cultural and natural assets of a poor rural community with limited growth options, made significant contributions in terms of both economic and livelihood benefits. The article concludes that small tourism operators can play a significant role in the alleviation of poverty through tourism. This case study makes a significant contribution to our understanding of pro-poor tourism development in countries such as South Africa.

All articles in this special issue provide interesting perspectives on a number of topics in the area of cultural tourism development, management, and marketing. This diverse set of articles will certainly appeal to both academics and practitioners.

The special issue has benefited from the help of many people. We are immensely grateful to the contributors and the reviewers who assessed the articles.

Building a Preliminary Model of Event Management for Rural Communities

ANTONELLA CAPRIELLO

Department of Business Studies and Environment, University of Piemonte Orientale, Novara, Italy

IAN D. ROTHERHAM

Tourism and Environmental Change Research Unit, Sheffield Hallam University, Sheffield, United Kingdom

This article considers a network-based stakeholder approach for marketing and managing community-run events and festivals with a focus on the implications for regional development. A qualitative case study method was adopted in order to explore selected social networks and stakeholders' power relationships. The case study was based on a series of local events in rural communities between the Orta and Maggiore Lakes in Italy. The empirical findings emphasize the importance of event organizers' skills and abilities in working with stakeholders. The commitment and trust of key players in the local hospitality and leisure industry were critical for success and depended on having shared goals. From the research a model for the event industry is proposed in which networking processes with stakeholders help explain organizers' problem-solving activities. The theoretical framework applied facilitates the analysis of key aspects related to event management such as strategic marketing planning, product innovation, and socioeconomic impact.

A preliminary version of this article was presented at the International Conference, "Cultural and Event Tourism: Issues & Debates," in November 2008, and was awarded the best paper in Event Tourism.

INTRODUCTION

The importance of festivals and events for promoting rural areas has been widely recognized in the tourism and event literature (Getz, 2005, 2007). When rooted in community and cultural development strategies, events can also strengthen feelings of belonging, create a sense of place, and encourage tolerance and diversity (Bowdin, Allen, O'Toole, Harris, & McDonnell, 2006). Thus, cultural events can be transformed into celebrations for the host community, especially through the contribution of representatives of local cultures and nonprofit organizations (Jafari, 2008). Although rural festivals need little financial support from the public sector (Janiskee & Drews, 1998), they may have low demand and low value (Getz, 2008, p. 407) and their economic impact can be uncertain (O'Sullivan & Jackson, 2002).

Given the importance of achieving socioeconomic aims in rural tourism and regional development planning, this article analyzes the impacts of event organizers' networking processes in marketing and managing community-run events and festivals. Informed by tourism and event literature, a case study was carried based on the rural region between the Orta and Maggiore Lakes in Italy. Through the analysis of the empirical findings a management model is proposed. This model is based on four propositions related to event organizers' skills and abilities in building relationships with stakeholders. In coherence with a network-based stakeholder approach (Gummesson, 2008), this contribution is particularly important since other studies have concerned specific issues related to event organization such as funding (Tomljenovic & Weber, 2004), innovation and product development (Mackellar, 2006), and knowledge sharing (Getz, 1998; Stokes, 2004).

The article structures as follows: first we review the literature on stakeholders and networking processes in accordance with the implications on event organization; the next section presents the research design followed by information regarding the case study and empirical findings, followed by the conclusion.

STAKEHOLDERS, NETWORKING PROCESSES, AND EVENT ORGANIZATION

The management literature has focused on the concept of *stakeholder*, even if the term remains vague (Jones & Wicks, 1999). Freeman (1984, p. 46) defined a stakeholder as "any group or individual who can affect or is affected by the achievement of the organizations' objectives." Clarkson (1994) instead, associated the concept to a condition of bearing a risky position, representing a narrower definition (Mitchell, Agle, & Wood, 1997). Donaldson and Preston (1995) proposed a broader nature of the "stake," considering it in connection with various groups' moral interests. Rowley (1997) employed a social network concept and proposed a stakeholder theory based on the presence of multiple and interdependent interactions in the stakeholder environment, whilst Mitchell et al. (1997) described the stakeholder identification in accordance with three attributes (power, legitimacy, and urgency).

In coherence with the described framework and through a cross-comparison case study, Getz, Andersson, and Larson (2007) developed the idea that festival organizations result from a set of managed stakeholders' relationships. They proposed typologies of stakeholders to help the analysis of the complex web of relationships related to event marketing and management. The relevant categories for the current study are: (a) facilitators provided cash grants, sponsorships, and in-kind support; (b) co-producers such as performers and associations involved through voluntary activities in creating the event experience; (c) suppliers acting as services providers inside the festival value chain; (d) the audience; and (e) the impacted including the local community and special interest groups.

In the light of the likely aims of community-run events and festivals, a network-based stakeholder approach can be applied, as in the event industry there is a constant need to moving from a "customer centricity" to a "balanced centricity" (Gummesson, 2008). In fact, the involvement of all stakeholder groups is a key element for a sustainable tourism development in rural communities (Bramwell, 1998; Sautter & Leisen, 1999). Additionally, in presence of public financial resources, a more holistic approach is needed to assess the overall costs and benefits (Dwyer, 2008).

In order to ensure economic efficiencies and to maximize success, event management is based on resource interdependencies between partners (Long, 2000, p. 58). Networks in regional communities are fundamental not only to explore new opportunities for marketing local industry (Mackellar, 2006), but also to create the prerequisites for regional product innovation (McCarthy, Moscardo, Murphy, & Pearce, 2007).

The event managers' skills and capabilities in building personal networks are a key element for event sustainability in the long run (Arcodia & Whitford, 2005). Person-to-person communication emerges as important in maintaining strong stakeholder relationships and limiting latent conflicts (Merrilees, Getz, & O'Brien, 2005). Some festival organizations work with stakeholders through informal personal relationships or with natural allies in the professional community (Getz et al., 2007). Andersson and Getz (2007) identified the importance of divergent strategies in dealing with both powerful and weak stakeholders. Furthermore, strategies for media and public relations should be coherent with the local authorities' orientation in terms of image and brand management (Mossberg & Getz, 2006). In particular, Getz and Fairley (2004) demonstrated the critical stakeholder interrelationship in events as being particularly important for effective media management.

In rural communities, collaborative processes can be created through round-tables and other participatory mechanisms (Stokes, 2008). Although interactions between actors are collaborative, there is frequently a need to reconcile partners' strategic objectives (Long, 2000). Additionally, in the tourism industry the benefits from cooperation among local actors can be limited by a low presence of the private sector (Araujo & Bramwell, 2002), and by stakeholders' position in terms of resource allocation and profit orientation (Bramwell & Sharman, 1999; Bramwell, 2006).

RESEARCH DESIGN

The case study was developed in coherence with grounded theory (Eisenhardt, 1989), allowing exploration of an observed phenomenon to produce possible explanations. Findings from case studies play "an important role in creating new knowledge, generating hypotheses or propositions and testing new existing theories" (Getz, 2007, p. 368).

A single case study was carried out in the rural communities between Orta and Maggiore Lakes located in the Province of Novara, Italy. The geographical context was selected in accordance with the aims of the study directed at gaining insights into event organizers' networking processes with local stakeholders. In fact, artists and writers living in the area and local associations represent the social capital, as they are actively involved in promoting the territory through events. A further feature is represented by the local institutions' commitment in marketing the rural communities with cultural initiatives and by means of a co-shared project branded under the name *"Un Cuore Verde tra i due Laghi"* ("A Green Heart Between the Two Lakes"). A more detailed description of the socioeconomic context is presented next.

In the first stage of the study, a dataset related to the relevant programs of events was established. As there was no existing comprehensive list available, both soft and hard copies of promotional materials were consulted. The materials were from a range of sources such as local tourist information offices and nonprofit associations. A total of 15 planned cultural events was identified, according to the typology of event forms proposed by Getz (2007). For the current study, 13 events organized by local actors (professional and volunteer associations, local public institutions) were selected. This decision was coherent with the purposes of study directed at assessing local actors' involvement and commitment in regional development. Thus, two events organized by the Province of Novara in the area were not considered.

The format and content of the selected events were analyzed for a period from June 2007 to September 2008. Thus, each event was evaluated in terms of its evolution and status (i.e., the first, second, or third time it had run). This was considered to be a key element in understanding the dynamics of event organizers' relationships (Halinen & Törnroos, 2005).

In the second stage, 24 interviews directed at various levels of decision-makers were carried out. Firstly, the interviews were targeted at seven event coordinators with a focus on the history of the organization and the features of the event such as its objectives, actors involved, programmed activities, and participant profiles. This enabled effective collection and collation of information on present and former relationships with stakeholders. Contextually, a purposeful sampling technique identified representatives of powerful stakeholder groups active in the geographical context (Patton, 1990). Representatives of stakeholder groups were identified by a "reputation approach" and the researchers contacted nominees suggested by knowledgeable informants. The latter were selected for their knowledge of tourism policy and planning in the region. These informants helped generate a list of potential interviewees known to be active in the region. These actors were mainly 10 hotel managers in the area, two banking foundations, two private sponsors of events, two public administrators, and the local retailers' association. Interviews ascertained stakeholders' involvement and commitment in event organization and local development.

In the third stage a triangulation process was adopted (Woodside & Wilson, 2003, p. 506), including participant observation of events and evaluation of written documents supplied by event organizations and tourist information offices. Additionally, the researchers also took part in three workshops organized by local municipalities, in order to analyze emerging issues in these communities and discuss the validity of the preliminary findings.

In keeping with the theoretical framework the identified convergence of themes and patterns helped guide data analysis (Miles & Huberman, 1994). In particular, following a content analysis research method (Kaplan, 1943; Holbrook, 1977; Kassarjian, 1977; Kepplinger, 1989; Kolbe & Burnett, 1991) critical and recurrent issues were identified and considered in evaluating empirical results. In accordance with these findings, four research propositions were formulated on which the proposed conceptual model is based.

THE CASE STUDY

The Socioeconomic Context

The rural communities between the two lakes (Figure 1) suffer from a significant depopulation related to traditional dependence on established sectors, particularly farm and craft industries. The strong natural distinctiveness of the region is associated with the presence of a unique woodland area with ancient trails connecting the communities between the two lakes.

The area is characterized by important architectural heritage related to the history of the territory and the dominance of the Catholic Church, but

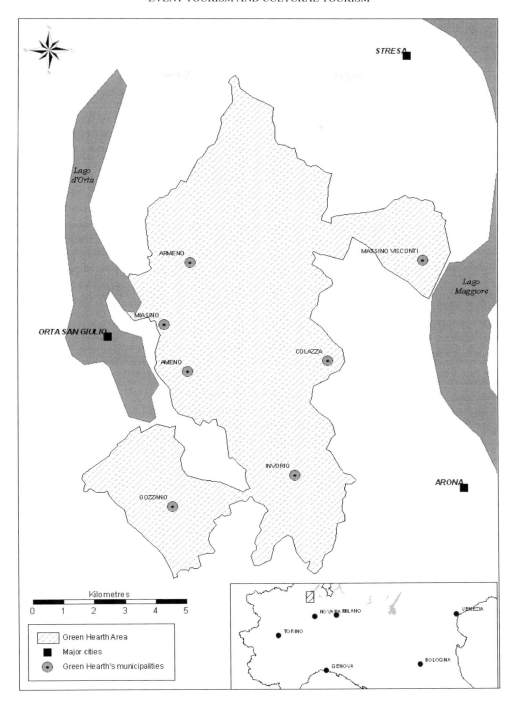

FIGURE 1 The geographical context.

maintenance and restoration operations have not yet been sustainable. The presence of artists and writers who have chosen to reside in the hills of the Orta Lake has helped trigger several cultural initiatives.

In the 18th and 19th centuries, private country residences were constructed by European noblemen and an entrepreneurial middle class from the Lombardy or Piedmont. Some of them, such as Palazzo Tornielli in Ameno and Villa Nigra in Miasino, are now selected as locations for local events.

After the Second World War the manufacturing industry developed with significant damage to vegetation in and around the Orta Lake. Yet, given the crises in the local manufacturing sector, the current tourism strategy is oriented to a relaunch of the Orta Lake.

In the studied geographical context, local institutions identified an opportunity to develop a shared project linking to local markets for leisure and tourism activities. The project also aims to co-ordinate the initiatives of locally active professional and voluntary bodies in promotional and management work. In January 2008, a partnership was established involving local municipalities, schools, religious bodies, and associations. Since then the geographical area represented by these municipalities was identified under the name "Cuore Verde fra i due Laghi", and now has the potential to promote itself through the "Green Heart" brand.

Event Organizers and Activities

The events aim to help market the area as a cultural district with support from local stakeholders. This is achieved through measures directed at embedding interest in conservation of natural and historical resources with potential benefits for the local economy. Seven associations were identified with 13 events occurring between June 2007 and September 2008 (Table 1).

There is a formal group, the Association *Asilo Bianco*, which actively promotes the area. It is located in Ameno and aims to promote contemporary arts through cultural initiatives (Events 1–6). The objectives of the association are to develop interest in arts through the discovery of local heritage (Event 3). A key aspect has been the creation of an international social network between artists and writers by means of the financial support of banking foundations. This collaboration has helped generate an events program and repopulate the area. In fact, workshops organized by artists and writers are oriented to establish relationships between residents and tourists (Event 4).

The *Ecomuseo* of the Orta Lake and Mottarone is an association of local museums, entities, and sites around the Orta Lake with a focus on folk culture, arts and nature. Supporting the aims as described increased the awareness of local heritage by visitors and residents (Event 7).

TABLE 1 Description of Events

Organizer	Event	Edition	Format and content
Asilo Bianco	1. Papers/Leaves and Writing	1st	Promotion of a tourist guide realized by international artists and writers hosted in the area.
Asilo Bianco	2. Contemporary Art Exhibition	1st	Promotion of the local heritage through contemporary art.
Asilo Bianco	3. Breakfast on the Grass	1st	Planned openings of local churches and historical houses with marketing actions for local productions.
Asilo Bianco	4. Mediterranean Frost—A Review of Swedish Literature	1st	Cultural exchanges in the area through Swedish literature
Asilo Bianco	5. Targeted Landscapes	1st	Exhibition of photographic proposals directed to redesign the Green Heart's municipalities.
Asilo Bianco	6. Opening Artists' Studios	4th	Explanation of artists' works and actions to enhance the value of local cuisine and farm productions.
The Ecomuseo of Orta Lake and Mottarone	7. Girolago	3rd	Cultural walks around the Orta Lake and directed at discovering local heritage.
La Finestra sul Lago	8. A Town with Six Strings	3rd	Musical and dancing performances.
La Finestra sul Lago	9. The Heavy Course	4th	Gastronomic events combining music and theatrical performances.
Ameno Blues	10. Ameno Blues Festival	4th	Music performances in local municipalities.
Proloco of Miasino	11. Miasino Classic Jazz Festival	8th	Music performances in Villa Nigra (Miasino).
Teatro delle Selve	12. Moving Theatre	8th	Open-air theatrical performances in local municipalities.
Poetry on the Lake	13. Poetry on the Lake Event	7th	Poetry readings, workshops, discussions, and competitions.

Note. Our data collection.

La Finestra sul Lago is an association promoting cultural events with different expressions of arts related to theatre, music, and gastronomy (Events 8 and 9). *Ameno Blues* is a nonprofit organization promoting interest in blues music through marketing and managing festivals. Since July 2005, the Blues Festival organized in Ameno and sponsored by the Novara Province has attracted around 400 people each year. Performances by several international artists from the United States and the association's semiexclusive rights have combined to progressively increase the reputation of the event among fans (Event 10). Similarly, to promote a local town, the *Proloco of Miasino* is a local volunteer association with 200 supporters that has organized an annual jazz festival since 2000. This event is attended by about 350 people and with a peak of 500 (Event 11).

The *Teatro delle Selve* was formed in 2001 to promote the theatre. A distinctive feature of the events is the selection of open-air theater locations in 10 towns around the Orta Lake. The initiatives aim to create a symbiotic relationship between people, nature, and culture (Event 12).

The Poetry on the Lake association is focused on developing interest in literature. Since 2001, they have organized an annual event supported by the British Council and UNESCO. This annual event is attended by around 100 participants from different countries (Event 13).

RESULTS AND DISCUSSIONS

Empirical Findings and Research Propositions

In the studied area the cross-comparison of event formats and contents indicate that event managers' aims are to market the region by combining the natural distinctness of the place with arts expressions. In relation to this objective, the assessment of activities reveals four critical issues based on actions related to funding, marketing and production, innovation, and socioeconomic impact.

EVENT FUNDING

For the analyzed events, dependence on public funding sources generated strong ties to public institutions. Some initiatives drew on local politicians' interests, and strengthened relationships with facilitators (Event 6, 10, and 11). One event organizer explained: "The first Blues Festival was organized in June 2005, given local administrators' passion for music. They perceived it as a way to reduce the anonymity of territory and animate the area" (organizer of Event 10). Private sponsorship from local firms only occurred in two cases (Events 5 and 13). It was also associated with event marketing activity through a co-branding action. One interviewee indicated: "Attracting tourists in the area is not our mission. Our sponsorship is associated with the nature and purposes of an event" (private sponsor). The public sector also acts as a facilitator in terms of supplying the venue, as indicated by one organizer: "In Miasino Villa Nigra belongs to the local municipality. And it is the most used location in accordance with planned actions directed at marketing this historical asset" (Event 11).

According to local associations, the potential for free entrance supported by public actors was counterproductive. It seems the event organizers are not able to effectively communicate the event quality and product position, as described by one event organizer: "The free entrance policy reduces the value of events and is a penalty for the hard work developed in managing events. And it is also risky given the presence of several initiatives with a divergent cultural level" (Events 8 and 9). Given the economical constraints, some artists take part for free, as described by one interviewee: "There is a crisis of financial supports. Except for some contributions from. . . . the events results from poetries' volunteer activities" (organizer of Event 12). However, all local associations had developed expertise in applying for resources offered by grant-aiding sources such as banking foundations.

The aforementioned empirical findings lead us to posit Proposition 1 as follows:

> *Proposition 1*: Financing of events is based on the involvement of facilitators and co-producers through informal relationships, and this social network leverages on the presence of common interests and achievement of co-shared aims with the mentioned stakeholders.

EVENT MARKETING AND PRODUCTION

Some of the events, for example Events 3 and 7, put significant investment into producing brochures and leaflets. Yet, since the importance of mainstream distribution channels tends to be undervalued, main tourist information offices in key locations such as Stresa or Orta did not stock these promotional materials. A private stakeholder explained: "Each tourism office offers only own materials related to its territory. This is not the way to promote tourism! With so many initiatives from different institutions that cost and do not produce measurable and real effects." This aspect is accentuated by fact that in the case study area there are several events that are not specifically related to the destination image. Moreover, the Green Heart brand is still weak and relatively unknown by the potential audience. Additionally, as one event organizer emphasized: "If you compare the promotional materials, each association has well designed brochures and leaflets. But there is a lack of a unique communication policy for the Green Heart area."

It also seemed that links to the media were ineffective; this was reflected in local newspapers with some positive and/or negative articles on the initiatives. Additionally, few event organizers cultivated relationships with key journalists. One event organizer stressed: "A significant promotional tool is the collaboration with two journalists specialized in music and gastronomy. They disseminate information related to our events through focused articles in specialized magazines" (Event 8 and 9).

Analysis indicates that marketing activity is mainly through collaborations with a selected group of suppliers, word-of-mouth advertising, and networking in local communities, as described by one event organizer: "Fundamental instruments to promote the event program are leaflets and brochures which are distributed by local retailers and hoteliers" (Event 11).

The study found that the associations' personal networks were considered central to their promotional strategies, and helped recruit event co-producers, as indicated by an interviewee: "The most important poets are selected through my personal links and word of the mouth adverting. I have very good connections in UK" (Event 13). Another interviewee said: "The initiatives were generated through a specific co-operation program involving the Swedish Minister of Culture and Embassy in Rome, and inviting international artists from Sweden, previously hosted by the Association" (Events 1, 2, and 4).

Our empirical findings lead us to suggest Proposition 2:

> *Proposition 2*: Event marketing and production are based on a co-operation with suppliers and host communities, and are strengthened on event organizers' personal networks with co-producers.

PRODUCT DEVELOPMENT AND INNOVATION

The comparison of events organized by individual associations and the annual sequence of particular events reveal that innovation processes and product development were supported by complex webs of weak ties created by event organizers. In the case of Event 3, the working group was directed at involving local suppliers and provided new opportunities to identify and combine key attractors in the area.

Personal networks are also important to recruit new artists, and the co-producers contributed to event program innovation in the area. According to one organizer: "The performers are selected in accordance with our previous contacts and a part of them is new each year" (Event 10).

There were positive attempts to relate leisure events to the existing economy. As the Novara Province has been promoting local farm production, there was a specific focus on marketing gastronomy during the events program. For Event 6, this activity was based on the involvement of local producers and adopted as a tool to reinforce the products' image. An interviewee described:

> The idea is to combine arts' expressions with territory, building a productive dialogue. An artistic packaging is a value added component for local foods, often sold in an industrial and anonymous manner. They are three products for the area between the two Lakes. We have created a link with local small producers which are characterized by high level of quality, but a limited market (Event 6).

In the described perspective, the local industry acts as a supplier for the event activity and contributes to product development and event value chain creation.

The previous discussion allows us to formulate the following proposition:

Proposition 3: Product development and event innovation are related to the event organizer's abilities and skills in networking processes with co-producers and suppliers, and stakeholders' involvement in rejuvenating the events program.

SOCIOECONOMIC IMPACT

Visitor surveys were not undertaken, though the event managers were able to identify participant profiles associated with the initiatives. There were higher levels of attendance for musical events, as the associations and their events are well known among fans. Relationship-based marketing strategies were developed to network with the audience and attract specific market segments (for example children and amateurs). In the case of Event 6, local artists opened their studios and explained their works to visitors. One organizer described:

> It is important to networking with the audience, in order to favor the understanding of contemporary arts. Beyond the aesthetical dimension, Leonardo's painting is difficult to understand too. What is instead really important is the artist's interest of talking about their activities and experiences. (Event 6)

Following a bottom-up approach in tourism development planning, Event 5 involved the audience in assessing and discussing photographic works related to development proposals. These proposals were collected from contestants among designers and architects, and were directed at redesigning the image of local towns in the area. The event organizer described the initiative:

> It is an invitation addressed to local institutions, operators, and citizens to think about the richness of local landscape in several communities, but also the expression of the need to regenerate the area through methods, tools, and plans. Microprojects for public spaces are presented by means of postcards. The best ones will be printed, distributed to the local population and presented through a local exhibition. (Event 5)

Social issues were considered important by event organizers. In order to achieve social inclusion objectives and enhance quality of life in the rural communities, they developed specific actions. In particular, the building of community ownership of events was important to avoid the creation of niche products, which might be marketed only to specific interested visitors. Emulation between local communities was also a key motivator for the entertainment-organizing group in each municipality, as described by one event organizer:

The basic principle of our event is the idea of a "slow walk" with the aims of rediscovering the life in rural communities. An additional purpose is to favor the recover of ancient ways and landscapes through a tangible contribution of local communities. The existence of the initiative is due to the cooperation between municipalities, local associations, and residents. They contribute to initiatives through work, financial resources, ideas, and voluntary activities. (Event 7)

In the case of Events 2 and 6, organizers considered provocative artistic displays in key locations in local towns as a strategic tool to involve the host community in the regeneration processes. However, some residents still find it difficult to understand the artists' behavior, as described by an event organizer:

A part of the local population belongs to the first migration (the 1950s) and finds it difficult to understand our initiatives. One day two artists, who are hosted by our association, decided to show the ancient process to produce soap. They started boiling water and grease in the town's place. Some were surprised, but others seeing smoke called firemen! (Events 2 and 6)

With Events 1 and 6, the program also included didactic laboratories organized in collaboration with schools. An interviewee explained: "In collaboration with a retailer and schools, an interesting educational program on environment will be developed in order to combine the different theatrical expressions with the discovery of local landscapes" (Event 12).

In tourism and leisure development, the potential economic impacts are often considered important by planners and funding bodies. Yet in terms of assessing the economic impacts, the event organizers tended to have developed only weak, sporadic, and sometimes selective dyadic relationships with private sector. For some well-known events (e.g., Events 8, 9, 10, 11, 12, and 13), organizers noted collaborations with the local hospitality industry. However, a representative of the hotel industry indicated: "The calendar of events is focused on the summertime with a mainly local visitor catchment area." And another hotelier highlighted: "I believe that the current provision is limited to attract tourism that exists thanks to natural landscape around the Maggiore Lake."

Although suppliers in event marketing and management are important, the involvement of small operators was a problem, as described in the case of Event 3:

The better results were obtained from operators who developed an aggressive marketing policy in their local stores. Yet, one operator refused the adherence but after the clientele' pressure on the initiative, he called back saying as an excuse that he did not receive enough details about the relevance of the program.

Moreover, the importance of co-shared project is a key aspect, as one stakeholder indicated: "It is an initiative that damages bars, restaurants, agritourism, and all of them who work actively in the tourism industry. A project which is not co-shared with operators" (Event 3). On the other hand, a representative of a public stakeholder noted: "The potential operators such as local restaurants, hotels, retailers find it difficult to follow our initiative. The medium average of productive firms is low." Thus, it seems that conflicts and turbulence were a limit on contributions to regional growth, whilst trust and commitment of local suppliers should be instead a key element for generating local development.

Additionally, given a relatively lower participation level of audiences, local events and festivals had less adverse environmental impact and so achieved the aims of conserving natural resources. Yet, in terms of expanding the audience, the maintenance of quality standards and the venue capacity for the events program are constraints, as described: "The amount of audience is linked to the selected location. This is often a historical courtyard, a churchyard or an unusual location where is not possible and wished a crowded place."

The empirical findings suggest Proposition 4:

Proposition 4: Achieving socioeconomic objectives through events is based on building community ownership of event through the involvement of host communities, on generating trust and commitment among local suppliers, and on developing marketing relationship strategies with audience.

Towards a Preliminary Model

In accordance with the four research propositions based on our findings, networking processes with stakeholders are a critical factor in understanding the event managers' problem-solving activities. In Figure 2, a model is proposed to summarize these assumptions, equating the position of event organizer to that of a focal organization. This theoretical framework is based on the stakeholders' categories proposed by Getz et al. (2007) and was previously presented in the literature review. However, the stakeholder "host community" is introduced, instead of considering a more ample category called "the impacted." Additionally, the position of suppliers is focused on the role played by the local industry in creating the event value chain and generating economic impact through cultural initiatives.

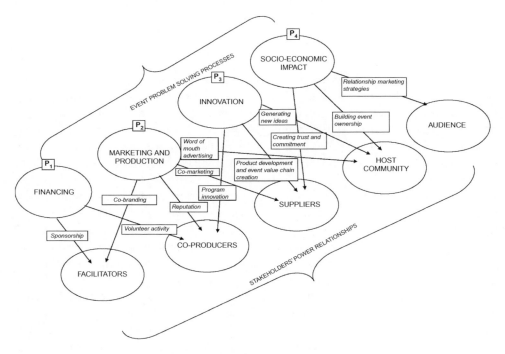

FIGURE 2 A preliminary conceptual model.

This decision relates to the need of observing and analyzing event organizers' abilities in involving host communities and their implications on regional development.

In accordance with our four research propositions, the described linkages are related to the following critical issues: event funding, event marketing and production, product innovation and development, and socioeconomic impact.

As indicated in Figure 2, the aims of networking processes depend on the nature of stakeholder. In particular, beyond the importance of the artists' reputation and the implications for promotion, event marketing and production benefit from a collaborative approach with facilitators and suppliers.

The model stresses the importance of building a sense of belonging and event ownership in host communities. In fact, the event organizers' social networks support their activities in presence of shared interests among local actors. Building trust and commitment in rural communities implies social cohesion, but stakeholders' power relations might be a constraint. In fact, divergent objectives and competition in terms of resource allocation generate tensions and conflicts, and increase the complexity of event organizers' problem-solving processes.

CONCLUSIONS

Although community-run events and festivals are often low demand, they have potential to achieve socioeconomic aims. Yet, in the analyzed area, the event experience is frequently built through the volunteer input of local stakeholders. With this concern in mind, the case study is focused on event organizers' networking processes to identify new strategies for attracting human and financial resources. There is a parallel with business marketing networks and innovation diffusion (Woodside & Biemans, 2005) and this indicates that event managers and associations are proactive in supporting regional development. However, protecting local heritage and promoting culture are not always a priority for the private sector, as business considerations tend to dominate over social and cultural aims. Thus, reflecting the theoretical framework of relationship marketing (Bucklin & Sengupta, 1993; Gundlach, Achrol, & Mentzer, 1995; Morgan & Hunt, 1994), the findings underline the importance of co-sharing a project among stakeholders.

The four propositions emphasize event managers' skills directed at leveraging through complex webs of informal relationships. This finding is significant, as destination development planners tend to consider events as priorities in their agendas. Thus, in the described context a prerequisite for any event policy is evaluating the event organizers' orientation and propensity towards networking processes and partnership mechanisms.

From a theoretical viewpoint, the model proposed benefits from a co-joint application of network and stakeholder theories and clarifies the roles of local actors in the event sector, focusing on the nature of relationships established in the leisure industry. It facilitates analysis of key aspects related to event management such as strategic marketing planning, product innovation, and socioeconomic impact. In addition, it is a complementary tool to formulate destination management and development policy, as it is directed towards understanding networking processes and stakeholders' power relationships with specific critical issues. This contribution is significant because current tourism policies tend to prescribe a collaborative orientation without assessing relationships among key players. The model reflects a sustainable development approach, but whilst minimizing adverse environmental impacts, the low levels of audience participation also limit socioeconomic benefits.

As with Wilson and Woodside (1999) and Yin (2003), our study was constrained by empirical findings being from a cross-comparison of events in a single context. Additionally, this preliminary model is not intended to represent the complex web of relationships inside the local communities.

Thus, further investigation is needed to make the model more robust. Additionally, this research was formulated in relation to an emerging destination and with a program of leisure and tourism events. Future studies will investigate the role of social networks in other geographical contexts. In particular, as the current priority of destination planners and marketers is to foster regional identity, it may be interesting to assess stakeholders' power relationships and interactions with traditional values of rural communities.

REFERENCES

Andersson, T., & Getz, D. (2007). Resource dependency, costs and revenues of a street festival. *Tourism Economics*, *13*(1), 143–162.

Araujo, L. M., & Bramwell, B. (2002). Partnership and regional tourism in Brazil. *Annals of Tourism Research*, *29*, 1138–1164.

Arcodia, C., & Whitford, M. (2006). Festival attendance and the development of social capital. *Journal of Convention and Event Tourism*, *8*(2), 1–18.

Bowdin, G., Allen, J., O'Toole, W., Harris, R., & McDonnell, I. (2006). *Events management* (2nd ed.). Oxford, England: Butterworth-Heinemann Elsevier.

Bramwell, B. (1998). Selecting policy instruments for sustainable tourism. In W. F. Theobald (Ed.), *Global tourism* (2nd ed., pp. 361–379). Oxford, England: Butterworth-Heinemann.

Bramwell, B. (2006). Actors, power and discourses of growth limits. *Annals of Tourism Research*, *33*, 957–978.

Bramwell, B., & Sharman, A. (1999). Collaboration in local tourism policymaking. *Annals of Tourism Research*, *26*, 392–415.

Bucklin, L. P., & Sengupta, S. (1993). Organising successful co-marketing alliances. *Journal of Marketing*, *57*(2), 32–46.

Clarkson, M. (1994, July). *A risk based model of stakeholder theory*. Proceedings of the Second Toronto Conference on Stakeholder Theory, Centre for Corporate Social Performance and Ethics, Toronto.

Donaldson, T., & Preston, L.E. (1995). The stakeholder theory of the corporation: Concepts, evidence, and implications. *The Academy of Management Review*, *20*(1), 65–91.

Dwyer, L. (2008). Economic evaluation of special events. In A. Aktas, E. Wickens, M. Kesgin, E. Cengiz, & E. Yenialp (Eds.), *International Tourism Conference 2008. November 5–9, 2008 Alanya TURKEY, Cultural and Event Tourism: Issues & Debates* (pp. 25–48). Ankara, Turkey: Detay Yayincilik.

Eisenhardt, K. (1989). Building theories case study research. *Academy of Management Review*, *14*, 532–550.

Freeman, R. E. (1984). *Strategic management: A stakeholder approach*. Boston, MA: Pitman.

Getz, D. (1998). Information sharing among festival managers. *Festival Management and Event Tourism*, *5*(1/2), 33–50.

Getz, D. (2005). *Event management and event tourism* (2nd ed.). New York, NY: Cognizant.

Getz, D. (2007) *Event studies: Theory, research and policy planned events*. Oxford, England: Elsevier.

Getz, D. (2008). Event tourism: Definition, evolution and research. *Tourism Management*, *29*, 403–428.

Getz, D., Andersson, T., & Larson, M. (2007). Festival stakeholder roles: Concept and case studies. *Event Management, 10*, 103–122.

Getz, D., & Fairley, S. (2004). Media management at sport events for destination promotion. *Event Management, 8*(3), 127–139.

Gummesson, E. (2008). Extending the service-dominant logic: From customer centricity to balanced centricity. *Academy of Marketing Science, 36*(1), 15–17.

Gundlach, G. T., Achrol, R. S., & Mentzer, J. T. (1995). The structure of commitment in exchange. *Journal of Marketing, 59*(1), 78–92.

Halinen, A., & Törnroos, J. (2005). Using case methods in the study of contemporary business networks. *Journal of Business Research, 58*, 1285–1297.

Holbrook, M. B. (1977). More on content analysis in consumer research. *Journal of Consumer Research, 4*(3), 176–177.

Jafari, J. (2008). Transforming culture into events: Faux pas and judicious deliberations. In A. Aktas, E. Wickens, M. Kesgin, E. Cengiz, & E. Yenialp (Eds.), *International Tourism Conference 2008. November 5–9, 2008 Alanya TURKEY, Cultural and Event Tourism: Issues & Debates* (pp. 25–48). Ankara, Turkey: Detay Yayincilik.

Janiskee, R. L., & Drews, P. L. (1998). Rural festivals and Community reimaging. In R. Butler, C. M. Hall, & J. Jenkins (Eds.), *Tourism and recreation in rural areas* (pp. 157–175) Chichester, England: John Wiley & Sons.

Jones, T. M., & Wicks, A. C. (1999). Convergent stakeholder theory. *The Academy of Management Review, 24*, 206–221.

Kaplan, A. (1943). Content analysis and the theory of signs. *Philosophy of Science, 10*, 230–247.

Kassarjian, H. H. (1977). Content analysis in consumer research. *Journal of Consumer Research, 4*(1), 8–18.

Kepplinger, H. M. (1989). Content analysis and reception analysis. *American Behavioral Scientist, 33*, 175–182.

Kolbe, R. H., & Burnett, M. S. (1991). Content analysis research: an examination of applications with directives for improving research reliability and objectivity. *Journal of Consumer Research, 18*, 243–150.

Long, P. (2000). After the event: Perspectives on organizational partnerships in the management of a themed festival year. *Event Management, 6*(1), 45–59.

Mackellar, J. (2006). Conventions, festivals, and tourism: Exploring the network that binds. *Journal of Convention and Event Tourism, 8*(2), 45–56.

McCarthy, B., Moscardo, G., Murphy, L., & Pearce, P (2007). Mining and chamber music: Terra Nova, exploring new territory in the development of music-tourism networks. In L. Andreu, J. Gnoth, & M. Kozak (Eds.), *Proceedings of the 2007 Advances in Tourism Marketing Conference*. Sueca, Spain: Publications de la Universitat de Valencia.

Merrilees, B., Getz, D., & O'Brien, D. (2005). Marketing stakeholders. Branding the Brisbane Goodwill Games. *European Journal of Marketing, 39*, 1060–1077.

Miles, M. B., & Huberman, A. M. (1994). *Qualitative data analysis* (2nd ed.). Thousand Oaks, CA: Sage.

Mitchell, R. K., Agle, B. R., & Wood, D. J. (1997). Toward a theory of stakeholder identification and salience: Defining the principle of who and what really counts. *The Academy of Management Review, 22*, 853–886.

Mossberg, L., & Getz, D. (2006). Stakeholder influences on the ownership management and management of Festival Brands. *Scandinavian Journal of Hospitality and Tourism, 6*, 308–326.

Morgan, R. M., & Hunt, S. D. (1994). The commitment–trust theory of relationship marketing. *Journal of Marketing, 58*(3), 20–38.

O'Sullivan, D., & Jackson, M. J. (2002). Festival tourism: A contributor to sustainable local economic development. *Journal of Sustainable Tourism, 10*, 325–342.

Patton, Q. M. (1990). *Qualitative evaluation and research methods*. Newbury Park, CA: Sage.

Rowley, T. J. (1997). Moving beyond dyadic ties: a network theory of stakeholder influences. *The Academy of Management Review, 22*, 887–910.

Sautter, E. T., & Leisen, B. (1999). Managing stakeholders: A tourism planning model. *Annals of Tourism Research, 26*, 312–328.

Stokes, R. (2004). A framework for the analysis of events- tourism knowledge networks. *Journal of Hospitality and Tourism Management, 11*(2), 108–122.

Stokes, R. (2008). Tourism strategy making: Insights to the events tourism domain. *Tourism Management, 29*, 252–262.

Tomljenovic, R., & Weber, S. (2004). Funding cultural events in Croatia: Tourism-related policy issues. *Event Management, 9*(1/2), 51–59.

Wilson, E. J., & Woodside, A. G. (1999). Degrees-of-freedom analysis of case data in business marketing research. *Industrial Marketing Management, 28*, 215–229.

Woodside, A. G., & Biemans, W. G. (2005). Modelling innovation, manufacturing, diffusion and adoption/rejection processes. *Journal of Business and Industrial Marketing, 20*, 380–393.

Woodside, A. G., & Wilson, E. J. (2003). Case study research methods for theory building. *Journal of Business and Industrial Marketing, 18*, 493–508.

Yin, R. M. (2003). *Case study research. Design and method* (3rd ed.). Thousand Oaks, CA: Sage.

When Fit Matters: Leveraging Destination and Event Image Congruence

MAGDALENA FLOREK

Department of Trade and Marketing, Poznan University of Economics, Poznan, Poland

ANDREA INSCH

Department of Marketing, University of Otago, Dunedin, New Zealand

This article develops a framework for conceptualizing and managing destination and event image congruence. Building on the foundations of Roth and Romeo's (1992) product–country image fit matrix, a framework for categorizing the interactions between destination and event image is presented that can be applied to leverage positive, relevant associations and rebalance less positive associations of both types of images. The usefulness of the matrix is shown through an in-depth case study of the image-rebalancing program of the FIFA 2006 host country Germany. This case and others demonstrate the suitability of the framework for managing, and more importantly leveraging, image congruence in this context. Implications for managers and researchers derived from applying the framework are also discussed.

INTRODUCTION

Opportunities to host events, especially so-called "mega-events," are hotly contested due to the economic benefits to be gained through tourism and related supporting industries. In addition, the trend in destination management to create new events and bid for existing ones also offers organizers the platform to modify and build the host destination's image or better communicate its identity (Getz, 1989). Among the most prized events that are targeted by destination managers include the Olympic Games, trade and political forums, and world expositions or fairs (DeGroote, 2005a). Thus, it is not uncommon for local governments to have agencies dedicated to promoting their destinations (towns, cities, regions, or countries) as locations for events. Like events, destinations differ in the attractiveness of their image, as well as their substance. In order to maximize the benefits for both event organizers and the host destination, logic would suggest identifying synergies and leveraging them. The infrastructure development options attached to hosting an event may be restricted or limited due to the location itself. However, the potential to build and enhance the image of the destination may be unlimited, depending on the synergistic effects of the image attributes of the host and event, akin to symbiosis. On the other hand, a regretful mismatch between the image of the host and the event could taint the image of either, or both, and in the long-term harm their reputations.

Despite a handful of studies on the influence of events on the images of their host destinations, a comprehensive framework of understanding the fit, or congruence, between the destination and event image is absent from published theory or practice of destination and tourism management. Thus, the central aim of this article is to develop and present such a conceptual framework that might be applied to identify and manage destination and event image congruence where fit matters.

To achieve this major aim, the first section reviews the relevant literature on the formation of destination image. This is followed by a review of research on events, in particular special or mega-events. Next, these two streams are integrated in the context of country-of-origin effect. This provides the basis for a decision-making matrix designed to aid managers to maximize or leverage image congruencies and address image incongruence, or mismatch. Finally, application of the matrix and its implications are detailed utilizing representative examples. Following these examples, an in-depth analysis of the image re-balancing program undertaken to resolve image mismatches for Germany hosting the 2006 FIFA World Cup is discussed.

DESTINATION IMAGE

A vast body of research in marketing focuses on the relationships between product and country images due to the economic implications of country images attached to exports. Less is known about how the images of certain products influence the country image (e.g., Florek & Conejo, 2007), or how they might simultaneously influence each other. Knowledge of the role and formation of country, or destination images, in buyer decision-making gives insight into the nature and composition of such images and guidance when attempting to promote products and the places they are produced in. Similarly, it helps to understand the relations between events and host destinations.

A destination's image is a cognitive category that describes subjective associations, knowledge, opinions, judgments and emotions about the destination (Kotler, Haider & Rein, 1993). It can be defined as "a mental or attitudinal construct developed on the basis of a few selected impressions from among the flood of total impressions through a creative process in which those selected are elaborated, embellished and ordered" (Reynolds, 1965, cited in Lee, Lee, and Lee, 2005, p. 840). Image, thus, is a relative concept in which objective information and facts are replaced by subjective opinions and judgments. Perception may thus vary among individuals depending, for example, on their experience with the destination (often based on single event), their knowledge about it, their experience with other places, attitudes, expectations, motivations, simplistic stereotypes they hold or their personal goals (Florek, Breitbarth, & Conejo, 2008).

Differences in images between individuals are related to the elements that compose them—cognitive (awareness, familiarity, and associations with an object), emotional (feelings and emotions towards an object) and behavioral elements (tendency of certain behavior towards an object). Gartner (1993) applied these components of image theory on tourist image formation and mentions: cognitive (internally accepted picture of destination attributes), affective (motives what is to be obtained from the destination), and conative (actions and behavior after cognitive and affective evaluations). The image concept assumes that if an individual has adequate knowledge of a destination together with positive emotions and judgments towards it, he, or she is willing to choose it (as well as related products) from others (Florek & Zyminkowski, 2002). This tendency might result in repeat visits, growing demand for commercial goods, or willingness to create more permanent ties with a destination. Formation of destination images is a multifaceted process whereby images are constantly built and modified through the interpretation of information from different sources. Thus, the images held by potential visitors, nonvisitors, and returned visitors will differ. Gunn (1972) explains this process in terms of a stage theory which is made up of the following three major steps: (a) *organic image*, which is formed by "independent" information delivered from nontourist sources (e.g., media, word-of-mouth, etc.); (b) *induced image*, that is shaped by promoted information (promotional campaigns, travel agencies, etc.), and (c) *modified-induced image* as a result of personal experience of the destination. At each stage there are possibilities to include relevant activities and types of information sources that might influence an individual's destination perception. This attempt to modify or change the intended image is more and more often referred to "destination branding" or "place branding," which is a process of implementing branding strategies and techniques to market a place or to differentiate it.

Destinations are analyzed from a tourism perspective and can be defined as an amalgam of individual products and experience opportunities that combine to form a total experience of the area visited (Murphy, Pritchard, & Smith, 2000). This is why destination image, like brand image, can be viewed as a summary construct (Min, 1989), meaning visitors (or broadly, external audiences) may abstract information about a destination from its products, celebrities, behavior of its residents, or events taking place. As Kim and Morrsion (2005) analyze, among the numerous image studies, differences in image perceptions appear between previsitors and postvisitors, before and after trips, before and after advertising campaigns, between first-time and repeat visitors, between visitors and nonvisitors, and before and after internationally significant political events. Over the long term, however, certain images might be difficult to shake or change, especially those experienced at certain stages of an individual's life. Papadopoulos & Heslop (1993, p. 477) therefore explained, "the challenge facing marketers is to ascertain the images consumers hold about the products and their origin countries and act accordingly by suppressing, presenting, enhancing or aggressively promoting them." This applies to special events in particular which attract huge attention and might hold symbolic significance and in turn form lasting associations between the images of the host and event.

EVENTS

Investing in promoting events as attractions has developed to feature in many destinations' tourism marketing strategies (Mules, 1998; Gnoth & Anwar, 2000; Getz, 1991, 1997). Even though the notion of events is well established (Martyn, 1969; Jones, 2001; De Groote, 2005a), it is their scale and strategic use which makes them appealing for host places, media, visitors, and others. Increasing competition among destinations to host events is directly related to the perceived positive social, economic, and cultural impacts that they can provide. Such benefits include the following as identified by Marris (1987): (a) tourism = amount, quality; (b) economic = other industries: amount; (c) technical = other industries: quality; (d) physical = environment, conservation; (e) social = family links, habits; (f) cultural = traditions, creeds; (g) psychological = pride, reputation; (h) political = local, national, worldwide.

Large scale mega-events, in particular, offer many direct and indirect economic benefits. For example, the benefits of hosting a world event such as the Olympic Games include tangible outcomes—economic growth, tourist revenues, and job creation, and intangible outcomes—national pride, world status, and offering a grand platform to promote the host destination (e.g., De Groote, 2005b). In the case of the Sydney Olympic Games held in 2000, it was estimated that 88% of the 110,000 international visitors who came to

Australia for the Olympics were likely to return to Sydney as a tourist. In addition, it was estimated that awareness of Australia, as a consequence of hosting the Olympics, as a destination was likely to be ahead 10 years what it would have been without hosting the Games (ATC, 2001).

As with the types of benefits and costs that might derive from staging a major event, the type, scale, and scope of such events also differs. Jago (2007) distinguishes: mega-events, special events, hallmark events, major events, festivals, and minor and small-scale events.

Overlapping and often used interchangeably is the notion of a mega-event or "hallmark event" (e.g., Ritchie, 1984). Particular differences among these events have been suggested (e.g., Roche, 2000), but their similarities are binding—the magnitude of their impacts on the host. In this way, Getz (in Fayos-Sola, 1998, p. 242) defines mega-events as:

> Planned occurrences of limited duration which have an extraordinary impact on the host area in terms of one or more of the following: tourist volumes; visitor expenditures; publicity leading to a heightened aware-ness and a more positive image; related infrastructural and organizational developments which substantially increase the destination's capacity and attractiveness.

In addition, Roche (2000) emphasizes the large-scale cultural (including commercial and sporting) features of such events, their dramatic character, popular appeal, and international importance.

Despite potential local benefits, some events, for example sports mega-events, have been largely developed by undemocratic organizations, like FIFA and the International Olympic Committee (see Jennings, 1996, 2006), in the interest of global motives rather than for the benefit of local host communities (Horne & Manzenreiter, 2006, cited in Florek et al., 2008). Still, destinations may use the appeal and characteristics of such events for their image building and modification purposes. As Getz (1989, p. 125) mentions, "there is clearly a trend to exploit events for tourism and to create new events deliberately as tourist attractions".Thus, event attraction and organization should be managed strategically, in order to maximize the synergies between the event and the destination. Deconstructing the relationship between event and destination image, Chalip and Green (2001, p. 350) suggest, "it is reasonable to expect that the particular effect of the image of events destination hosts will depend on the images that are compatible (or incompatible) with the event." The authors follow the view that image effects of the hosted event depend on the link and compatibility of features of the destination and the event's characteristics (Chalip & McGuirty, 2004; Chalip, Green, & Hill, 2003). The effects might be mutual: the destination and the event may benefit from each other depending on their image congruence. The next section explains the linkages and interactions between host and event image constellations.

COUNTRY OF ORIGIN EFFECT IN THE CONTEXT OF EVENT AND DESTINATION

Consumers construct destination images, among others, by generalizing information from different products of the same destination (city, region, or country). The products (or more specifically the brands) are thus perceived to have similar attributes related to this destination (Han, 1989). The relation is known as country-of-origin effect (COO) and is widely discussed in the literature (see Papadopoulos & Heslop, 2002).

According to Ahmed et al. (2004, p. 104), consumers "make decisions about the quality of products based on a systematic process of acquisition, evaluation and integration of product information or cues that can be intrinsic or/and extrinsic." The COO concept assumes that consumers with no prior experience or knowledge of a product's intrinsic attributes tend to rely on extrinsic attributes when evaluating a product (Skaggs, Falk, Almonte, & Cárdenas, 1996; Johansson, 1989). The intrinsic attributes relate to the physical composition of the product and extrinsic ones encompass the brand, price, package, seller, warranties, and country of origin.

According to Hong and Wyer (1989), COO information can affect product evaluation, firstly through influencing interpretation of other available product attributes; secondly, by providing a heuristic basis for evaluation without considering other attributes; thirdly, by acting as an attribute in itself; and finally, through influencing the attention paid to other attributes affecting their impact.

Analogously, the image of a destination can affect the event being organized via specific perception of some features of the event (e.g., influencing the perception of organization capacity, safety of the event, etc.), acting as the dominant feature of the event (e.g., "typical American event"), acting as one of the features of the event (e.g., by transferring characteristic atmosphere for the destination), and lastly, influencing the way the other features of the event are perceived (e.g., through stereotypic opinions).

Janda and Rao (1997) argue that a person's perception of a country may be represented as a hierarchical structure. At a general level country image is made up of stereotypes that can then be progressively refined to contain typical product categories, typical products (particular domain of a specific country), and particular brands. Brands originating from a particular country thus create intangible assets or liabilities that are shared by brands originating from the same country. This dependence might be important in the case of events, where the perception of the host destination will influence the perception of particular types of events (e.g., sport, cultural, and business).

COO is also considered in the context of country branding and its role in creating or enhancing a country, or more universally, destination brand (Florek & Conejo, 2007). Gnoth (2002) stated that particular products might signal benefits that, in turn, might be associated with the destination brand. According to Tellström et al. (2006), the geographical area is used to promote a product but the product also promotes the geographic area. In a similar vein, the reverse to Janda and Rao's (1997) approach suggested that through product category, particular products, or brands, destination image and its brand might be modified, strengthened or even created (Florek & Conejo, 2007). Consequently, strategic commercial products or flagships might serve as a basis for at least enhancing a destination brand. In this context, events are also a part of a destination's offer and they might be considered as destination "products" or even brands (especially if the event is organized regularly). Similarly to traditional products, for which COO is referred to, the image of the destination the event takes place in, might influence the perception of the event itself. Secondly, with even more power to communicate destination identity (reflected in destination image) than regular products and brands, the authors argue that events influence the external perception of the host destination (which may vary depending on whether participation is active or passive through media transmission). The mechanism and analysis of these mutual relations provide destination and event mangers with relevant information about necessary actions and tools as well as possible benefits from destination and event image congruence.

Two theories have been used to explain how product–country relations affect consumer behavior. Han (1989) suggests that the country–product interface may work in either or both directions as a "halo construct" (country image is used to evaluate products about which people know little) or as a "summary construct" (knowledge about a country's products is abstracted to the image of the country itself). Consequently, when consumers are not familiar with a country's or destination's products or are unable to determine their quality prior to purchase because of lack of information, the country image serves as a halo from which consumers infer a product's attributes and quality. As consumers become familiar with a country's products, country image may become a summary construct that summarizes a consumer's beliefs about product attributes. The halo effect operates in low familiarity countries. The summary construct, in turn, is operant in high familiarity countries (Han, 1989). In the discussed context, destination awareness and familiarity will therefore influence the possibility of using destination perceptions when organizing and/or hosting events.

Many studies suggest that the importance given to COO is not universal and varies across countries (e.g., Papadopoulos & Heslop, 1993; Klein, Ettenson, & Morris, 1998), product category (e.g., Kaynak & Cavusgil, 1983; Wall, Liefleld, & Heslop, 1991), consumer segment (e.g., d'Astous & Ahmed, 1995), nationality of subjects (e.g., Hong & Yi, 1992), involvement in the product class (e.g., d'Astous & Ahmed, 1992), countries' similarity (e.g.,

Wang & Lamb, 1993; Kaynak & Cavusgil, 1983), influence of ethnocentrism (e.g., Lantz & Loeb, 1996), and research methods and techniques used (e.g., Parameswaran & Yaprak, 1987).

Verlegh and Steenkamp (1999, cited in Tellström et al., 2006) note that COO should be understood in broader terms than just a cognitive cue for product quality. It relates also to emotions, identity, and autobiographical memories that transform COO into an image attribute. COO can also be viewed as the mental representations of a destination's people, products or culture (Askegaard & Ger, 1996, cited in Verlegh & Steenkamp, 1999). The consumer effect of COO has symbolic and emotional meaning (Li & Wyer, 1994), COO might thus determine a brand's desirability for symbolic reasons since products and especially brands chosen by consumers often serve as symbolic acquisition and communication of social distinctions and particularly status (Douglas & Isherwood, 1979). It might be assumed that these interrelations are valid for events as well and they can enrich the emotional value of destinations.

MATCHING DESTINATION IMAGE AND EVENT IMAGE

Categorizing the image of a destination and the image of an event according to how they are perceived overall allows their images to be defined as positive (possessing attributes that are in the majority perceived as positive) or negative (mostly negative opinions). Based on this classification, the relevant type of fit between the event and host destination can be identified. This concept derives from the premises of Roth and Romeo's (1992) product–country fit matrix.

In the context discussed, it is expected that if a host destination is perceived to have a positive overall image and the event it is hosting also has a positive image, the visitors will be more willing to attend the event (see Figure 1). Several examples are discussed next to illustrate each situation presented in Figure 1.

Favorable Match: Nobel Prize Award Ceremonies

An example of a favorable match between destination and event images are Stockholm and Oslo hosting the Nobel Prize Award Ceremonies. The Nobel Prizes in the specific disciplines (chemistry, physics, physiology or medicine, and literature) and the Prize in Economics, which is commonly identified with them, are widely regarded as the most prestigious award one can receive in those fields. The Nobel Peace Prize is presented in Oslo, Norway, and the remaining Nobel Prizes and the Prize in Economics are presented in Stockholm, Sweden, all at the same time at the annual Prize Award Ceremony on December 10—the anniversary of Alfred

		Destination image	
		Positive	Negative
Event image	Positive	Favorable match	Unfavorable match
	Negative	Favorable mismatch	Unfavorable mismatch

FIGURE 1 Destination and event images according to image dimensions.

Nobel's death. Both cities strengthen their images by hosting the prestigious, world-famous events. Stockholm's image communication, centered on the message, "Stockholm—The Capital of Scandinavia," uses the "Home of the Nobel Prize" attribute among others (see SBR, 2008). Stockholm has a strong reputation being ranked as 26th in Anholt's City Brands Index (Anholt-GMI CBI, 2006), with an image as safe, clean, and having a superior standard of public amenities; and 25th in the Top 50 European cities according to the European Cities and Regions Of The Future (FDI Intelligence, 2008). The event's positive symbolic dimension and the city image provide further favorable associations and reinforcement for both.

Unfavorable Matches: 2008 Olympic Games and 2002 Miss World Contest

The recent example of an unfavorable match situation is Beijing, China and the 2008 Olympic Games. When China made its bid for the Games, the biggest sporting mega-event based on the positive values of the Olympic movement, the vice president of the Beijing Olympic bid committee argued, "By allowing Beijing to host the Games, you will help the development of human rights" (Segal & Economy, 2008). During the evaluation process in May 2008, the International Olympic Committee reported that the "Beijing Games would leave a unique legacy for both China and sport as a whole" (Barnet, 2001). According to Segal and Economy (2008), hosting the event was supposed to be a chance for China to showcase the country's rapid economic growth and modernization to the rest of the world, and domestically, to give the opportunity for the Chinese government to demonstrate the Communist Party's competence as well as affirm the country's strong status. Hosting the Olympic Games gave China the chance to portray itself as a "peace-loving" country. Consequently, the Games focused international attention on nearly every aspect of the People's Republic of China, including the regime's flawed human rights record. After the dramatic events in Tibet, many foreign athletes, politicians, and celebrities joined the chorus of China's critics. Demands for political liberalization, greater autonomy for Tibet, increased pressure on Sudan, better environmental protection (there was the immediate concern for many Olympians whether Beijing could ensure clean air and safe food for the duration of the Games), and an improved product-safety record threaten to put a damper on the country (Segal & Economy, 2008).

In the case of Nigeria, their event heightened world attention to the already unfavorable country image. On December 7, 2002 Nigeria hosted the Miss World Contest. Although the event presents some controversy (especially among feminists), in general it is communicating positive messages ("charity work is integral to the Miss World ethos and part of the brief to contenders in each country is that they volunteer their time or fundraise for charity," Miss World, 2008). After the leading Nigerian newspaper said the Prophet Mohamed would have married one of the contestants in the Miss World pageant, Islamic Militants burnt down the regional offices of the publisher in Kaduna. At least 105 people were reported killed in the fighting between Christians and Muslims in Kaduna and the violence spread to Abuja, the capital, where the Miss World Pageant was to have had its finale (Cowell, 2002). The Nigerian *Umma* (the Muslim brotherhood) declared a "serious religious emergency" and issued a statement calling on the government to stop the pageant. The flare-up added to raging controversy over Nigeria's staging of the showbiz event. Many contestants threatened to boycott the pageant to protest against a Muslim woman in northern Nigeria being sentenced to death by stoning for adultery. Islamists, who called the pageant "a parade of nudity" threatened to disrupt the event that was hosted during the holy month of Ramadan. As a result, the finale gala was moved to London. The idea and nature of the event clearly mismatched the country culture and identity and caused negative publicity.

Favorable Mismatch: Global Marijuana March

An example of an event with a negative image that is hosted in many destinations that generally have a positive image is the annual Global Marijuana March to demand an end to marijuana prohibition. Marches take place in small towns and large cities across the United States (which accounted for 118 of the 232 cities listed by organizers), Europe (66 cities), Latin America (21 cities), and Canada, as well as in Australia, New Zealand, Ireland, Israel, and Japan. Demonstrations ranged from handfuls of people in small American towns to more than 20,000 in Toronto (the world's largest Global Marijuana March). The vast majority of marches are peaceful and noncontroversial, but there were dozens of arrests in Australia, Buenos Aires, and in

Eastern Europe, where the Russian and Bulgarian authorities cracked down on marchers (Drug War Chronicle, 2007).

Unfavorable Mismatch: Nuclear Testing in North Korea

Among countries having a controversial reputation that are inclined to negative events is North Korea and its involvement in nuclear tests. On October 9, 2006, the Democratic People's Republic of Korea announced that it conducted a nuclear test. After several days of evaluation, U.S. authorities confirmed that the underground explosion was nuclear, but that the test produced a low yield of less than 1 kiloton (Chanlett-Avery & Squassoni, 2006). On October 14, 2006, the United Nation Security Council unanimously approved limited military and economic sanctions against North Korea (North Korean Nuclear Test, n.d.). North Korea remained defiant, insisting that any increased pressure on the regime would be regarded as an act of war (Chanlett-Avery & Squassoni, 2006). Negative economic effects were seen throughout the region after the test. South Korea's KOSPI index fell 2.4% and the Japanese yen fell to a 7-month low against the U.S. dollar, while the price of oil on the world market rose and several stock markets in Asia from Singapore to Manila traded lower possibly due to the tests (North Korean Nuclear Test, n.d.).

Obviously, destinations try to avoid organizing events of negative or controversial image (however sometimes their occurrence is unexpected and destinations can only react to soothe their consequences). More useful thus, is the analysis of the importance of product (event in this case) category components with the perceived image of the country of origin (host destination) along the same elements as Roth and Romeo's (1992) suggested in their framework. A desirable product–country match occurs when important dimensions (features) for a product category (e.g., technical aspects) are also associated with a country's image and its perceived strengths (e.g., highly skilled workforce). As Roth and Romeo (1992) found in their study, when a strong, favorable match between the country and product exists, a COO effect is likely to occur, positively affecting product evaluation and willingness to buy a product from a particular country will be high. On the other hand when a mismatch is identified, COO should have little impact on willingness to buy. Thus, "perceptions vary depending on how well the country's perceived production and marketing strengths are related to the product category" (Roth & Romeo, 1992, p. 493). Ahmed et al.'s (2004) research indicated that a country may have positive COO perception for some product categories but a negative one for others.

The fit between a product and its important features and analogical elements of the destination image should therefore be analysed in the case of a particular product category. A lot of well-known examples confirm that many countries specialize in and thus are famous for producing a particular product or brand. In contrast, a general positive image of a country may not bolster the international marketing of its product as Ahmed et al. (2004) concluded.

Based on the concept and even closer to the individual level, the authors suggest analyzing the fit of particular (important, less important, or unimportant for audience) features or elements of the single event with their relevant perceptions of the host destination. Such an approach will guide relevant decisions as regards to which elements need to be stressed, which ones improved and which should be ignored (see Figure 2).

A favorable match occurs when the destination is perceived positively in the areas that are also important features for the event. Consequently, events with features that positively correlate with the destination image will strengthen the image of this destination. On the other hand, the positive image of a destination together with the elements important for the event will enhance the attractive image of the event itself. In this case marketers of either the event or destination should use the positive link and promote the important and positive aspects of both.

An unfavorable match reflects the situation where components important from the visitors' or observers' point of view are not perceived as attractive destination assets. The situation might be improved by real modification of those features and delivering appropriate information about the change; in this case the positive change (experienced during the event or communicated appropriately), can influence the positive changes in perceptions of the destination. If it is impossible, the negative aspects should be avoided in communication. Otherwise the negative perception of destination features might hurt the perception of the event.

		Destination image elements	
		Positive	Negative
Event components	Important	**Favorable match:** Strengthen, promote	**Unfavorable match:** Improve, modify and inform or avoid in communication
	Not (or less) important	**Favorable mismatch:** Use as a support, use as added value, communicate	**Unfavorable mismatch:** Ignore in communication

FIGURE 2 Implications of country and event category elements matches and mismatches.

An event–destination mismatch exists when the event's features are less or unimportant to bring benefit for the audience. If particular features are not associated with the event but are still positively evaluated in the case of the destination (favorable mismatch), they might be used as additional benefits enhancing the image of the event. Whereas the reverse sequence suggests that the event itself is a good means to communicate the other, positive aspects of a destination that could become more important in the future.

Negative perception of some aspects of a destination which are simultaneously not or less important in the case of a particular event (unfavorable mismatch) should be ignored to avoid negative mutual influence. Obviously, if it is possible, their improvement might play similar role as in the case of favorable mismatch and event itself might serve as a good platform to communicate the positive change.

In the next section, the case of Germany and its hosting of a sports mega-event is discussed to demonstrate the practical implications of destination and event image congruence.

Image Rebalancing: Germany

As place-branding consultant Simon Anholt suggests, Germany has a positive but unbalanced international image (Anholt, 2006). According to a survey by the Pew Global Attitudes Project, 89% of French people and 79% of Russians have a favorable view of Germany (Pfanner, 2005), but its image is double-sided.

On the one hand, Germany is well known for its exceptional reputation as a manufacturer of top-quality goods and brands (e.g., Audi, BMW, Siemens, Braun), and recognized investment potential. On the other hand, despite being positive in functional areas, Germany is not associated with warmth, hospitality, beauty, culture, or fun. As Anholt (2006, p. 7) concluded: "Germany is perceived as a factory, heavily weighted on the 'hard' side of economics, production and politics, and rather light on the 'soft' side of people, culture and landscape."

Germany's image seems to be primarily caused by the perception of its residents who are traditionally considered serious and disciplined (Geoghegan, 2006); efficient, organized, and reliable but not entertaining; spontaneous and in general likeable (Anholt, 2006). They are perceived as hard working, punctual, businesslike, and competitive but not really having a sense of humor (Kotarski, 2006; Purvis, 2006, in Florek et al., 2008). Also, the unfavorable aspect of the country perception relates to Second World War associations, which still weighs on Germany's image and exasperates Germans. The other problem is related to Germans themselves and their inner sense of self-regard. For example, Germany's president diagnosed the country was entering a "collective depression" in 2004 (Crossland, 2006, in Florek et al., 2008).

According to the Anholt Nation Brand Index, the position of Germany is very strong (2nd place in 2006 and 2007 quarterly rankings). It is interesting, however, to see the scores of particular components (according to six dimensions used in the ranking methodology). In the third quarter of 2006, Germany was evaluated very high as a producer of high quality export products (3rd place—close to Japanese and American goods). The position of Germany in aspects of heritage and culture was also high (4th among all countries being analyzed) as well as in investment and immigration (6th) and governance (8th). Relatively poor results were achieved in dimensions related to people and tourism (both 12th position). Germans were evaluated ambiguously: on the one side as a country of well-qualified employees and specialists, and on the other side respondents pointed out they did not see Germans as their playmates. Germany, having potential that comes from beautiful and interesting cities, is not well known for tourism. More detailed results (for the year 2005) for Germany also recorded high scores in science and technology, sport, and education (Nowosielski, 2008).

In 2006 Germany, with its image legacy, hosted the FIFA World Cup—the world's largest and most important football event and one of the biggest sport events. Some of the event's components could be seen as important and some as less or unimportant from the external audiences' perspective. They can be simultaneously viewed as positive and negative when referring to the particular host destination (Germany, in this case). Relevant attributes, based on a scan of the related literature and research results on German culture, international marketing, and tourism, are placed in corresponding cells of the proposed matrix (Figure 3).

		Germany's image	
		Positive	Negative
Event's components	Important	Safety, efficiency, reliability, hard working people, outstanding infrastructure	Stiff atmosphere, boring and unapproachable people, expensive
	Not (or less) important	Tourism assets, culture, economic prosperity, governance, democracy, outstanding technology, education, high quality goods	World War Two associations

FIGURE 3 Country and event matches and mismatches for the 2006 FIFA World Cup and Germany.

Germany's positive associations that go hand-in-hand with the important elements of the sporting mega-event were already supported by visitors before the event. Research on Germany's image among New Zealand football supporters before and after attending the World Cup (Florek et al., 2008) revealed that there was substantial agreement in terms of the appropriateness of having the event in Germany (50% very much agreed and 33% agreed), and a64% of respondents already expected it to be very well organized. At the same time, Germany and the event were expected to be very expensive by 31% of the sample and expensive by 47%.

To change the negative and to enhance less important (often unknown) but positive associations and assets, Germany used the event to present itself as a hospitable, joyful, and modern nation, bursting with ideas (Purvis, 2006). A series of activities were used to achieve this goal:

- The German government spent nearly 4 billion Euros to improve its already sufficient infrastructure: terminals, roads, and stadiums (Tokarski & Groll, 2006). This effort encompassed also a surge in new buildings, museums, and exhibitions with the purpose of positioning Germany as the European center of design beyond the duration of the event (Boyes, 2006).
- German police made the event completely safe in a friendly manner and tolerant, nonintrusive approach (Crossland, 2006) to avoid militaristic associations (Tokarski & Groll, 2006). An innovation was inviting police officers from other countries to help patrol stadiums, facilitate fan interaction, and improve cooperation between national police forces (German Police, 2006).
- The initiative "Land of Ideas" accompanied the sporting event and targeted two groups: prospective tourist and TV audiences to enhance the image of Germany as an open and friendly country, and potential investors to strengthen Germany's past accomplishments, innovation, performance, and competitive potential (Land of Ideas, 2006). The initiative's tone was light and dynamic, with the help of German celebrities, to show a German sense of humor (Boyes, 2006).
- The German government designed a 30-million Euro program around the football theme consisting of 48 projects in diverse areas (Bundesministerium des Innern, 2005). Art and culture initiatives helped highlight Germany's diversity, creativity, and talent (Tokarski & Groll, 2006).
- In order to address the unfavorable perceptions of Germans, the federal government developed the National Service and Friendliness Campaign that was implemented under the slogan, "Germany Rolls out the Red Carpet," targeting the service sector and general residents. The aim of the campaign was to highlight the strong commitment to service leading to nicer reception, stay, and experience during the World Cup. All members of the service value chain from airports, train stations, hotels, and public transport to taxi services were trained in workshops offering advice

on intercultural relations, tolerance, sensibility, hospitality, and foreign languages (GFG, 2006).

Several studies have been conducted to examine if a positive change in perception of Germany occurred after the event once the above initiatives were implemented. At the beginning of 2008, the German National Tourist Board (GNTB, 2008a) commissioned IPK International to analyze Germany's image as a travel destination. The representative survey examined international attitudes towards 13 aspects that contribute to a country's appeal. According to research results, for almost all countries, the highest scoring statement for Germany was "quick and easy to get to" (78% of people agreed). In second place came "interesting historical attractions" (with an average of 63%), which found most agreement from respondents in neighboring countries, followed by "attractive destination for city breaks" (with an average of 60%). In a variety of countries, a high percentage of people agreed that Germany had "excellent shopping opportunities" and was a "cosmopolitan and friendly country." It also scored highly for the quality of its hotels.

Research carried out by TNS Infratest on behalf of the German National Tourist Board confirmed, "destination Germany had successfully capitalised on the opportunity provided by the World Cup to enhance its image" (GNTB, 2008b). The first stage of the survey was carried out in November 2005, the second 2 months after the Word Cup (the survey sample consisted of fans who traveled to Germany from the seven countries whose teams were in the final round). Results show that Germany's image improved in the intervening period, with 55% of Dutch, 48% of Italian, and 55% Brazilians describing Germany as "cosmopolitan and hospitable" (higher compared to the first stage by 8%, 5%, and 20% respectively). After the 2006 FIFA World Cup, 60% of the French respondents and 63% of Italians described Germany as an "ideal host country" (a 7- and 12-point increase). For Italians, for example, the host country's image improved significantly in all categories, especially in terms of its importance for culture-related holidays and city breaks and in their assessment of German hotels (both up by 11%). Quality of the hotels was also appreciated by Japanese visitors (increase of 11%). Value for money was perceived to be better after the event, rising by 9% in the Italian group and 4% among Swedes. At the second stage of the survey, 7% more Swedes questioned said that Germany has "exciting nightlife" (GNTB, 2008b).

Another study carried out by Florek et al. (2008) among football supporters from New Zealand revealed that the overall evaluation of Germany was much more favorable after than before the event. In all, 77% of respondents had a very positive perception compared to 19% before their visit. Germany was almost twice as better perceived as a good place to host the event (93% very much agreed compared to 50% before). Germany was also better evaluated in terms of organization. Before the event, 64% of respondents expected it to be very well organized, while after the event this perception increased to 87%. After their visit to Germany, New Zealand fans found the event very safe and without hazards (80%). The only measure that showed an average decrease was "Germany and the event are expensive," showing that respondents found Germany and the event to provide better value for money than expected. In general, respondents thought that a visit to Germany provides good value for money, with 66% having somewhat agreed and 17% very much agreed. The majority of image-related opinions showed a significant positive change before and after the World Cup. Those of the most positive changes in opinion are: safety of event, friendliness and approachability of Germans, a multicultural atmosphere, as well as good and friendly German service. The in-depth profile of participants, none of whom had been to Germany before, suggests that their perceptions of Germans changed because they overcame some of their skepticism about the unap-proachable nature of German people and instead had positive first-hand experiences (Florek et al., 2008).

Results from these studies support the positive influence of the German initiatives surrounding the event. The improvement of unfavorable aspects, utilizing the less important, but positive elements, and strengthening the already positive associations led to the perception that Germany is a pleas-ant place to travel. According to Anholt (2006), Germany took advantage and left its controversial past behind in order to achieve a more balanced national image, demonstrating its softer attributes such as being warm and welcoming. The World Cup has definitely helped not only to soften and boost Germany's image, but has also shown its potential as a destination for fun and friendliness. As a result, in the third and fourth quarter of 2007, Germany occupied the number one spot in the Nation Brands Index for the very first time. For example, for consumers in Brazil and the United States, Germany's greatest improvements are in tourism strong points such as cul-ture, friendliness, and natural beauty. In Switzerland, Germany scored higher than other countries for its heritage, contemporary culture and friendliness (GNTB, 2008b).

SUMMARY AND CONCLUSIONS

Destination and event managers face an increasingly complex task of ensur-ing the places and spectacles they promote hold favorable images in the minds of potential visitors, attendees, and observers. The interrelationships and interdependencies between the two overlapping sets of images are the ingredients from which impressions are formed, revised, or reinforced. As a starting point, understanding the favorable and unfavorable matches or mismatches, similarly to product–country relations (Roth & Romeo, 1992), is vital for event organizers and destination (city or country) brand managers. Such analysis and the decision-making tool developed in this article can provide information about what kind of events might be effective in the destination branding process as well as how the image of the host destination might influence the success of securing and organizing an event and its post evaluation.

The destination–event image fit matrix is not a stand-alone tool for shaping destination images. From a long-term strategic perspective, it can be used as part of event portfolio analysis to aid managers when deciding which events transfer positive associations to the destination and which ones do not enhance or reinforce the destination's image. Finally, as the case of Germany's hosting of the 2006 FIFA World Cup demonstrates, destination marketers must devote sufficient resources to ensure that the image of the event does not eclipse that of the destination through careful selection of appropriate communications tools and market research to measure intended image transfer effects.

REFERENCES

Ahmed, Z. U., Johnson, J. P., Yang, X., Fatt, C.K., Teng, H. S., & Boon, L. C. (2004). Does country of origin matter for low-involvement products. *International Marketing Review, 21*(1), 102–120.

Anholt, S. (2006). How Germany won the World Cup. *Anholt Nation Brands Index Special Report—Q3 Report,* 2006. Retrieved from http://www.insightcafe.com/reports/NBI_Q3_2006.pdf

Anholt-GMI CBI. (2006). *How the world views its cities* (2nd ed.). Retrieved from http://www.citybrandsindex.com/downloads/cbi2006-q4-free.pdf

Australian Tourist Commission. (2001). Australia's Olympics, special post games tourism report. Sydney, Australia: Author.

Barnet, K. (2001). *Beijing stretches its image to fit through the Olympic Rings.* Retrieved from http://www.brandchannel.com/features_effect.asp?pf_id=50

Boyes, R. (2006, June 3). Fussball and Volk—Germans seize their chance to rebrand a nation. *The Times.* Retrieved from http://www.timesonline.co.uk/article/0,,13509-2208825,00.html

Bundesministerium des Innern. (2005). *Die Welt zu Gast bei Freunden. Fünfter Fortschrittsbericht des Stabes WM 2006 zur Vorbereitung auf die FIFA Fußball— Weltmeisterschaft 2006.* Berlin, Germany: Author.

Chalip, L., & Green, B. C. (2001). Event marketing and destination image. *American Marketing Association Conference Proceedings, 12,* 346–351.

Chalip, L., Green B., & Hill, B. (2003). Effects of sport event media on destination image and intention to visit. *Journal of Sport Management, 17,* 214–234.

Chalip, L., & McGuirty, J. (2004). Bundling sport events with the host destination. *Journal of Sport Tourism, 9,* 267–282.

Chanlett-Avery, E., & Squassoni, S. (2006, October 24). North Korea's nuclear test: Motivations, implications, and U.S. options. *CRS Report for Congress*. Retrieved from http://www.fas.org/sgp/crs/nuke/RL33709.pdf

Cowell, A. (2002, November 23). Religious violence in Nigeria drives out Miss World event. *New York Times*. Retrieved from http://query.nytimes.com/gst/fullpage.html?res=9A06E3D81339F930A15752C1A9649C8B63

Crossland, D. (2006, July 10). From humourless to carefree in 30 days. *Der Spiegel*. Retrieved from http://www.spiegel.de/international/0,1518,426063,00.html

d'Astous, A., & Ahmed, S. A. (1992). Multi-cue evaluation of made-in concept: A conjoint analysis study in Belgium. *Journal of Euromarketing, 2*, 9–29.

d'Astous, A., & Ahmed, S. A. (1995). Comparison of country-of-origin effects on household and organizational buyers. *European Journal of Marketing, 29*(3), 35–52.

De Groote, P. (2005a). A multidisciplinary analysis of world fairs (expos) and their effects. *Tourism Review, 60*(10), 12–19.

De Groote, P. (2005b). Economic and tourism aspects of the Olympic Games. *Tourism Review, 60*(3), 20–28.

Douglas, M., & Isherwood, B. (1979). *The world of goods: Towards an anthropology of consumption*. New York, NY: Basic Books.

Drug War Chronicle. (2007, November 5). *Global marijuana marches take place in more than 200 cities worldwide*. Retrieved from http://stopthedrugwar.org/chronicle/2007/may/10/feature_global_marijuana_marches

Fayos-Sola, E. (1998). The impact of mega events. *Annals of Tourism Research, 25*(1), 241–245.

FDI Intelligence. (2008). *European cities and regions of the future*. Retrieved from http://www.fdimagazine.com/cp/10/FDI_052-055_0208-2.pdf

Florek, M., Breitbarth, T., & Conejo, F. (2008). Mega event = mega impact? Travelling fans' experience and perceptions of the 2006 FIFA World Cup host nation. *Journal of Sport & Tourism, 13*, 199–219.

Florek, M., & Conejo, F. (2007). Export flagships in branding small developing countries: The cases of Costa Rica and Moldova. *Place Branding and Public Diplomacy, 3*(1), 53–72.

Florek, M., & Zyminkowski, T. (2002). Transfer wizerunku regionu na wizerunki przedsiebiorstw. [Transfer of image on companies' images]. In L. Zabinski, & K. Sliwinska (Eds.), *Marketing: Koncepcje, badania, zarzadzanie* [Marketing: Conceptions, research, management], (pp. 358–363). Warsaw, Poland: Polskie Wydawnictwo Ekonomiczne.

Gartner, W. C. (1993). Image formation process. *Journal of Travel and Tourism Marketing, 213*, 191–215.

Geoghegan, T. (2006, December 4). Berlin gets into World Cup mode. *BBC News*. Retrieved from http://news.bbc.co.uk/1/ni/world/europe/4897642.stm

German National Tourist Board. (2008a). *Germany's image in 2008. "Destination Germany" held in high regard around the world*. [Press release]. Retrieved from http://www.germany-tourism.de/pdf/13_Image.pdf

German National Tourist Board. (2008b). Second phase of GNTB survey completed. World Cup boosts image of "Destination Germany." [Press release]. Retrieved from http://www.germany-tourism.de/pdf/PI_DZT_FIFA-D-Image_english.pdf

German Police. (2006). *Die Welt zu Gast bei Freunden*. Retrieved from http://www. bundespolizei.de/cln_029/nn_484498/DE/Home/Startseite/Sport/FIFA__WM__ 2006/__WM2006__anmod.html__nnn=true

Getz, D. (1989). Special events—defining the product. *Tourism Management, 10*(2), 125–137.

Getz, D. (1991). *Festivals, special events and tourism*. New York, NY: Van Nostrand Reinhold.

Getz, D. (1997). *Event management and event tourism*. New York, NY: Cognizant Communications.

Gnoth, J. (2002). Leveraging export brands through a tourism destination brand. *Journal of Brand Management, 9*, 262–289.

Gnoth, J., & Anwar, S. A. (2000, August). New Zealand bets on event tourism. *Cornell Hotel and Restaurant Administration Quarterly*, 72–83.

Gunn, C. A. (1972). *Vacationscape: Designing tourist regions* (2nd ed.). New York: Van Nostrand.

Han, C. M. (1989). Country image: Halo Or summary construct? *Journal of Marketing Research, 26*, 222–229.

Hong, S. T., & Wyer, R. S. Jr (1989). Effects of country-of-origin and product-attribute information on product evaluation: An information processing perspective. *Journal of Consumer Research, 16*, 175–187.

Hong, S. T., & Yi, Y. (1992). Cross-national comparison of country-of-origin effects on product evaluations. *Journal of International Consumer Marketing, 4*(4), 49–71.

Horne, J., & Manzenreiter, W. (2006). An introduction to the sociology of sports mega-events. *The Sociological Review, 54*(2), 1–24.

Jago, L. K. (2007). *Special events and tourism behaviour: A conceptualisation and an empirical analysis from a values perspective* (Unpublished doctoral dissertation). Department of Hospitality, Tourism and Marketing Faculty of Business, Victoria University.

Janda S., & Rao, C. P. (1997). The effect of country-of-origin related stereotypes and personal beliefs on product evaluation. *Psychology & Marketing, 14*, 689–702.

Jennings, A. (1996). *The new lords of the rings: Olympic corruption and how to buy gold medals*. London, England: Pocket Books.

Jennings, A. (2006). *Foul! The secret world of FIFA: Bribes, vote rigging and ticket scandals*. London, England: HarperSport.

Johansson, J. K. (1989). Determinants and effects of the use of "made-in" labels. *International Marketing Review, 6*, 27–41.

Jones, C. (2001). Mega-events and host-region impacts—determining the true worth of the 1999 Rugby World Cup. *International Journal of Tourism Research, 3*, 241–251.

Kaynak, E., & Cavusgil, S.T. (1983). Consumer attitudes towards products of foreign origin: Do they vary across product classes? *International Journal of Advertising, 2*, 147–157.

Kim, S., & Morrsion, A. M. (2005). Change of images of South Korea among foreign tourists after the 2002 FIFA World Cup. *Tourism Management, 26*, 233–247.

Klein, J. G., Ettenson, R., & Morris, M. D. (1998, January). The animosity of model of foreign product purchase: An empirical test in the People's Republic of China. *Journal of Marketing, 62*, 89–100.

Kotarski, K. (2006, July 8). World Cup has done much to dispel stereotypes of Germany. *Vancouver Sun.* Retrieved from http://www.canada.com/vancouversun/news/travel/story.html?id=0532ef4a-4ea7-4f4b-ab9a-8340f8c030bb&p=1

Kotler P., Haider D. H., & Rein, I. (1993). Marketing places—attracting investment, industry, and tourism to cities, states, and nations. New York, NY: The Free Press.

Lantz, G., & Loeb, S. (1996). Country of origin and ethnocentrism: An analysis of Canadian and American preferences using social identity theory. *Advances in Consumer Research, 23*, 374–378.

Lee, C., Lee, Y., & Lee, B. (2005). Korea's destination image formed by the 2002 World Cup. *Annals of Tourism Research, 32*, 839–858.

Li, W. K, & Wyer, R. S. (1994). The role of country of origin in product evaluations: Informational and standard of comparison effects. *Journal of Consumer Psychology, 3*, 187–212.

Land of Ideas. (2006). Official Web site. Retrieved from http://www.land-der-ideen.de/CDA/projekte,22,0„de.html

Marris, T. (1987). The role and impact of mega-events and attractions on regional and national tourism development. *Revue de Tourisme, 4*, 3–12.

Martyn, H. (1969). The influence of sports on international tourism. *Business and Society, 9*(2), 38–44.

Min, H. C. (1989). Country image: Halo or summary construct? *Journal of Marketing Research, 16*, 222–229.

Miss World. (2008). *Official Web site.* Retrieved from http://www.missworld.com/index.php?option=com_content&view=article&id=166&Itemid=111?=en

Mules, T. (1998). Events tourism and economic development in Australia. In D. Tyler, Y. Guerrier, & A. Robinson (Eds.), *Managing tourism in cities: Policy, processes and practice* (pp. 195–214). Chichester, England: Wiley.

Murphy, P., Pritchard, M. P., & Smith, B. (2000). The destination product and its impact on traveller perceptions. *Tourism Management, 21*, 43–52.

North Korean Nuclear Test. (n.d.). In *Wikipedia.* Retrieved July 4, 2008, from http://en.wikipedia.org/wiki/2006_North_Korean_nuclear_test

Nowosielski, M. (2008). German model nation branding: Implications for Poland. In J. Czaputowicz (Ed.), *Polityka zagraniczna Polski Unia Europejska—Stany Zjednoczone* [Foreign Policy of Poland: European Union, United States, Neighbok] (pp. 195–214). Poland: Warsaw, Wydawnictwo Polski Instytut Spraw Międzynarodowych.

Papadopoulos, N., & Heslop, L. (1993). Product–country images: Impact and role in international marketing. New York, NY: International Business Press.

Papadopoulos, N., & Heslop, L. (2002). Country equity and country branding: Problems and prospects. *Journal of Brand Management, 9*, 294–314.

Parameswaran, R., & Yaprak, A. (1987, Winter). Cross-national comparison of consumer research measures. *Journal of International Business Studies,* 35–49.

Pfanner, E. (2005, September 11). On advertising: Kicking off a new image in Germany. *International Herald Tribune*. Retrieved from http://www.iht.com/articles/2005/09/11/business/ad12.php

Purvis, A. (2006, June 12). Germany's new pitch. *Time International Asia*. Retrieved from http://find.galegroup.com/gtx/infomark.do?contentSet=IAC-Documents&type=retrieve&tabID=T003&prodID=A147481953&source=gale&srcprod=AONE&userGroupName=otag.&version=1.0

Ritchie, B. (1984). Assessing the impact of hallmark events. *Journal of Travel Research*, *23*(1), 2–11.

Roche, M. (2000). *Mega-events and modernity—Olympics and expos. The growth of global culture*. London, England: Routledge.

Roth, M. S., & Romeo, J. B. (1992). Matching product and country image perceptions: A framework for managing country-of-origin effects. *Journal of International Business Studies*, *23*, 477–497.

Segal, A., & Economy, E. C. (2008, July/August). China's Olympic nightmare. What the games mean for Beijing's future. *Foreign affairs*. Retrieved from http://www.foreignaffairs.org/20080701faessay87403-p30/elizabeth-c-economy-adam-segal/china-s-olympic-nightmare.html

Stockholm Business Region. (2008). Official Web site. Retrieved from http://www.stockholmbusinessregion.se/templates/indexpage____39345.aspx?epslanguage=EN

Skaggs, R., Falk, C., Almonte, J., & Cárdenas, M. (1996). Product–country images and international food marketing: Relationships and research needs. *Agribusiness*, *12*, 593–600.

Tellström, R., Gustafsson, I.-B., & Mossberg, L. (2006). Consuming heritage: The use of local food culture in branding. *Journal of Place Branding*, *2*(2), 130–143.

Tokarski, W., & Groll, M. (2006). Die FIFA Fußball—WM 2006 in Deutschland: Ohne Staat und Politik läuft nicht viel! *Wissenschaftsmagazin der Deutschen Sporthochschule Köln*, *1*, 2–6.

Verlegh, P. W. J., & Steenkamp, J.-B. E. M. (1999). A review and meta-analysis of country-of-origin research. *Journal of Economic Psychology*, *20*, 521–546.

Wall, M., Liefleld, J., & Heslop, L. A. (1991). Impact of country-of-origin cues on consumer judgments in multi-cue situations: A covariance analysis. *Journal of the Academy of Marketing Science*, *19*(2), 105–113.

Wang, C., & Lamb, C. Jr. (1983). The impact of selected environmental forces upon consumers' willingness to buy foreign products. *Journal of the Academy of Marketing Science*, *11*(2), 71–84.

Innovation and Creativity in Festival Organizations

MIA LARSON

Centre for Tourism, School of Business, Economics and Law, University of Gothenburg, Gothenburg, Sweden

This study contributes to understanding processes of innovation and creativity in festival organizations. The focus is on the internal work of renewing the festival. Three case studies of Swedish festival organizations demonstrate how festival workers attempt to renew the festival product. Processes of renewal include various ways of encouraging new ideas and creative solutions, such as brainstorming, imitation of similar products, and influences from the external environment. Two main processes of renewal were identified: institutionalized and emergent. The study further elaborated on the emergent process of renewal, thus identifying incremental and improvised renewal. Different factors contributing to or hindering innovations were distinguished; the demands of potential visitors, the management's view on renewal, the team's view on renewal, the organizational culture, and change of managers and staff.

INTRODUCTION

Many Swedish festivals are established, having been in existence for 10 to 30 years. They go through what is called a product life cycle—that is, introduction, growth, maturity, and finally decline and stagnation or new growth (Allen, O'Toole, McDonnell, & Harris, 2000). Organizing a festival that has already been held several times before involves a set of problems of another form than those of a festival that is being arranged for the first time. In the beginning it is often happy amateurs and enthusiasts for the festival's theme who play the primary roles. As the festival matures, a professionalization takes place in which specialized persons are engaged for marketing, finance, and composing the program. There occurs an institutionalization of the festival in which the festival's value and existence no longer need to be justified; it is accepted and regarded by the surrounding community as natural and in many cases indispensable (Edström, Beckérus, & Larsson, 2003). Once the festival is seen as an institution, its audience and stakeholders have clear notions about what the festival stands for, and this means that changing its direction becomes more difficult. Stability and continuity are maintained, then, at the cost of a lower inclination to change (Edström et al., 2003).

Consequently, how the recurring festival can be reinvented in order to get visitors to return and to attract new visitors is an important question. Forestalling a decline in attendance requires development and reinvention of the festival product, a process in which new and creative ideas are generated in the festival organization in parallel with adaptations to social trends (Larson, 2003). How this innovation take place is the focus of this article.

The primary questions are the following:

• How does innovation work take place in a festival organization?
• What factors contribute to and counteract innovation?

Material from three case studies of three festivals—the Great Lake Festival (*Storsjöyran*), the Malmö Festival (*Malmöfestivalen*), and the Göteborg Party (*Göteborgskalaset*) will be examined to shed light on these questions. The festivals are all annual city festivals that have existed for at least a decade.

PROJECTS AND INNOVATION

Unique and Repetitive Tasks

Lundin and Söderholm (1995) see unique and repetitive tasks as representing two fundamentally different types of tasks that involve specific conceptions of how and why actions in temporary organizations are performed. Table 1 displays how Lundin and Söderholm characterise unique and repetitive tasks.

When repetitive tasks are being performed the actors know what is to be done, why they are to be done, and who is to do them. The people in the work group have similar experiences, since they have performed similar tasks previously and will be repeating the tasks in the future. For this reason the work group shares a common interpretation of the situation (Lundin & Söderholm, 1995). Tasks in a recurring project tend to become increasingly

TABLE 1 Unique and Repetitive Tasks (Lundin & Söderholm, 1995, p. 441)

	Repetitive tasks	Unique tasks
Goal	Immediate, specified	Visionary, abstract
Experience	Own or codified by professions	Others' or none
Competence	In codes and tacit knowledge	Diverse or unknown, requires flexibility and creativity
Leadership/Owner of temporary org.	Low or middle managers	Top management
Development process	Reversible	Irreversible
Evaluation	Result oriented	Utility oriented
Learning	Refinement	Renewal

"scripted"[1] (or coded) and assume an increasingly automatic course, since situations are interpreted stereotypically by the work group to an increasing degree (cf., Gioia & Poole, 1984). The situation looks different in a recurring project in which the work group (or a single individual) has been replaced, because the task is new (unique) for the new work group (or individual).

When unique tasks are being performed no one has immediate knowledge of what is to be done. Unique tasks, therefore, require entrepreneurship of a more genuine type, because predetermined actions and behaviors are absent to a great extent. What are needed here are visionary, flexible, and creative actions along with a more deliberate search in the collected experiences of other areas (Lundin & Söderholm, 1995). Unique, or new, tasks are performed preferably without scripts (cf., Gioia & Poole, 1984). It is primarily through unique tasks that more radical innovation occurs, while the innovation that comes about through repetitive tasks consists of refining previously accomplished work processes or products.

The Innovation Paradox in Repetitive Projects

Lundin (1998) maintained that people who work in recurring projects on a routine basis, such as in construction and building, usually have a clear image of how the project can and should be run, based on extensive experience in the specific area. It might be expected that because the project is recurring, previous knowledge and experience will generate knowledge and learning over time. It has been found, however, that perceptions of projects are often stable across certain organizational fields and are simultaneously stable over time (Lundin, 1998; Kadefors, 1995). Lundin said that despite the fact that every new project begins with new stipulations, in which people have the possibility to exploit previous experiences of how a project can be managed, these possibilities for learning often are not utilized, and the method of working is largely repeated from project to project—even mistakes tend to be repeated (cf., Winch, 2000).

The innovation paradox (see e.g., Ekstedt, Lundin, & Wirdenius, 1992; Lundin, 1998; Ekstedt, Lundin, Söderholm, & Wirdenius, 1999) thus means that despite the fact that recurring projects would seem to have the potential for developing and reinventing work processes and by this means generating innovation of the product, this does not happen. Instead, the work becomes institutionalized (Kadefors, 1995) and people largely keep to the method that worked previously. Thus, in temporary organizations built up around a repetitive task, implementation without rethinking and readjustment is often inherent in the work culture: disruptions are simply not tolerated in the work group for economic reasons. The "stick to the plans" imperative becomes institutionalized in such settings. (Lundin & Söderholm, 1995, p. 448).

The innovation paradox can be observed in various industries where projects are perceived as some form of repetition (Lundin, 1998), such as in the events industry. If the project is conceived of as repetition, the way the project is run and what the project accomplishes will tend to have the character of repetition. Innovation, thus, has to do in large part with individuals' conceptions, ideas, and intentions (Ekstedt et al., 1992). According to the Eksteat et al. (1992), learning processes on the group level in recurring projects do not lead to innovation and development because the work processes tend to be institutionalized.

The theoretical point of departure in this section has dealt with unique and repetitive tasks. It is chiefly through unique tasks that innovation originates. This occurs through visionary, flexible and creative actions. Repetitive tasks instead result, in the best case, in the refinement of established products through institutionalized work processes. Studies have shown that recurring projects (where chiefly repetitive tasks are performed) often have difficulty transferring learning from project to project, and thus developing work processes that foster innovation. This is due to the work group's perceiving the project as a repetition of tasks performed previously. For this reason, new methods of working are not tested in the form, for instance, of creative improvisation.

The studied festivals presented in this article are recurring projects for their operationally responsible organizations. The innovation paradox, so-called, that has been previously discussed can be expected to be highly relevant. In the summer of 2004, the 11th Göteborg Party was held and the Malmö Festival celebrated its 20-year jubilee. The first Great Lake Festival was launched in 1983. The operational work in the Great Lake Festival is led and performed largely by the same people every year. Six of the seven driving spirits who started the festival in 1983 are still involved. People in both the Malmö Festival and the Göteborg Party have remained for quite a few years; on the other hand, a number of changes of directors have taken place. How the work of reinventing the festivals is done, and how the institutionalization process that may lead to the innovation paradox can be understood in the festivals, is discussed next.

THE CASE STUDIES

The Great Lake Festival

The Great Lake Festival is arranged by the Great Lake Partnership Company, which in turn is owned by the management company Dizzy Production AB. The company is a functions and production company whose activity is based mainly on producing the festival, but smaller events are produced as well at other times of year. Five people are employed full-time, while most people are employed on a project basis for about 2 to 4 months. The festival turned over 16 million Swedish kronor in 2002, of which some 75% came from ticket revenues and 25% from vendors and sponsors.

The Great Lake Festival is basically a music festival with a regional identity. In its first years, the performers were principally local and regional talents. Later on, as the festival grew larger, the organizers raised the level of ambition and increasingly contracted nationally and internationally known performers. From the festival's beginnings, the owners have had a high level of ambition that involves an endeavor to become northern Europe's best and most interesting folk festival. Every year about 50 artists perform on some nine stages. The festival evenings with performer programs go on from Thursday to Saturday and at that time admission is charged to the festival grounds. But the festival sets its mark on Östersund for 10 days, when the "restaurant row" is open and activities of all kinds are arranged. The number of paid visits to the festival has stood at about 50,000 to 59,000 since 1998. The festival week as a whole draws about 300,000 visits.

Despite the fact that many artists have performed at the Great Lake Festival several times, there is an ambition to reinvent the repertoire from year to year. The festival offers a wide variety of performers, everything from local talents to international superstars, from punk to pop ballads. There are a great many other activities as well, such as restaurants, a funfair, theatre, cultural installations, and sport competitions.

The Malmö Festival

The Malmö Festival is a nonprofit organization within the City of Malmö. The festival is organized by the Events Division, which is part of the City Environment Department of the Office of Streets. Thirteen people work with the festival. They work with other events during the year as well. The festival turned over about 18 million Swedish kronor in 2004. About 50% of festival costs are financed by the City of Malmö, while about 30% is obtained through sponsorships. The City of Malmö decides from year to year on the size of the budget the festival will have at its disposal.

The Malmö Festival began in 1984 and since then has been held in central Malmö in August every year. The festival is aimed chiefly at Malmö residents. It is meant to be accessible to everyone by being free, by reflecting multicultural Malmö, and by offering something for all ages and tastes. The key terms for the festival are *encounters, diversity,* and *experiences.* The festival's current director says that the objective is not to be the best or biggest festival in the world, but to be a festival for everyone in Malmö that can be produced for a reasonable sum of money.

The festival draws about 1.4 million visits in the course of 8 days. Measurements commissioned by the Malmö Festival show that about 75% of Malmö's residents attend the festival and 95% of them want to return the following year (www.malmofestivalen.se). In all, some 6,000 people take part in working with the festival. Its local support is strongly rooted and its principal contributions come from businesses and voluntary associations.

Music is one of the foremost reasons many people visit the Malmö Festival. From some 15 stages, more than 900 hours of free entertainment is offered. The stage programs include everything from opera to hip-hop and hard rock. In addition, cultural expressions, both narrow and broad, are everywhere at the festival in film, music, theatre, performance, poetry, literature, and much else. The Malmö Festival also offers a large selection of food from different parts of the world.

Staff members experience the festival's quality as becoming increasingly better in terms of both program and production. This is a result of the festival's having been allocated more resources in recent years. All of those interviewed believed that the festival would survive for many years to come.

The Göteborg Party

The Göteborg Party is a project conducted in Göteborg & Co., which in turn is commissioned by the Municipality of Göteborg. The budget work begins in January, and each year a decision has been taken by the municipality to pay the project grant. The Göteborg Party has two people employed full-time and about nine project staff members for approximately 6 months. The festival turns over about 20 million Swedish kronor, of which the municipality contributes half. The remaining portion is paid through rentals of vending sites (about 5 million) and through sponsors (about 5 million).

The festival's breakthrough came in connection with the 1995 Athletics World Championship, when it dominated the entire centre of Göteborg. Since then the festival has worked primarily with the same form. The basic idea is to create a party for Göteborg's residents and their guests. In the course of 9 days the Göteborg Party has about 1.5–1.9 million visits, which corresponds to about 500,000 visitors.

The festival goes on at 11 different sites with different emphases—everything from dance-band music to children's parties and cultural events. *Kungstorget* (King's Square) is the meeting place for adults, where there are a great many different restaurants and food shops as well as a stage with a comprehensive program. An abundance of activities is to be had at the festival, such as golf, Sweden's sauna championship match, a photography competition, a mini-car rally, a vintage auto exhibition, and demonstrations by cooks. Liseberg Amusement Park stays open for festival visitors and offers popular performers. The opening fireworks with music are a tradition.

The festival stirs feelings in Göteborg and has both opponents and admirers. Criticism of the lively street life in the evenings grew in the late 1990s, and for that reason there was an overhaul in 1999, with a new project director and a decision to concentrate more on activities for young people. Since 2000, the festival has developed to focus more on culture.

METHODOLOGY

The study was performed as a qualitative case study. The focus of this research method is on understanding the dynamics of a specific phenomenon (Eisenhardt, 1989). Gummesson (1988) differentiated between two types of case studies: drawing general conclusions from a limited number of cases or drawing specific conclusions from a single case. Merriam (1994) posited that sometimes it is only by considering a single event or a single case that we can gain a complete picture of the interaction among different factors or actors in a given situation. In this study, three cases were used to arrive at specific conclusions about how festival innovation is carried out.

Case studies are particularly suited to practical, workaday problems such as questions, situations, or difficulties that arise in connection with reinvention. Attention is directed at how groups of people manage problems of various types and make it possible to shed light on the problems from an overall perspective. One of the end products in a case study is description, meaning that the description of the studied phenomenon is dense and comprehensive (Merriam, 1994). The result is also to bring previously unknown (or unconscious) conditions and variables into focus, which may lead to a new perspective on that which is studied. In turn, this leads to the formulation of new concepts that clarify these conditions.

The case descriptions consist of descriptions of observations; direct quotations of various individuals on their experiences, attitudes, opinions, and thoughts; excerpts from the organizations' documentation; and second-hand information about the event, such as newspaper articles. These descriptions, quotations, and excerpts constitute raw data. The information plumbs the depths and yields detailed pictures.

The majority of the Great Lake Festival case study was carried out between March and July 1998, and thus primarily sheds light on the festival project that resulted in the Great Lake Festival held July 2–5, 1998. The historical retrospectives depicted stem from the informants' stories about the evolution of the festival as they interpreted it in 1998. Further observations were performed during the 1999 festival due to the contacts established with people in the Great Lake Festival office when a study of festival attendees was performed (see Faulkner, Fredline, Larson, & Tomljenovic, 1999; Tomljenovic, Larson, & Faulkner, 2001).

The Great Lake Festival office had five members of staff in January 1998, four of them full-time. In-depth personal interviews were conducted with these individuals. Also interviewed were a member of the board who had been involved in the Great Lake Festival since its inception and three individuals who worked with ticket management, press relations, and advertising. Additional interviews were held with the managing director in 1998 and 1999. In order to update the material, yet another interview was held with the managing director (the same person as in the previous interviews) in December 2004. Documentation for the festival was also collected and participatory observations were made at meetings and in the course of day-to-day work on about 10 occasions. There were also more informal talks with members of the Great Lake Festival staff.

Six interviews of four different individuals in the core work group were held at the Malmö Festival (including two with the managing director) in 2003 and 2004. One of the interviews was conducted by students (Tamara Bubalo and Anna Nilsson) at the Graduate Business School of the Göteborg University School of Business, Economics and Law. Four interviews were held at the Göteborg Party between 2003 and 2004, with the former festival director, the current festival director and two members of staff. One staff member was interviewed by students (Roosa Anttonen, Emmi Sarrivara, and Päivi Klemm).

The interviews lasted between 60 and 150 minutes. They were recorded on tape and transcribed. Documentation from newspapers and the Internet was collected during the period the case studies were performed.

The case studies of the Malmö Festival and the Göteborg Party were less extensive than the study of the Great Lake Festival. Fewer people were interviewed, which may have made the results less representative of the respective festival organizations than the results of the Great Lake Festival study. Here, the results are more oriented towards the views of festival directors on festival reinvention, as their interviews make up the bulk of the empirical material.

INNOVATION PROCESSES IN THE FESTIVAL ORGANIZATIONS

Innovation in Work Processes

The work group in the Great Lake Festival took a positive approach to changing and innovating the operational work. In connection with marketing the festival, for instance, a cooperative project with a festival in Norway was established with the aim of sharing information about marketing channels, such as press cultivation and ticket sales. Another clear instance of innovation in marketing was a novel idea for attracting journalists to the festival.

Comprehensive strategies in the festivals have changed as well. The Great Lake Festival previously had an ideology that involved the festival's not representing commercial interests. Therefore they had sponsors to the least possible degree. This ideology changed in about 1997, and they established relationships with some sponsors, such as Spendrups (a brewery). The Malmö Festival, too, has invested more in working with sponsors in recent years and is concentrating on bringing more money in via sponsors in the future. They have engaged an agent to help them in this work.

Balance Between Unique and Repetitive Tasks

Many of the people who work in the festival organizations have worked together for many years. The work with the festival changes over time, partly because any given person gradually gains more experience of the work, but also because the festival organization and its partners accumulate more knowledge and experience over the years. Similar problems arise from year to year, which involves successive learning. Many tasks eventually become repetitive and are consequently managed with increasingly strong scripts. This incremental refinement of work processes also leads to refinement of the various elements of the festival product.

> In terms of organization I go a lot by the year before. There's a lot of routine there, of course. As long as it's working well and you see that nothing's about to get out of hand so you'll have to change things. (Staff member, Great Lake Festival)

When the work with the basic components of the festival, such as ticket management and toilets, is routinized, operational efficiency is generated in the work. Routinization involves the work's being institutionalized. But at the same time there was an ambition in the Great Lake Festival to reinvent the festival every year, which broke up the routine repetitive tasks to some extent.

> We work hard at finding innovation. It's not easy, it's extremely hard. Partly, the performers are switched each year. But the thing we've got to be able to say to ourselves every year is that we've found something new, that we have reinvented ourselves. Then the infrastructure itself, that's the way it is, we've got the stage in the square, and it's standing there and the toilets are standing there, that's the same, of course. It's

what's actually on offer that has to be reinvented. (Staff member, Great Lake Festival)

Because the staff were working consciously with developing the festival, it was not possible to routinize the work entirely. They let go of previous methods of working and embarked on new areas of which they had no experience. Consequently, some of the repetitive tasks were abandoned in favor of unique tasks. A conscious effort to reinvent the various subproducts of the festival thus meant that the work processes were being reinvented at the same time.

One instance of such reinvention is the entry of the President of Jämtland into Stortorget (the main square) to give his speech. This happens every year in a different way—some of the more spectacular entrances have been on an elephant and in a zeppelin. The project work group is thus forced to be very creative at finding new solutions every year. The festival-goers have high expectations of a spectacular entrance, and when this succeeds the festival has the chance not only to satisfy its public but also to receive a lot of media attention.

With every year, however, the staff experienced that it was becoming more difficult to find unique solutions and develop novel ideas. Back in 1998 the managing director expressed the difficulty with reinvention.

> We improvised more before. A few years ago there were more big revolutionary decisions that we took under tight time constraints. Now these decisions are on a lower level and deal with less important things. The risk of course is that we get stuck in the same rut. (Managing director, Great Lake Festival)

In 2003 and 2004, the Great Lake Festival work group did not work much with innovation because they had so many other tasks over and above the festival.

> During the past 2 years we have had a snag in that we've had a lot of external commissions. In that case, it's easy to do what we did last year. We've gone on like that for a couple of years. On the other hand, maybe it's not all bad if it lies fallow, since later, when you want to begin, it's really fun. But you can't have such stagnation that the market notices it. (Managing director, Great Lake Festival)

Organizational Culture

Many of the people who were working in the Great Lake Festival in 1998 had taken part previously. The driving spirits who started the festival were still involved with it in some way, although (except for the managing director) they only had positions on the board of directors without attendant operational duties. The work group was permeated by a shared identity and a shared commitment that were based on a genuine interest in music and a feeling for the region of the country where the festival is held. These people's expectations about the work were therefore relatively similar and most had a good general sense of each other's tasks.

The individuals had thus been working together for a relatively long time and had evolved shared norms for the project work (cf., Lundin & Söderholm, 1995). An organizational culture had been developed that provided conditions for collective action. Organizational culture is an established concept in business economics and management, but it is viewed in various ways depending on whether it is seen as a metaphor or an objective phenomenon. Schein (1985), who was one of the first to use the concept, defined it as:

> A pattern of basic assumptions—invented, discovered, or developed by a given group as it learns to cope with its problems of external adaption and internal integration—that has worked well enough to be considered valid and, therefore, to be taught to new members as the correct way to perceive, think, and feel in relation to those problems.

The shared expectations and experiences in the festival organizations created the basis for shared commitment (cf., Lundin & Söderholm, 1995; Wikström, 2000). At the same time, there was room in the work group to express differing views. These differing views gave rise to a dynamic in the work group with a great deal of discussion, which in turn fostered fresh ideas.

> The members of the staff have more or less the same outlook on how the work should be carried out. . . . But we don't have it exactly, and that's a huge advantage. That's what the danger is, if everyone has exactly the same outlook and the same intentions. If so, then there's often going to be this taboo pronouncement, "We'll do it like last year." So that's not good, of course. No, but most often we'll sit and discuss things, sometimes quite loudly. Nobody needs to feel ashamed of having an opinion and nobody thinks "I'm scared to say things". (Staff member, Great Lake Festival)

The work group had continual meetings in which a great deal of time was taken to develop and reinvent the festival by together trying to generate innovations. This took place through shared brainstorming.

> It can take lots of meetings without us coming upon anything. We just sit and brainstorm, but in the end maybe you produce one thing. (Staff member, Great Lake Festival)

Staff members in the Malmö Festival's work group also experience there being an open atmosphere for ideas, with a lot of new thinking taking place. The director works on getting the staff to think in new pathways.

> You question. And you come out with other suggestions. You turn questions over. Shall we do what we did last year? Why, you ask. I see it as no more complicated than that. (Managing director, Malmö Festival)

Changes in the Work Group

CHANGE OF DIRECTOR

The managing director of the Great Lake Festival has worked with the festival since its start, one of seven friends who got the festival going. In 1997 he took over the post of director from one of these friends. There have not been many changes of director in the Great Lake Festival during the organization's history.

The Malmö Festival, on the other hand, has had many directors in recent years. The present director came in as the third director in 2003 alone. The directorship situation generated uncertainty in the organization in regard to the direction it was working towards. Staff experienced 2004 as an off year, where the new managing director was feeling out how he wanted to develop the festival. He has already had an effect on the festival, however, through a strong focus on music. The Malmö Festival's goals are experienced as changing with its director.

> Kina was more of a marketing person and Per is more of a music person. She didn't have that much experience working with performers, so Per is putting a lot of time and energy into us bringing performers in properly. While Kina worked more towards sponsors, more externally directed. (Staff member, Malmö Festival)

The director of the Malmö Festival has also implemented organizational changes. One staff member pointed to five areas that have been changed in terms of organization: more structured organization, clearer division of labor, more documentation and formality, shorter meetings, and more openness. He was also perceived as bringing in more professionalization of the festival work, such as in the area of security.

The Göteborg Party's most recent director took charge in April 2004. She had been working as the festival's program coordinator for the previous

3 years. Unlike the director before her, she had a background in culture and music.

CHANGE OF STAFF MEMBERS

When new individuals come into the work group, the rules of the game change as new expectations and experiences enter. The expectations and ability of individuals are related to their previous knowledge and experience (Lundin & Söderholm, 1995). Thus, when new people enter a work group, new solutions to problems often appear, which in turn may yield innovation. An instance of one such piece of business in the Great Lake Festival had to do with representatives from the festival going round every year knocking on the doors of the people who lived near the festival grounds to resolve any problems the festival might cause its neighbors. Previously, it had been the festival's owners who did this. The younger co-workers took over the task.

> So now they're resolving the problems in their way. And this is our way of seeing to it that rejuvenation of the festival happens. (Owner, Great Lake Festival)

The core work group of the Great Lake Festival has been composed in recent years of five people. Three of them have been in this work group for many years, while the other two have worked with the festival previously, though less intensively. The Göteborg Party employs two people full-time to work with the festival. For about half a year an additional nine people are employed on a project basis. The Malmö Festival has a similar structure, which consists of a small work group employed full-time. A number of project staff members and consultants are engaged. The staff turnover in the festival work groups is low. The majority of people stay for many years. Because the work is seasonal, however, a small number of project workers do change.

The owners of the Great Lake Festival have previously discussed the importance of letting younger people take part in the more comprehensive strategy discussions. Of the festival's visitors, 16% were younger than 31 (Tomljenovic, Larson, & Faulkner, 2001). It was particularly important, therefore, to be able to read the preferences of this group.

ANALYSIS

Proactive and Reactive Festival Innovation

The challenge for all three of the studied festivals has to do with designing the festival product to suit a broad target group. The Malmö Festival and the

Göteborg Party in particular have this goal, which can be explained by the fact that they are financed by municipal funds which all taxpayers ultimately pay. A condition for achieving the festivals' goal of reaching everyone is to reinvent the festival.

Since all of the festivals are established and have existed for a long time, there is already a well-established program structure with places for activities. Many new ideas have already been tested and implemented or discarded. For this reason, there are few radical changes of, but more incremental adjustments to, the festival. Even innovation in work processes occurs relatively slowly and in small increments. Innovation work in the Malmö Festival and the Göteborg Party appears to occur relatively reactively, that is, as a response to a reaction or event coming from outside, such as adapting the program in response to a negative evaluation in a market research study or developing the security work in response to accidents at other festivals. This can be seen as a way to handle changeable and complex surroundings, that is, reducing contextual uncertainty (Christensen & Kreiner, 1997). Innovation work thus has to do with the ability to perceive tendencies in the market that has a demand for the event product, and adapting the product accordingly.

The Great Lake Festival instead has a more proactive approach to innovation in which the work of reinvention is constantly present in the work of the festival. Their ambition is to "be ahead of the market." Instead of merely adapting the event to its environment, the Great Lake Festival has the goal of reconstructing the market by achieving creative, innovative products. Thus, contextual uncertainty can be reduced both through feeling and responding to the demands of the environment and through generating an innovative and creative event product whose components and constellation are innovative, in this way giving rise to changes in the surrounding world.

Figure 1 shows how (a) individuals in the event organization perceive market trends, that is, changes in market demand, and design the festival accordingly. At the same time, the people in the event organization generate a market through creative innovation work; that is, they create experiences

FIGURE 1 Proactive and reactive innovation work in festivals. Adapted from Larson (2003).

for visitors and cooperating partners that they have previously been unable to imagine and have therefore not demanded.

It is important, however, to discuss whether it is relevant for all festivals to work with reinventing their product. Many festivals live on traditions that the festival-goers expect to be repeated year after year, like the October Festival. None of the studied festivals has had a permanent reduction in number of visitors, despite the fact that some years the festivals have been largely the same as they were in previous years. The Great Lake Festival has more to lose in the short term, however, if a misjudgement of the market causes them not to reinvent themselves, since they are dependent on ticket revenues. The Göteborg Party and the Malmö Festival do not encounter this immediate effect, since both are financed by municipal funds. In the long term, however, the festivals lose their legitimacy if fewer visitors come.

In contrast to innovation in the festival product, innovation in work processes can be seen as necessary for improving or maintaining the organization's internal efficacy. Increased specialization and professionalization can be discerned in all of the studied festivals.

Planned and Emergent Innovation Work

INSTITUTIONALIZED INNOVATION PROCESSES

The innovation work of the festivals is largely intentional, that is, consciously planned. The staff's conceptions of the project work, above all in the Great Lake Festival, are composed of a strong awareness of trying constantly to reinvent the product. The work is formulated in the work group's shared development of novel ideas around the festival, which occurs largely in the form of brainstorming at formal and informal meetings. The new ideas are discussed in the work group and a concrete but relatively unspecified and informal plan of action is developed for the new tasks. After this it is up to the separate individuals (and in the final stage—the small work groups) to implement the tasks.

Some of the tasks are implemented with little change in work process relative to previous years. In that case, innovation in the festival product occurs as a result of repetitive tasks, that is, a form of institutionalized innovation. The work of engaging performers and renting vending sites every year can be seen as a form of planned and institutionalized innovation that plays out in a similar way from year to year. This is due to the high degree of professionalism in the work group in connection with performing these tasks, where many years of experience in the industry helps reduce operational and contextual uncertainty, for example the uncertainty for the individuals or work group in operationally implementing the project task, and the inherent uncertainty of the environment (Christensen & Kreiner, 1997). The work of reinventing the performer line-up and vending sites may thus be seen as a repetitive task performed in an institutionalized process.

EMERGENT INNOVATION PROCESSES

Other tasks in the innovation work are carried out to a greater degree through an emergent process. Innovation occurs in situations when the work group (or the individual) reacts to changed circumstances, such as a perceived change in audience demand or an immediate potential problem, through ad hoc decisions. The emergent innovation work is done not only reactively but also proactively, when people try to implement novel ideas with which they lack previous experience. Solutions to problems emerge here as a result of the work group (or the individual) learning more about the task.

The staffs of the festivals often proceed from a roughly defined conception of the tasks to be performed. Implementation goes through a process in which—as people learn new things, run into unexpected barriers or get new ideas about how the task should be performed—the original idea is reformulated and refined. Design and implementation of the tasks thus overlap. The following quotation illustrates the emergent work:

> Then the entire time, of course, a certain degree of planning comes along with it. It goes all the way from when you start thinking about the Great Lake Festival all the way until you're done. Even on the final days you're making preparations for certain things. And when changes come, it can be, well, wham. There's a basic plan of course, and then there are changes in planning and then there's a sort of precision planning and then there's the doing of it. (Staff member, Great Lake Festival)

The emergent work thus involves realizing the novel ideas that emerge in the work group. The tasks can be characterized as genuinely unique in the cases where people do not have experience of similar tasks. Tasks that have not been performed before include a degree of uncertainty, which means that the implementation of some of them does not succeed. Sometimes the new task is postponed until a future festival.

> For instance, the water display in Magistrate's Park which we really want to do and the idea exists, all the contacts exist, but there's no money for it. And then we had the Water Works, which was prepared to go in and pay for it, and then later they backed out, and so then we had to shut the whole thing down again, it was fairly late in the spring. (Staff member, Malmö Festival)

The emergent work emphasizes learning in situations with uncertainty or complexity. The learning in one project (one year's festival) is transferred to later projects (festivals in subsequent years).

I experience that I'm learning new things all the time, how this works. So that there are lots of question marks and you're thinking "How's this one, and this one?" But every day when you run into a problem you're forced to find a solution and then you're learning something new. I think it's all the time. (Staff member, Great Lake Festival)

The previous discussion has shown that different tasks in the innovation work of the festivals have different elements of emergent design. The project design has varying degrees of mix between planned action and instinctive reaction (cf., Rehn & Wikström, 1999). Some of the innovation work is relatively planned, but it is often emergent to a high degree. The incremental and the improvised are different forms of emergent design.

INCREMENTAL PROCESSES AND IMPROVISATION

Important features of the emergent innovation work are that it is performed under time pressure and in a turbulent environment. In this context, changes are often made in small steps that respond to emerging possibilities (Fulop & Linstead, 1999). These processes are fragmented, development-oriented, and largely intuitive (Quinn, 1978). Lindblom (1959) speaks of incremental processes as "muddling through" despite the lack of formal organization. Seen from a long-term perspective, the innovation work in the festivals can be understood as largely incremental with elements of occasional major leaps (in which radical reinvention occurs, such as the Great Lake Festival's ideological shift in the 1990s which involved initiating cooperation with sponsors, or the Göteborg Party's overhaul of the festival in 1999 when greater concentration on young people came about). Incremental processes, however, provide room for innovation in the form of refinement above all (Quinn, 1985). More radical reinvention does not occur in these processes. Moreover, changes tend to take place over time without predetermined time frames.

But from a more short-term perspective, it is more fruitful to talk about improvisation than incremental change as a means of understanding innovation work in festival organizations. This is due to the fact that the time factor is more focused in connection with improvisation. The time that the festivals had at their disposal was often perceived as very limited. The work became progressively more intense over the course of the project (cf., Packendorff, 1993). When there is next to no time for consideration, reflection and planning, the people improvise.

Organizational improvisation leads one to think about the metaphor of jazz (see e.g., *Organization Science*, 1998; Rehn & Wikström, 1999; Hatch, 1999). In jazz performances, order and control are suddenly broken and a new order created (Weick, 1998). The musicians are working with creative processes at the same time that a steady tempo is maintained. The reaction to different actions must be immediate, and the consequences are irrevocable. Improvisation handles the unforeseen and embraces action in the present without predetermined stipulations. Accordingly, improvisation is without planning—something is created in the heat of the moment (Weick, 1998). However, the practitioners (the musicians) must learn to conjure up short- and medium-term goals at the same time the music is being played (Berliner, 1994).

Improvisation thus brings about an outcome that is unique to each creation (such as a piece of music or a festival), because processes in the improvisation give rise to new creative ideas that transform previous knowledge, creating new from the old. Weick (1998) shows clearly that spontaneity and intuition are important dimensions of improvisation. On the other hand, the improvisers are relying on their knowledge, previous experience and discipline (Berliner, 1994), something that distinguishes good improvisation from bad. Thus, good improvisation is produced by people with previous experience and with knowledge on the subject in question (cf., Moorman & Miner, 1998; Crossan, White, Lane, & Klus, 1996).

Brown and Eisenhardt (1995) maintained that product work groups with product-design processes that are more experimental and improvisational develop products more rapidly. Improvisation is thus a means to manage limited time, but also a means to manage a turbulent environment.

> You have to zig-zag your way forward, between A and B, but in this, you've got room to improvise. (Staff member, Great Lake Festival)

Like jazz improvisation, innovation work takes place with narrow time frames and contextual uncertainty. The innovation and reinvention arise not just as a reaction to a change in the surrounding world but are also consciously evoked, for instance through planned brainstorming. To generate innovation, people try to think in new pathways and break up those scripts that the individuals have created. This can happen through improvisation by creative individuals with good experience and knowledge of the task.

Improvisation in connection with totally unknown situations (cf., Weick, 1993) or improvisation that is performed by inexperienced individuals, however, can be regarded as risky. Since there is nothing to relate the performance of the actions to, it is more likely that the improvisation will fail. Experiences of failure, on the other hand, are used to learn for later festivals. Activities that cannot be carried out, or fail in some other way, are sometimes adjusted and tried again at the next festival.

Improvisation can be seen as a means to manage contextual uncertainty and limited time, but also as a work form that consciously generates innovation. A work environment like the one in the Great Lake Festival's work group, which encourages and allows creative, improvisational work processes, can lead to generating creative products. All improvisation needs a positive atmosphere and an organizational culture that does not punish mistakes or criticize unnecessarily (Crossan et al., 1996). The work group in the Great Lake Festival is prepared in the highest degree to work consciously with innovation and not stagnate. The staff have a great deal of scope for action, even at a late stage, when it comes to innovating, refining or hitting upon and carrying out completely new activities.

The emergent innovation work on the festivals can thus be characterized as more or less improvised. Through improvisation the work group manages time pressure and a turbulent environment in which unforeseen events occur. The improvised processes also give individuals and work groups scope to unleash their creativity and test novel ideas and methods of working, which may lead in the long run to reinvention of the festival.

Factors that Foster and Counteract Innovation

The previous discussion described how creative processes come about in the studied festivals. Next are various factors that could be seen in the study to foster or counteract innovation.

An exacting market that demands innovation causes the festival to have greater incentive to reinvent itself. The festivals conduct market research studies in which they evaluate how their audience experiences the festival, which provides information for development.

The commissioning agent's approach to innovation has an effect on innovation. To be able to implement major changes, the work groups in the Göteborg Party are dependent on decisions by Göteborg & Co.'s board of directors. This is sometimes experienced as taking a long time. The decision-making paths for the Great Lake Festival, which is a private company, are not as long.

The festival workers' approach to innovation has an effect on what form of innovation occurs. The Great Lake Festival's work group saw reinvention as a natural part of its work and as an important competitive strategy. The Malmö Festival and the Göteborg Party also saw the importance of reinventing themselves, but emphasized that it was more a matter of cautious innovation in which tradition was maintained.

An organizational culture that fosters innovation could be seen in the Great Lake Festival. The managing director encouraged novel ideas, and in the entire evaluation process a place was provided for brainstorming and discussing new suggestions. This could be seen in the Malmö Festival and the Göteborg Party as well, though not to the same extent. The new director of the Malmö Festival, however, expressed the intention to change the attitude towards innovation by getting the staff to reflect more.

Recurring festivals are developed to survive in the long term. Product development has a tendency to become increasingly organized, since the people and organizations involved tend to adopt an increasingly shared perspective through their relatively long-term relationships. When the relationships last too long, however, they may bring about stagnation and a lack of flexibility and innovation (Nooteboom, 2001). Accordingly, balancing long-term stability with changes that lead to reinvention is a challenge for the festival organization. Replacing the festival director and people in the work group may be changes of this kind.

Changing the director can constitute a step in a new direction for the festival, as the examples of the Malmö Festival and also to some degree the Göteborg Party show. Every person brings their own experiences, interests, and competencies. In the case of the Malmö Festival, the new director brought a greater focus on the festival's musical selection, while the Göteborg Party's new director contributed a focus on culture.

Innovation can also happen through changes in staff. New staff members can contribute new ideas and knowledge as well as directors can. At one juncture, the owners of the Great Lake Festival had even thought about selling the festival to younger talents. Staff turnover in the inner work group has been low in all of the studied festivals. On the other hand, new people come in as project staff members or consultants.

CONCLUSIONS

Projects, as a work form, involve some form of innovation. The studied recurring festivals constitute examples of projects in which innovation occurs. In the Great Lake Festival innovation formed a natural part of the work in 1998. Every year the work group of the Great Lake Festival endeavored to find new ways to develop and reinvent the festival, such as new activities and new ways to decorate the festival grounds. Creativity and improvisation were important processes in the project work for the purpose of achieving innovation. A festival's innovative powers may change over time, however, due to a change in internal or external circumstances (cf., Salavou, 2004). A development of this kind could be seen in the Great Lake Festival in 2003 and 2004, when some degree of stagnation occurred. The other two studied festivals, the Göteborg Party and the Malmö Festival, saw reinvention as less important. Innovation work here has more to do with fine-tuning and slow development with preservation of traditions.

Innovation work can be described like the music-making in a jazz group. Through the fact that most of the people in the festivals' work groups had been working with their particular festival for many years, there was a great deal of experience and knowledge of the work, just as jazz musicians have many years' knowledge of music. Part of the innovation work is institutionalized and is performed in a similar way from year to year, and consequently is planned. Even as a jazz tune has a basic beat that is repeated, a festival consists of components that are refined and repeated every year. As in a jazz group, everyone knows what is to be done, and this routine work is done individually and at a steady tempo. At the same time, a creative process breaks the routine, creating interesting and unusual components. In order to manage uncertainty, such as turbulence in the environment and time pressure, improvisation occurs. Improvisation therefore may occur proactively, for the purpose of developing new ideas. The project work can thus be seen like jamming in a jazz group; that is, a fundamental "bass beat" is blended with each member's scope to improvise and "do their thing." At the same time, openness exists for external actors, or new group members, to enter in and contribute for a longer or shorter period of time. In this way the festival is reinvented.

Innovation work in festivals can be characterized as ad hoc, emergent, and more or less improvised, something that facilitates and fosters innovation. This type of organizing, according to Dimmock and Tyce (2001), is assigned to the initial phases of a festival's evolution into a professional organization (cf., Getz & Frisby, 1988; Frisby & Getz, 1989). The study suggests that this type of organizing constitutes important characteristic features in the professional organizing of a festival in all its phases.

According to previous research on repetitive projects, it appears to be simpler to do the same thing from project to project instead of rethinking matters and doing new things (cf., the discussion on the innovation paradox). March (1995) discussed a similar idea in the concept of the "success trap." March said that when an organization succeeds, it repeats the actions that were experienced as having brought about the success whereas other good ideas or technologies are not tried. The success trap leads to the organization's not experimenting enough.

This can lead to internal efficiency in the work (cf., Kadefors, 1995), but there is also a risk that the routine work stifles the creativity and the new thinking (cf., Westley & Mintzberg, 1989) required to reinvent the festival product for the purpose of increasing the festival's attractiveness over time. The study of the festivals describes innovation in recurring projects. Tasks in the recurring projects have features both of standardization and of a unique and innovative character. It is possible to discern adaptation to the surroundings in the form both of the exploitation of existing ideas and knowledge through refinement and routinization (especially in the Malmö Festival and the Göteborg Party) and of the experimentation with novel ideas for the purpose of finding alternatives to the old ones (especially in the Great Lake Festival; see March, 1995, discussion of exploitation and exploration). Actions and behaviors are not as highly institutionalized as studies of building projects, for instance, have shown. Learning is transferred from project to project and people work more or less actively with innovation. The results of this study thus show that the innovation paradox does not square fully with this type of recurring project. The Malmö Festival and the Göteborg Party appear closest to being able to be described with the help of the innovation paradox, since staff members were more skeptical towards innovation. In recurring projects like festivals, then, innovation occurs in the form of creative, emergent and improvised processes, which in turn bring about reinvention of the festival product.

The innovation work of the festivals can be seen as an important strategic issue since they can be assumed to have a product life cycle, which means that they can be expected to be less popular in the future. Accordingly, staying up-to-date with market development and constantly innovating are an important survival strategy. Maintaining the entrepreneurial spirit (cf., Hjorth & Johannisson, 1997) expressed as creativity, spontaneity and commitment, which often characterize the work in a project that is being performed for the first time (or one of the first times), while the work group also maintains a strong conception of the importance of innovation, creates the conditions to counteract institutionalization processes and thus stagnation of the festival. Through improvised innovation processes people also have the possibility to respond to market changes that occur within a very narrow time frame. The project work group in the Great Lake Festival tries to avoid getting caught in situations that are too stereotypical by finding new roads to the reinvention of product and process. Traditional means of planning and evaluating project work are not aimed at. As a consequence, emphasis is not on organization and control; instead, creativity, spontaneity, and action through intuition are encouraged, that is, action-oriented improvisation that focuses on new possibilities, ideas, and innovations.

NOTE

1. A script is a scheme that is held in memory and describes events or behaviors (or sequences of events or behaviors) appropriate to a particular context (Gioia & Poole, 1984).

REFERENCES

Allen, J., O'Toole, W., McDonnell, I., & Harris, R. (2002). *Festival and special event management* (2nd. ed.). Milton, Australia: John Wiley & Sons Australia.

Berliner, P. F. (1994). *Thinking in jazz: The infinite art of improvisation*. Chicago, IL: University of Chicago Press.

Brown, S. L., & Eisenhardt, K. M. (1995). Product development: Past research, present findings, and future directions. *Academy of Management Review, 20*, 343–378.

Christensen, S., & Kreiner, K. (1997). *Projektledning—att leda och lära i en ofullkomlig värld* [Project management—to lead and learn in an imperfect world]. Lund, Sweden: Academia Acta.

Crossan, M. M., White, R. E., Lane, H. W., & Klus, L. (1996, Spring). The improvising organization: Where planning meets opportunity. *Organizational Dynamics,* 20–35.

Dimmock, K., & Tiyce, M. (2001). Festivals and events: Celebrating special interest tourism. In N. Douglas & R. Derret (Eds.), *Special interest tourism: Context and cases* (pp. 355–383). Brisbane, Australia: John Wiley & Sons Australia.

Edström, A., Beckérus, Å., & Larsson, B.-E. (2003). *Evenemangsföretagande* [Managing events]. Lund, Sweden: Studentlitteratur.

Eisenhardt, K. M. (1989). Building theories from case study research. *Academy of Management Review, 14*(4), 532–550.

Ekstedt, E., Lundin, R. A., Söderholm, A., & Wirdenius, H. (1999). *Neo-industrial organising, renewal by action and knowledge formation in a project-intensive economy.* London, England: Routledge.

Ekstedt, E., Lundin, R. A., & Wirdenius, H. (1992). Conceptions and renewal in Swedish construction companies. *European Management Journal, 10,* 202–209.

Faulkner, B., Fredline, E., Larson, M., & Tomljenovic, R. (1999) A marketing analysis of Sweden's Storsjöyran Festival. *Tourism Analysis, 4,* 157–171.

Frisby, W., & Getz, D. (1989, Summer). Festival management: A case study perspective. *Journal of Travel Research,* 7–11.

Fulop, L., & Linstead, S. (1999). *Management: A critical text.* London, England: MacMillan Press.

Getz, D., & Frisby, W. (1988, Summer). Evaluating management effectiveness in community-run festivals. *Journal of Travel Research,* 22–27.

Gioia, D. A., & Poole, P. P. (1984). Scripts in organizational behavior. *Academy of Management Review, 9,* 449–459.

Gummesson, E. (1988). *Qualitative methods in management research.* Lund, Sweden: Studentlitteratur.

Hatch, M. J. (1999). Exploring the empty spaces of organizing: How improvisational jazz helps redescribe organizational structure. *Organization Studies, 20*(1), 75–100.

Hjorth, D., & Johannisson, B. (1997). Entreprenörskap som skapelseprocess och ideologi [Entrepreneurship as a process of creation and ideology] (Working Paper No. 1997:2). Available from SIRE (Scandinavian Institute for Research in Entrepreneurship).

Kadefors, A. (1995). Institutions in building projects: Implications for flexibility and change. *Scandinavian Journal of Management, 11,* 395–408.

Larson, M. (2003). *Evenemangsmarknadsföringens organisering: Interaktion mellan aktörer på ett politiskt torg* [Organizing the marketing of events: Interaction between actors in a political market square]. Östersund: ETOUR Scientific.

Lindblom, C. E. (1959). The science of "muddling through." *Public Administration Review, 19,* 78–88.

Lundin, R. A. (1998). Temporära organisationer—några perspektivbyten [Temporary organizations—Some shifts of perspective]. In B. Czarniawska (Ed.), *Organisationsteori på svenska* [Organization theory] (pp. 194–214). Malmö, Sweden: Liber Ekonomi.

Lundin, R. A., & Söderholm, A. (1995). A theory of the temporary organization. *Scandinavian Journal of Management, 11,* 437–455.

March, J. G. (1995). The future, disposable organizations and the rigidities of imagination. *Organization, 2,* 427–440.

Merriam, S. B. (1994). *Fallstudien som forskningsmetod* [The case study as a research method]. Lund, Sweden: Studentlitteratur.

Moorman, C., & Miner, A. S. (1998, July). The convergence of planning and execution: Improvisation in new product development. *Journal of Marketing, 62,* 1–20.

Nooteboom, B. (2001, July). Business networks. Presented at EGOS Colloquium 2001 Lyon, Subgroup Evolutionary Perspectives. Lyon, France.

Organization Science (1998). 9(5).

Packendorff, J. (1995). Inquiring into the temporary organization: New directions for project management research. *Scandinavian Journal of Management, 11,* 319–333.

Quinn, J. B. (1985, May/June). Managing innovation: Controlled chaos. *Harvard Business Review,* 73–84.

Rehn, A., & Wikström, K. (1999). *Kind of grey—playing the live jazz of project management* (Working Paper No. 1). Turku, Finland: Research Group for Project-Based Industry, Åbo Akademi University.

Salavou, H. (2004). The concept of innovativeness: Should we need to focus? *European Journal of Innovation Management,* 7(1), 33–44.

Schein, E. H. (1985). *Organizational culture and leadership.* San Francisco, CA: Jossey Bass.

Tomljenovic, R., Larson, M., & Faulkner, B. (2001). Predictors of satisfaction with festival attendance: A case of Storsjöyran Music Festival. *Tourism, 49,* 123–132.

Weick, K. E. (1993). The collapse of sensemaking in organizations: The Mann Gulch disaster. *Administrative Science Quarterly, 38,* 628–652.

Weick, K. E. (1998). Improvisation as a mindset for organizational analysis. *Organization Science, 9,* 543–555.

Westley, F., & Mintzberg, H. (1989). Visionary leadership and strategic management. *Strategic Management Journal, 10,* 17–32.

Wikström, E. (2000). *Projekt och produktiv kommunikation—en studie om sammanhållande dynamik* [Projects and productive communication—A study on cohesive dynamics]. Göteborg, Sweden: Bokförlaget BAS.

Winch, G. M. (2000). The management of projects as a generic business process. In R. A. Lundin & F. Hartman (Eds.), *Projects as business constituents and guiding motives* (pp. 194–214). Norwell, MA: Kluwer Academic Publishers.

Multiple Stakeholder Perspectives on Cultural Events: Auckland's Pasifika Festival

TINA BUCH, SIMON MILNE, and GEOFF DICKSON

New Zealand Tourism Research Institute, Auckland University of Technology, Auckland, New Zealand

Cultural festivals can assist local communities in showcasing cultural attributes and can offer the chance to strengthen a sense of identity. The Pasifika Festival, held annually in Auckland, New Zealand, is a celebration of the city's Pacific Island communities. Drawing on audience and stallholder surveys, and interviews/meetings with festival organizers, this article provides a multiple stakeholder perspective on the festival experience and what it means to those who are part of it. The article also addresses the important question of how to conduct robust, cost-effective research in large festival settings, focusing on the use of online survey tools.

INTRODUCTION

The staging of festivals is not a new phenomenon. Traditionally, across all cultures there have always been reasons to celebrate, socialize, honor, and remember (Douglas, Douglas, & Derrett, 2001). Organized by and for local communities to celebrate cultural identity and/or leisure activities, there was little to link festivals to tourism (Getz, 1989). However, with the growing economic significance of tourism, researchers and policymakers are placing increased emphasis on local festivals because of their perceived contribution towards the "destination marketing mix" (McKercher, Sze Mei, & Tse,

2006). In this way, and with the assumption of their effective implementation, cultural festivals can showcase a destination's heritage, traditions, ethnic backgrounds, and cultural landscapes (Getz, 2008; McKercher et al., 2006).

Auckland is a multicultural city and this is reflected in the variety of migrant festivals on offer. Auckland is also known as the world's largest "Polynesian city," as two thirds (67%) of New Zealand Polynesians live in the Auckland region (Statistics New Zealand, 2007). Alongside other cultural festivals such as the Diwali Festival of Lights (Indian community), and the Auckland Lantern Festival (Chinese community), Auckland hosts the annual Pasifika Festival (Pacific Island communities).

The Pacific Island migrant communities of New Zealand are a cultural grouping that has managed to raise their profile in the arts, leisure, and cultural arena, even though they continue to be economically marginalized. Many Polynesians (e.g., Samoans, Tongans, Cook Islanders) came to New Zealand in the 1960s and 1970s to work in low paid, blue collar, and service activities. Problems with "overstayers," growing unemployment and the country's declining manufacturing base, led to a generally negative images of Pacific Islanders being conveyed by the media (Kolo, 1990). During the 1990s, contemporary Pacific Island culture started to gain recognition in New Zealand with the emergence of the Polynesian version of hip-hop (Colchester, 2003), high-profile entertainers, and the growing number of Polynesians participating in elite sport, especially Rugby Union.

Pacific Island migrant communities have clearly brought a Pacific flavor to New Zealand and Auckland in particular. *Pasifika* has become the term for anything of Pacific origin in New Zealand—whether it be music, fashion, art, design, or style. For many, Pasifika culture now represents something that is "cool" and "trendy." This is evidenced by successes such as the BroTown television show, a prime-time animated comedy depicting the "positive representation of Polynesian ethnicity with larger-than-life comedic renderings" (Earl, 2005, p. 9). Interest in things Pasifika is also evidenced by the Otara Market, a Polynesian market held weekly in the economically disadvantaged, multicultural South Auckland suburb of Otara being positioned as a tourist attraction.

While the rise of cool Pasifika has been positive, Pacific Island migrant communities remain at risk of cultural erosion and language loss. As many are the children of migrants, they are often trapped in a dilemma of identities (Franklin, 2003). The term Pasifika now groups all Pacific Islanders into one, yet the Pacific Island cultures are many and diverse. It becomes difficult for the young Polynesians to fit traditional values into modern life. Most are now brought up with internet and cell phones, but are still expected to retain "sharing" and "giving" family values and obey the decisions of elders (Perrott, 2007).

Auckland City Council (Auckland City) is the organizer of the Pasifika Festival. Auckland City's events strategy seeks to "support Auckland's unique identity, and Pacific flavour" and "contribute to a strong sense of place through arts, culture and recreation" (Auckland City Council, 2005, p. 3). Auckland City seeks to support community-focused events that support social interaction, community involvement and help to build stronger community networks. Auckland City collaborates with Tourism Auckland to create awareness of events and festivals, with the aim of building Auckland's image as a vibrant and dynamic city.

Previous festival and event research has normally taken a single stakeholder perspective focusing exclusively on the visitor. This research departs from that norm and utilizes a multiple stakeholder perspective to examine the Auckland Pasifika Festival from an audience, stallholder and organizer's perspective. The research illustrates the value of taking a multiple stakeholder approach by examining the overall value of a cultural festival from multiple dimensions (i.e., economic, cultural, and social) and multiple perspectives (i.e., stallholders, audience, and organizer). The article examines the profile of the audience and the stallholders with a focus on demographics, motivations for attending, and levels of satisfaction. This article also provides a methods contribution focusing on the use of online research tools for festival research.

The article utilizes data from 6 years of audience surveys, 2 years of stallholder surveys, and interviews and meetings with the festival organizers. This study is part of an ongoing research program conducted by the New Zealand Tourism Research Institute (NZTRI) in partnership with Auckland City. This study has limitations and therefore caution should be taken in any generalization of the findings to other festivals and events. Using a nonprobability sample, the findings may be specific to this case study only. However, the results form the basis for further study into multiple festival stakeholders using online research tools.

FESTIVALS AND CULTURE: A REVIEW

A wide array of events tourism research has emerged over the past two decades, with the majority of studies focusing on sport events, conventions, and festivals (Getz, 2008). Academic interest in event tourism was clearly evident in the 1980s, and during the 1990s the field took off with a number of high profile publications (Getz, 1991; Hall, 1992). In the new millennium the events industry has seen a boost not only in terms of the number of events and festivals on offer, but also in the increased volume of academic publications and programs offered at tertiary institutions around the world. Economic impacts and related policy were the prevalent research topic in the 1990s and early 2000s. In more recent years the field has broadened to include social and environmental impacts, with all three areas being integrated into a "triple bottom line" approach (Dwyer, Mellor, Mistilis, & Mules,

2000; Fredline, Raybould, Jago, & Deery, 2005). This prompted Getz (2008) to argue that the events and festival literature had now reached the "maturity" stage.

As with any type of event, festivals come in a variety of shapes and sizes. A three-tiered typology of events is provided by O'Sullivan and Jacks (2002). "Home-grown" events are small scale and are managed by volunteers for the benefit of the locals. "Tourist-tempter" events are aimed specifically at attracting tourists to stimulate economic development. "Big-bang" events are generally large-scale events that work as a marketing tool aimed at stimulating sustainable, local economic development as well as entertainment. The impacts from smaller events are likely to be less significant than the impacts generated from "mega-events," "but are more likely to be generally positive than potentially very negative" (Higham, 1999, p. 87). Mega-events are characterized by their large size or high economic yield and heightened image, which they bring to the host destination. They are short-term events of a set duration. Major events have similar consequences yet on a smaller scale. Hallmark events are normally distinguished as holding certain perceptions such as tradition, attractiveness, image, and publicity, and can over time become a destination's competitive advantage (Getz, 1997, 2008).

Historically, festivals were staged for the benefit of the local community and not tourists (Getz, 1989). Festivals were held for a variety of reasons including religious purposes, to celebrate a social event or a successful harvest, to honor someone or simply for leisure (Douglas et al., 2001). Therefore, the driving purpose for festivals was for social benefits and not for economic benefits. However, in recent years, local and traditional festivals are being used as a destination marketing tool. More focus is being placed upon special interest tourists, such as cultural tourists, who are keen to explore authentic cultural tourism products. Cultural festivals appear well placed to cater for such demand.

The tension between festivals being designed for local or nonlocal (i.e., tourist) consumption is not straightforward. McKercher et al. (2006) studied three short-duration cultural festivals in Hong Kong to investigate if they were seen as tourist attractions. They discovered that very few international tourists attended these festivals despite being marketed as tourist attractions to the international market. This was attributed to tourists being unaware of the festivals prior to arrival and the difficulty of scheduling the festival into a preplanned itinerary. Other studies have also shown that locals or domestic visitors comprise the majority of festivals' attendees (Chang, 2006; McMorland & Mactaggart, 2007). This may well be because local festivals are developed by minority communities and may be quite localized or personal in nature, with limited appeal to mainstream tourists (McKercher et al., 2006). However, this approach fails to recognize that many tourists may want to experience "the local." Another issue arises where the community may not want to promote their local festivals. In their study of the

Queenstown Winter Festival, Milne, Clark, Buch, and Macario (2007) identified that many local residents felt that commercial pressures had resulted in the festival focus shifting from local residents to nonlocals. There are cautionary notes to positioning festivals for nonlocal audiences. Getz (1991) notes that if festivals are manipulated for extrinsic (i.e., economic development or profit) rather than intrinsic reasons, they will be viewed primarily as tourist attractions. This will place them at risk of losing their authenticity and as a result, interest and support of local community decreases. Similarly, Quinn (2006) states that if festivals are treated merely as events, they may end up becoming "staged attractions."

Festivals "are the outward manifestation of the identity of the community and provide a distinctive identifier of place and people" (Derrett, 2003, p. 57). As such they foster community development, cultural traditions and provide leisure opportunities (Getz, 1991). Festivals also provide a means of sharing and enhancing a community's social and cultural values: "offering connections, belonging, support, empowerment, participation, and safety" (Derrett, 2003, p. 52).

While festivals have a social dimension, they are also noted for their ability to become a vehicle for (re)establishing a sense of cultural identity, as well as reviving and maintaining traditional cultures (McKercher et al., 2006; Sofield & Sivan, 2003). Such events may also be an avenue for migrant communities to strengthen their sense of identity. Migrant communities may utilize "culture for reinforcement of self-worth, community assertiveness and financial gain through the commodification of that culture for touristic purposes" (Cave, Ryan, & Panakera, 2003, p. 373). Getz (2008, p. 53) has noted that "communities without ancient traditions and festivals to celebrate are often motivated to create them for the purpose of establishing traditions and providing a sense of roots." A cultural festival is one way for a community to publicize their culture and present a sense of identity to "outsiders" (Derrett, 2003; McMorland & Mactaggart, 2007).

One question that remains of interest to researchers is why people attend events. Motivational studies have been conducted on music events (Bowen & Daniels, 2005; McMorland & Mactaggart, 2007), arts and cultural festivals (Chang, 2006; Van Zyl & Botha, 2004), and across multiple events (Nicholson & Pearce, 1999, 2001). Crompton and McKay (1997) identified six motives stimulating visitors to go to festival-type events: cultural exploration, novelty or regression, to recover equilibrium (rest and relaxation or escape), known-group socialization, external interaction or socialization, and family togetherness. The motive of cultural exploration was identified by Chang (2006) as the most important factor leading people to attend an aboriginal cultural festival in Taiwan. Family togetherness, socialization, and event novelty aspects were also identified by Van Zyl and Botha (2004) in their motivational study of residents to the annual Aardklop National Arts Festival in South Africa. When examining visitor motivations of those attending traditional Scottish music events, McMorland and Mactaggart (2007) identified enjoyment, entertainment, social interaction, and support of Scottish music as the most important motivational factors.

However, the most important pull factors (or seeking factors) at that festival were atmosphere, food and beverage, and entertainment. Chhabra, Healey, and Sills (2003) found that people visiting the Flora Macdonald Scottish Highland Games in North Carolina primarily sought authentic Scottish goods, authentic Scottish food, outdoor recreation and information on Scottish heritage. Nicholson and Pearce (2001) compared visitor motivations at four New Zealand events and found that the dominant reason for attending varied according to the theme of each event. For example, people attending Warbirds over Wanaka came to "see the planes" while "music" was the motivation for the Gold Guitar Awards. The opportunity for social interaction also differed for each event with some emphasizing "fun" and "partying" aspects, while others highlighted "friends and family" elements. In summary, the main motivations that underpin festival attendance are: cultural exploration; festival novelty; and social interaction with family, friends, and others; as well as pull factors such as authentic food and entertainment.

Festival research has traditionally focused on the visitors or audience as the unit of analysis, not the stallholders. A few examples of research on stallholders include the study of stakeholders at the Greek Festival of Sydney (Spiropoulos, Gargalianos, & Sotiriadou, 2006). These authors developed a framework categorizing stallholders from both a functional perspective such as marketing and production, and an ethnic-oriented perspective (e.g., Greek, Greek-Australian). This framework may assist sponsors, policymakers, and event managers to better identify the roles and impacts of each stakeholder. Ruting and Li (2006) examine the "Bundanoon is Brigadoon" Scottish Highlands festival held in the Southern Highlands, Australia. They consider the Festival's impacts, implications for Bundanoon's place identity and motivations of visitors by interviews with local businesses, stallholders and visitors. The research reports that stallholders attended the Festival both because of the atmosphere and economic prospects.

Festival studies have mainly focused on visitor consumption and expenditure rather than on the stallholder production end of the festival equation. To address this, Frost and Oakley (2007) sought to integrate the concepts of financial and cultural entrepreneurship. The authors argue that festivals act as a temporary marketplace with low entry barriers. "They are often seen as providing opportunities for recent migrants, both to explore traditional cultural expressions such as dance or music and in areas like food retailing" (Frost & Oakley, 2007, p. 1).

Frost and Oakley's (2007) research focuses on the Carnaval del Pueblo and the Brick Lane Festival. These events are managed by communities in close cooperation with local authorities. Originally developed for London's Colombian community, the Carnaval now embraces the wider Latin American community and non-Latino groups and traders. However, this has created some resentment among Latino stallholders as "they see a dilution of the Latin American character of the event as bad for business" (Frost, n.d., p. 4). The Brick Lane Festival is popular within London's Bangladeshi population. For stallholders, the festival is a temporary space and they use the festival as "an accessible marketing opportunity, rather than as a showcase for cultural heritage" (Frost & Oakley, 2007, p. 5).

Limited research has focused on or included the perspective of the festival organizers. A study by Gursoy, Kim, and Uysal (2004) focused on the way event organizers view the impacts of festivals and special events on a host community. Their study showed that event organizers generally perceive festivals as contributing to community cohesiveness as opposed to being major contributors to the local economy. Jackson, Houghton, Russell, and Triandos (2005) noted in the development of their do-it-yourself kit for measuring economic impacts that the festival organizers only saw the economic impacts as part of the motivation for staging a festival. The majority specified increased tourism because of increased awareness created by the festival, and also included cultural, social, and other community development outcomes. Mayfield and Crompton (1995) developed a standard instrument for identifying the reasons why community organizations stage a festival in order to answer the question "is the rationale for staging a festival consistent with the benefits that visitors receive from it?" The authors also noted the need for a multiple stakeholder approach; it would be possible to get a better fit between the various stakeholders' needs by combining the instrument for organizers with a similar instrument for visitors.

THE AUCKLAND PASIFIKA FESTIVAL: CASE AND METHOD

The Auckland Pasifika Festival is held in March every year. The Festival was first conducted in 1993, initially attracting an audience of 30,000 and 150 stallholders. The 2-day Festival now attracts an estimated 225,000 people and over 300 stallholders. Pasifika opens with a Friday night concert, followed by a Saturday focused on celebrating the art, cultures, and lifestyle of Auckland's Pacific Island communities. The Festival is open for Maori and Pacific Island stallholders only. Some 10 Pacific Island nations (i.e., Tangata Whenua, Cook Islands, Fiji, Kiribati, Niue, Samoa, Tahiti, Tokelau, Tonga, and Tuvalu) present their culture in village settings which offer insights into cultural practices and ceremonies, traditional food, arts and crafts, and music and performances. The Pasifika Festival cannot be classified under any one of the three typologies as identified by O'Sullivan and Jackson (2002): home-grown, tourist-tempter, and big-bang. Pasifika shares similarities with the home-grown typology, as it is primarily staged for the benefit of the local communities, but differs from this category because of its size and involvement of paid staff as provided by Auckland City. The Festival may instead be classified as a recurring major event.

Auckland City conducted an audience survey at the Pasifika Festival between 2003 and 2007. In 2007, the NZTRI piloted an online stallholder survey. In 2008, NZTRI was commissioned to conduct research on both stallholders and audience. This article is based on a review of the findings of 6 years of audience surveys and 2 years of stallholder surveys. The aims of the audience survey are to get a better profile of the festival audience focusing on: (a) demographics; (b) reasons for attending; (c) level of awareness; and (d) satisfaction and expectations. The stallholder survey aims to create a greater understanding of the festival stallholders by providing descriptive data regarding (a) who the stallholders were; (b) reasons for being a stallholder; and (c) satisfaction levels and thoughts on how the festival could be improved. Another aim of the research in 2007/8 was to test the effectiveness of an online data collection for the audience and stallholder surveys. The criteria for measuring effectiveness would be reduced costs and increased response rates.

The audience surveys carried out by Auckland City during 2003 to 2007 were conducted using traditional paper-based surveys. Groups of volunteers approached the festival audience and asked them to complete a survey. In 2008, the research utilized mixed procedures with both clipboard surveys and a Web survey. Fully briefed research assistants were positioned around the festival grounds throughout the day of the 2008 festival. A key interview criterion was the need to have been at the festival for a minimum of half an hour. Research assistants were instructed to aim for a broad range of respondents. If a festival attendee agreed to participate, they were given two options: (a) complete the paper-based survey on the spot or (b) add their e-mail address to a list and a link to the survey would be emailed to them postfestival by the organizers. In an effort to boost response rates and promote the Web-based survey, a small incentive was offered to complete the survey online. A total of 371 paper-based surveys were completed and 677 valid e-mail addresses were collected. Responses were received from 214 of the e-mails, providing a response rate of 32% for the online component of the audience survey.

A link to the online stallholder survey was sent via e-mail to Auckland City's database of stallholders. Over half of the 353 stallholders were registered with an e-mail address, and for those without e-mail addresses, a paper-based survey option was also available. A total of 51 stallholders completed the survey online providing a response rate of 30%. Four paper-based surveys were also received from stallholders.

Previous studies of festivals stallholders and attendees have generally relied on traditional surveying methods: face-to-face interviews, onsite self-administered questionnaires, mailed questionnaires, and telephone surveys (Chang, 2006; Chhabra et al., 2003; Nicholson & Pearce, 2001). McMorland and Mactaggart (2007) distributed surveys via e-mail, yet limited studies in this field of research seem to have taken a Web-based approach. Previous research conducted by NZTRI, however, has utilized online surveys for arts festivals (Dickson & Buch, 2008; Milne & Clark, 2006) and community festivals (Milne et al., 2007). In his summary of recent academic event literature, gap assessment, and thoughts on future research methods, Getz (2008) did not consider Web-based approaches.

While the popularity of Internet surveying continues to grow, there are still concerns as to whether the data collected over the Internet are as reliable as traditional forms of surveying (Best, Krueger, Hubbard, & Smith, 2001; Schonlau, Fricker, & Elliott, 2002). While the Web is still being evaluated as a tool for scientific research, some researchers have acknowledged Web-surveying as being as reliable as paper-based surveys (Ballard & Prine, 2002; Denscombe, 2006; Gosling, Vazire, Srivastava, & John, 2004).

Dickson and Milne (2008) argued that Web-based approaches have an important role to play in building closer relationships between communities, businesses, and events. A key advantage of Internet surveys is that they are less labor intensive than traditional methods. Internet survey data are automatically downloaded into a database, there are no cost and time going into coding the data and subsequently entering the data into a database, as with traditional survey modes. Research shows that a response rate of at least 25% is achievable for online surveys in an event setting; however, response rates will be more successful where a database of participants' email addresses is provided to researchers. Research conducted by NZTRI has successfully achieved response rates of 25% to 44% (Milne, Dickson, & Buch, 2006a, 2006b) in cases where an email database was available.

FINDINGS AND DISCUSSION

This section outlines the key trends from surveys conducted at the Auckland Pasifika Festival. The results are based on six audience surveys conducted between 2003 and 2008, and stallholder surveys conducted in 2007 and 2008. Complementing these are four unstructured interviews completed in the context of a meeting with the festival organizers before and after the 2007 and 2008 festivals. During the meetings, aims and objectives of the festival were discussed along with the history of the festival and any constraints and challenges facing the organizers, which provided the researchers with a good understanding of the festival context. SPSS software provided the descriptive statistics. Open-ended questions were analyzed using a thematic analysis.

AUDIENCE

Consistent findings are identified across the six audience surveys. The Pasifika Festival attendees are more likely to be residents from within the

Auckland region. Less than 5% of attendees are international tourists. This supports previous research which has concluded that local cultural festivals should not be regarded as tourist attractions (Chang, 2006; McKercher et al., 2006; McMorland & Mactaggart, 2007). It is not clear the extent to which the disconnect between these festivals and the itineraries of international tourists can be overcome. However, the logical starting point is to ensure that festival organizers collaborate with their local tourism agencies to discuss ways and means of promoting these events as tourist attractions, especially for tourists seeking an authentic and interactive experience.

The festival audience is generally younger, with the average population aged 39 or under. Samoans have consistently been the largest single group among the audience, followed by Cook Islanders. This is not surprising given that Samoans and the Cook Island Maori comprise the two largest Pacific Island migrant communities in New Zealand (Statistics New Zealand, 2007). In 2008, 64% of the audience surveyed indicated that they belong to Pacific Peoples or Maori in terms of ethnic groupings. This is also consistent with other research which has identified over-representation of the relevant ethnic community amongst festival attendees (Frost, n.d.; Spiropoulos et al., 2006).

Repeat visitation is high. At least three quarters of the audience have attended the Festival in previous years. Consistency in the quality of service provided is vital to maintain existing festival-goers and future markets (Chhabra et al., 2003). This is made even more important because word of mouth communication is one of the main informal marketing channels of the Pasifika Festival. Each year the audience has rated the Festival as being "very good" or "excellent." Continued high levels of satisfaction among the audience throughout the years and the large proportion of repeat visitors, suggest that the festival organizers are successful in creating a positive festival experience.

Festival attendees are more likely to travel to the Festival with family, friends, or a partner than by themselves or with an organized group. This fact also underscores the motivation aspect of socialisation, that is "a family day out to catch up with friends and relatives" (Crompton & McKay, 1997; Van Zyl & Botha, 2004).

Throughout the years (2005–2007), people have attended the Pasifika Festival primarily for the food, entertainment and music, culture, and people or atmosphere. In 2008, the audience attended the Festival to (in rank order): (a) experience diverse cultures; (b) experience Pacific Island food; (c) view performances and music; (d) have a family day out to catch up with friends and relatives; and (e) experience the fun and enjoyable atmosphere. Audience comments also reflect that the Pasifika Festival is a cultural eye-opener for people from different ethnic backgrounds:

> Had the time this year and I want to expose my daughter to the multicultural society we in New Zealand live in, especially as we are a multicultural family ourselves.

These findings are consistent with the literature on motivations for attending a festival that has focused on cultural exploration, family togetherness, and socialization (Chang, 2006; Crompton & McKay, 1997; Van Zyl & Botha, 2004). The desire to experience local, traditional food has also been highlighted by Chhabra et al. (2003) and Frost and Oakley (2007).

The Pasifika Festival is predominantly a cultural event, focusing on Pacific Island cultures and traditions. Thus it makes sense that the audience comes to experience culture including cultural performances, music, and food (see Nicholson & Pearce, 2001). Comments from the audience also demonstrate how the festival can act as an avenue for emerging new talents:

> I love Pasifika, getting to see all the new Pacific talent that's out . . . especially seeing our youth getting involved as well with their hip-hop dance.

Generally, the majority of the audience attends the festival for at least 4 hours and spends $40 or more, predominantly on food, drinks, and handicrafts. Because the majority of this money comes from people residing in the region, the local (spatial) impact of the event is not large. However, the family ownership of the stalls, ensures that any "new money" introduced to the community has the potential for secondary impacts (Milne et al., 2007; Mules & Faulkner, 1996).

Stallholders

The majority of the stalls provide food, drinks, or handicrafts. Stallholders report that they benefit personally from the festival in a number of ways. Listed in order of frequency, these benefits are: good for business; meet people, family and friends; enjoyment; cultural pride; learn about other cultures; brings us together; strengthen own culture; and highlight Pacific Island cultures.

Some stallholders attend the festival to promote their business and gain publicity among potential customers. While many stallholders merely break even or make a small profit, the larger benefit appears to be in terms of exposure and publicity. This aspect was also reflected on by Frost and Oakley (2007). They argued that a festival is a temporary marketplace with low entry barriers, which can be an easy opportunity for ethnic entrepreneurs to enter their products into the market.

Stalls are generally very family-oriented operations, reflecting the centrality of extended families to Pacific Island values and traditions. The majority of any profit made goes to family in New Zealand or is remitted to relatives overseas. The family togetherness motivation is highlighted in other literature (Crompton & McKay, 1997; Van Zyl & Botha, 2004). Frost and Oakley's (2007, p. 6) observation that some stallholders run a "food or craft stall with family or friends simply as a way of joining in with the celebration, while making a little extra cash at the same time" is certainly applicable for many of those running stalls at Pasifika.

Stallholders also attend simply for the enjoyment of the experience. The majority of stallholders (84%–89% in 2008) is returning from previous years and plan to return again. The levels of satisfaction among stallholders are high with most (76% in 2008) rating the festival as "very good" or "excellent."

While Pasifika stallholders attend the festival due to marketing opportunities they also, contrary to the literature (Frost & Oakley, 2007), see the festival as a cultural opportunity. The Pasifika stallholders identify intangible aspects (e.g., cultural exploration) as being important elements of their participation. It was often stressed that being part of the festival increases cultural pride and helps strengthen their cultural identity. As the comment from this stallholder illustrates:

> Learn a lot more about other Pacific cultures especially my own as I found out my language and culture goes a lot deeper than I know.

The findings that festivals can revive and maintain traditional culture are supported by the literature (McKercher et al., 2006; Sofield & Sivan, 2003). The same can also be said for the event's ability to promote a sense of identity for migrant communities (Cave et al., 2003). Some stallholders also reflected upon the positive exposure that Pacific Island cultures are given through the Pasifika Festival:

> Personally I love the positive light that this sheds on the Pacific peoples as I evidence a lot of negativity towards our people via media and in daily life. I like the fact that there are a lot of other cultures in New Zealand who attend this event which tells me that they are genuinely interested in our cultures, traditions, language but more importantly WHO WE ARE.

The stallholders support the festival organizer's aim to build Pasifika community capabilities and entrepreneurship. Stallholders recognize the festival as an opportunity for small Pacific Island businesses to develop and grow, as a way of sharing and showcasing traditions, as uniting the Pasifika community and being good for Pacific Island cultures. Some comments from the stallholders highlight these issues:

> It is important that Pacific Islanders realize their potential through business ventures and I believe that the Pasifika Festival achieves that, not to mention the opportunity to showcase our individual islands.

> It's a time to celebrate our cultures and traditions and share our language with New Zealanders and to keep (culture) alive.

Organizers

Interviews and meetings with the festival organizers provide a different stakeholder angle to the research. The Pasifika Festival organizers have for a number of years recognized the value of conducting audience surveys at the festival. Recently, they also acknowledged the need for a stallholder perspective in order to gain a more complete picture of festival stakeholders. Outcomes from both the audience and the stallholder surveys are used by the organizers to make changes and plan for future festivals.

Both audience and stallholders exhibit different motivations for attending and therefore the Festival should be marketed thematically to suit both stakeholder groups. Nicholson and Pearce (2001) stated that the uniqueness of the event must be highlighted as well as the opportunity for socialization enhanced, providing care is taken to identify the type of socialization (like-minded enthusiasts or family time).

The festival organizers have a policy that favors authentic Pacific Island (including Maori) stallholders. It is important to the organizers that the current stallholders are supportive of this initiative. The organizers are concerned that welcoming non-Pasifika stallholders would detract from the uniqueness of the festival and contradict with the original purpose—a concern also noted by Frost (n.d.).

The Pasifika festival organizers' aim for the Festival is to develop capabilities within Auckland's Pacific Island communities. They aim to achieve this by profiling emerging artists and developing new talent, increasing the level of involvement of youth groups, transferring more responsibility to the village coordinators and by encouraging the use of technology and the Internet. Generally, household access to the Internet is comparatively lower among Pacific Peoples than for the rest of New Zealand (Statistics New Zealand, 2004). As part of building the community's Internet capabilities, the organizers have pushed for the introduction of the online survey tools to complement (and possibly eventually replace) the traditional paper-based surveys.

Given the organizers' intention to change and develop the festival, it would be interesting to monitor the drivers of these changes, the level of community engagement regarding these initiatives, and ultimately, the extent to which these initiatives are embraced by stallholders and attendees alike. A longitudinal study of this nature has the potential to improve our understanding of all these issues.

Methods and Contributions

This study has adopted a different approach to data collection compared to the majority of other studies of events and festivals. The use of an online survey in combination with traditional paper-based surveys represents the exploratory dimension of the study. The use of a mixed-methods approach in this study has proven to be successful. The Web-based surveys of audience and stallholders received good response rates of 30% or more which is similar to previous NZTRI research on festivals and events (Dickson & Buch, 2008; Dickson, Milne, & Buch, 2007).

Web-based surveys have most successfully been adopted in research with an available sampling frame of e-mail addresses, as this ensures an easy and cost-efficient administration of the survey to potential participants (Dickson & Milne, 2008). However, for an open-gate event it becomes more difficult to administer the surveys. For that reason, an investigative approach was taken collecting e-mail addresses from the festival audience and subsequently e-mailing them a link to the survey. This approach had both drawbacks and advantages.

The drawbacks include the difficulty in deciphering the e-mail addresses as people tend to write it fast and hence unclear which will result in some bounced e-mails. In this case, 677 out of 723 e-mail addresses were valid. Some concern was evident beforehand as to whether or not people would willingly give out their e-mail address considering the general increase in spam e-mails. But most people had a positive attitude and were happy to participate. Filling in the survey online after the festival gave people the chance to just enjoy their time at Pasifika.

The 371 paper-based audience surveys received complemented the online responses. Most of these respondents agreed to fill in the survey later in the day whilst seated for lunch and after they had experienced most parts of the festival.

The online stallholder survey followed the successful format suggested by Dickson and Milne (2008) as the festival organizer already had a database of e-mail addresses available. The only drawback to this method was that only over half of the stallholders were listed with an e-mail address. To avoid excluding the remaining stallholders, stallholders were able to request a paper survey at the Council. This was done by just four stallholders, perhaps an indication that this method would involve too much effort from participants to simply complete a survey. Due to funding and contractual arrangements with the client it was not practical for the researchers to trace the remaining stallholders and facilitate the completion of the questionnaire. Hence, if the organizers succeed in encouraging the use of the Internet among stallholders then the online survey could become an even more effective tool in the future.

CONCLUSIONS

The Auckland Pasifika Festival celebrated its 16th anniversary in 2008. The festival is one of the largest community events in the Pacific and is acknowledged as a successful event because of its growing popularity and positive impact on the Auckland community.

This article has built on and added to previous research by describing the festival audience and their motivations for attendance. It has also added some insights into the motivations and benefits for festival stallholders. The article has confirmed the arguments that cultural festivals can contribute to both maintaining and reviving cultures, as well as strengthening community identity (McKercher et al., 2006; Sofield & Sivan, 2003). The Auckland Pasifika Festival appears to have the ability to create those characteristics for Pacific Islanders in Auckland. The festival may also shine a positive light on the Pacific Island migrant communities, thus mitigating the negative media coverage that exists.

Limited research has involved the perspective of stallholders. Thus we recommend that future research shift some of the focus from the festival audience or visitor to the stallholder to incorporate a multiple stakeholder approach. It is important to get a stallholder perspective as this brings a deeper insight into their motivations and behaviors, and their perspective is equally as important to understand as the visitor's perspective. Combining the audience and organizer perspectives makes it possible to discover synergies and divergences and therefore receive a more holistic picture of a festival.

It is also important to investigate the perspective of stallholders given that festivals can provide useful analytical studies of entrepreneurs from diverse backgrounds (Frost & Oakley, 2007). We suggest that future research explore other ethnic cultural festivals and how they contribute to maintaining or reviving culture among migrant communities.

One of the Pasifika Festival organizers' aims is to encourage the use of the Internet among Pacific Peoples. Using Web-based surveys is certainly a way forward to encourage the use of the Internet both among the audience and stallholders. We argue in this article that future research should incorporate these cost effective Web-based approaches to further validate and profile the use of these methods.

In conclusion, festivals are about people—the people that produce them and the people that attend them. It is important, both in research and in practice, that these variables in the festival equation are given equal attention.

REFERENCES

Auckland City Council. (2005). *Auckland City events strategy*. Retrieved from http://www.aucklandcity.govt.nz/council/documents/events/docs/strategy.pdf

Ballard, C., & Prine, R. (2002). Citizen perceptions of community policing: Comparing internet and mail survey responses. *Social Science Computer Review*, *20*, 485–493.

Best, S. J., Krueger, B., Hubbard, C., & Smith, A. (2001). An assessment of the generalizability of internet surveys. *Social Science Computer Review*, *19*, 131–145.

Bowen, H., & Daniels, M. J. (2005). Does the music matter? Motivations for attending a music festival. *Event Management*, *9*, 155–164. doi:10.3727/152599505774791149

Cave, J., Ryan, C., & Panakera, C. (2003). Residents' perceptions, migrant groups and culture as an attraction—the case of a proposed Pacific Island cultural centre in New Zealand. *Tourism Management*, *24*, 371–385. doi:10.1016/S0261-5177(02)00110-3

Chang, J. (2006). Segmenting tourists to aboriginal cultural festivals: An example in the Rukai tribal area, Taiwan. *Tourism Management*, *27*, 1224–1234. doi:10.1016/j.tourman.2005.05.019

Chhabra, D., Healey, R., & Sills, E. (2003). Staged authenticity and heritage tourism. *Annals of Tourism Research*, *30*, 702–719. doi:10.1016/S0160-7383(03)00044-6

Colchester, C. (2003). T-shirts, translation and humour: On the nature of wearer-perceiver relationships in South Auckland. In C. Colchester (Ed.), *Clothing the Pacific* (pp. 167–191). Oxford, England: Berg.

Crompton, J. L., & McKay, S. L. (1997). Motives of visitors attending festival events. *Annals of Tourism Research*, *24*, 425–439. doi:10.1016/S0160-7383(97)80010-2

Denscombe, M. (2006). Web-based questionnaires and the mode effect: An evaluation based on completion rates and data contents of near-identical questionnaires delivered in different modes. *Social Science Computer Review*, *24*, 246–254. doi:10.1177/0894439305284522

Derrett, R. (2003). Making sense of how festivals demonstrate a community's sense of place. *Event Management*, *8*, 49–58. doi:10.3727/152599503108751694

Dickson, G., & Buch, T. (2008). *2008 ERUPT Lake Taupo Festival audience Web-survey* (Commissioned report to ERUPT Lake Taupo Festival Trust). Auckland, New Zealand: New Zealand Tourism Research Institute.

Dickson, G., & Milne, S. (2008). Measuring the impact of micro-events on local communities: A role for Web-based approaches. In J. Ali-Knight, M. Robertson, A. Fyall, & A. Ladkin (Eds.), *International perspectives of festivals and events—paradigms of analysis* (pp. 253–263). London, England: Elsevier.

Dickson, G., Milne, S., & Buch, T. (2007). *Evaluating the economic impacts of the 2007 Ironman New Zealand on Taupo* (Commissioned report to Destination Lake Taupo). Auckland, New Zealand: New Zealand Tourism Research Institute. Retrieved from http://www.nztri.org/node/104#attachments

Douglas, N., Douglas, N., & Derrett, R. (Eds.). (2001). *Special interest tourism*. Brisbane, Australia: John Wiley & Sons Australia.

Dwyer, L., Mellor, R., Mistilis, N., & Mules, T. (2000). A framework for assessing "tangible" and "intangible" impacts of events and conventions. *Event Management*, *7*, 175–189.

Earl, E. (2005, July). *Brand New Zealanders: The commodification of Polynesian youth identity in television advertising*. Paper presented at the Annual Meeting of the Australian and New Zealand Communication Association, Christchurch, New Zealand.

Franklin, M. I. (2003). I define my own identity: Pacific articulations of "race" and "culture" on the Internet. *Ethnicities*, *3*, 465–490. doi:10.1177/1468796803003004002

Fredline, L., Raybould, M., Jago, L., & Deery, M. (2005). Triple bottom line event evaluation: A proposed framework for holistic event evaluation. In J. Allen (Ed.), *The impacts of events: Proceedings of the International Event Research Conference held in Sydney July 2005* (pp. 2–15). Lindfield, Australia: Australian Centre for Event Management.

Frost, N. (n.d.). *Carnival, culture and capital: The future of Creative Enterprise?* Retrieved from http://www.city.ac.uk/celeb_ent/dps/futureofcreativeent.pdf

Frost, N., & Oakley, K. (2007). *Celebrating enterprise: Ethnic entrepreneurs and festival-based businesses.* Retrieved from http://www.city.ac.uk/celeb_ent/dps/futureofcreativeent.pdf

Getz, D. (1989). Special events: Defining the product. *Tourism Management*, *10*, 125–137. doi:10.1016/0261-5177(89)90053-8

Getz, D. (1991). *Festivals, special events and tourism.* New York, NY: Van Nostrand Reinhold.

Getz, D. (2008). Event tourism: Definition, evolution and research. *Tourism Management*, *29*, 403–428. doi:10.1016/j.tourman.2007.07.017

Gosling, S. D., Vazire, S., Srivastava, S., & John, O. P. (2004). Should we trust Web-based studies? A comparative analysis of six preconceptions about internet questionnaires. *American Psychologist*, *59*, 93–104. doi:10.1037/0003-066X.59.2.93

Gursoy, D., Kim, K., & Uysal, M. (2004). Perceived impacts of festivals and special events by organizers: An extension and validation. *Tourism Management*, *25*, 171–181. doi:10.1016/S0261-5177(03)00092-X

Hall, M. (1992). *Hallmark tourist events: Impacts, management and planning.* London, England: Belhaven.

Higham, J. (1999). Commentary—Sport as an avenue of tourism development: An analysis of the positive and negative impacts of sport tourism. *Current Issues in Tourism*, *2*(1), 82–90.

Jackson, J., Houghton, M., Russell, R., & Triandos, P. (2005). Innovations in measuring economic impacts of regional festivals: A do-it-yourself kit. *Journal of Travel Research*, *43*, 360–367. doi:10.1177/0047287505274649

Kolo, F. (1990). An incident in Otara: The media and Pacific Island communities. In P. Spoonley & W. Hirsh (Eds.), *Between the lines: Racism and the New Zealand media* (pp. 120–122). Auckland, New Zealand: Heinemann Reed.

Mayfield, L., & Crompton, J. L. (1995). Development of an instrument for identifying community reasons for staging a festival. *Journal of Travel Research*, *33*, 37–44. doi:10.1177/004728759503300307

McKercher, B., Sze Mei, W., & Tse, T. S. M. (2006). Are short duration cultural festivals tourism attractions?. *Journal of Sustainable Tourism*, *14*, 55–66.

McMorland, L.- A., & Mactaggart, D. (2007). Traditional Scottish music events: Native Scots' attendance motivations. *Event Management*, *11*, 57–69. doi:10.3727/152599508783943246

Milne, S., & Clark, V. (2006). *The local economic impact of the Wanganui Blooming Artz Festival* (Commissioned report to Wanganui Blooming Artz Festival Trust).

Auckland, New Zealand: New Zealand Tourism Research Institute. Retrieved from http://www.nztri.org/node/84

Milne, S., Clark, V., Buch, T., & Macario, L. (2007). *The 2006 Lindauer Queenstown Winter Festival: Local impacts* (Commissioned report to Destination Queenstown). Auckland, New Zealand: New Zealand Tourism Research Institute. Retrieved from http://www.nztri.org/node/96#attachments

Milne, S., Dickson, G., & Buch, T. (2006a). *The ARC 12 & 24 Hour Adventure Race and local economic impacts on Whangamata.* Auckland, New Zealand: New Zealand Tourism Research Institute. Retrieved from http://www.nztri.org/node/88

Milne, S., Dickson, G., & Buch, T. (2006b). *The Taupo Special K Women's Triathlon: Local economic impacts.* Auckland, New Zealand: New Zealand Tourism Research Institute. Retrieved from http://www.nztri.org/node/88

Mules, T., & Faulkner, B. (1996). An economic perspective on special events. *Tourism Economics, 2,* 107–117.

Nicholson, R., & Pearce, D. G. (1999). Who goes to events: A comparative analysis of the profile characteristics of visitors to four South Island events in New Zealand. *Journal of Vacation Marketing, 6,* 236–253. doi:10.1177/135676670000600304

Nicholson, R., & Pearce, D. G. (2001). Why do people attend events: A comparative analysis of visitor motivations at four South Island events. *Journal of Travel Research, 39,* 449–460.

O' Sullivan, D., & Jackson, M. J. (2002). Festival tourism: A contributor to sustainable local economic development?. *Journal of Sustainable Tourism, 10,* 325–342.

Perrott, A. (2007, August 4). Pasifika: Identity or illusion? *New Zealand Herald.* Retrieved February 2, 2008, from http://www.nzherald.co.nz/section/6/story.cfm?c_id=6&objectid=10455473

Quinn, B. (2006). Problematising "festival tourism": Arts festivals and sustainable development in Ireland. *Journal of Sustainable Tourism, 14,* 288–306.

Ruting, B., & Li, J. (2006). *Tartan, bagpipes and kilts: A large Scottish festival in a small Australian town.* Sydney, Australia: University of Sydney.

Schonlau, M., Fricker, R. D., & Elliott, M. N. (2002). *Conducting research surveys via e-mail and the Web.* Santa Monica, CA: Rand.

Sofield, T. B., & Sivan, A. (2003). From cultural festival to international sport— the Hong Kong Dragon boat races. *Journal of Sport Tourism, 8,* 9–20. doi:10.1080/14775080306242

Spiropoulos, S., Gargalianos, D., & Sotiriadou, K. (2006). The 20th Greek Festival of Sydney: A stakeholder analysis. *Event Management, 9,* 169–183. doi:10.3727/152599506776771535

Statistics New Zealand. (2004). *Household access to the Internet article.* Retrieved from http://www.stats.govt.nz/products-and-services/Articles/hhold-access-inet.htm

Statistics New Zealand. (2007). *QuickStats about culture and identity.* Retrieved from http://www.stats.govt.nz/census/2006-census-data/quickstats-about-culture-identity/quickstats-about-culture-and-identity.htm?page=para016Master

Van Zyl, C., & Botha, C. (2004). Motivational factors of local residents to attend the Aardklop National Arts Festival. *Event Management, 8,* 213–222. doi:10.3727/1525995031436818

Special Events: A Framework for Efficient Management

MARIOS D. SOTERIADES and IRINI DIMOU

Department of Tourism Industry Management, Technological Educational Institute (TEI) of Crete, Heraklion, Greece

Academic literature suggests that events have a positive contribution to the host area, including both tangible and intangible outcomes. This study reviews the related literature, identifies key issues in events tourism management, and highlights the need for a systematic framework for managing events. The aim is to propose a conceptual framework that enhances efficient events management, in order to optimize their contribution to wider development objectives. From a destination perspective, it is suggested that a value-chain approach and a network analysis could provide an appropriate basis for this exploration model and would contribute to efficient events management, in order to optimize beneficial outcomes.

INTRODUCTION

The links between tourism and events have expanded considerably and both of them now stand among the largest and fastest growing industries in the global economy (Higham & Hinch, 2002). In the recent years, events have increasingly been incorporated into strategy development, decision-making, and marketing of many tourism destinations around the world (Bramwell, 1997; Gnoth & Anwar, 2000; Stokes, 2008). Events are an important source of primary income generation, present multiple opportunities for achieving and increasing awareness through media coverage, and often have a positive impact on the image of the host destination (Bowdin McDonnell, Allen, & O'Toole, 2001; Getz, 2008). Consequently, events have become an integral component of the tourism industry in many regions, as they can serve as an additional competitive advantage to attract visitors to a destination. Since the 1990s, many cities and destination marketing organizations have engaged in the systematic planning, development, and marketing of events as tourist attractions, image-makers, or catalysts for other developments. Events can help raise money, foster community development or the arts, provide leisure opportunities, and make excellent communications tools. As argued in Getz (1997), the popularity and specialness of festivals and events are closely related to their ability to achieve multiple goals. Various authors (e.g., Burgan & Mules, 2001) suggest that the benefits resulting from events include positive image, inward investment, tourism promotion through media coverage and the televising of event, and income generation. These might be objectives that justify the event. One of the most crucial issues of event tourism is appropriate planning and efficient management and marketing. (Getz, Andersson, & Larson, 2007; Mackellar, 2006; Stokes, 2006). Planning is a starting point to event organization, as it sets the objectives to work towards, optimizes the use of human and physical resources, and encourages stakeholders to determine their role and work cooperatively (Bramwell, 1997). Efficiency means having a comprehensive approach to influence all parameters and factors considered as being crucial for events success. A strategic approach is needed in order to consistently ensure higher standards of event product delivery and to appeal to ever more demanding customers.

The objective of this article is to propose a framework that would lead to successful event management. This conceptual framework would enhance the effectiveness of events management, in order to optimize their long-term contribution to broader development objectives. Initially, this study reviews the related literature and identifies key issues in events management, highlighting the need for a systematic and holistic framework for managing events (Masterman, 2004; Stokes, 2008). It is suggested that a value-chain approach (Porter, 1998) and a network analysis (Mackellar, 2006; Stokes, 2006) could provide an appropriate basis for this framework. The value-chain approach becomes quite crucial in the management of tourism-related activities, such as the staging of events, since the customer experiences the chain at first hand, and thus managers should take all necessary actions to ensure overall customer satisfaction (Yilmaz & Bititci, 2006). More specifically, the value-chain of an event destination illustrates the number of various actors involved in offering all event-related services. Furthermore, the strategic management approach emphasizes the importance of devoting more attention to analyzing the external and internal environments and formulating appropriate strategies (Chon & Olsen, 1990). A relational theory within strategic management that has more recently started to be applied to event management is network analysis (Mackellar, 2006; Stokes, 2006). A network consists of a set of firms, which seek for partners that would assist them gain some control over their environment. In order for a participating firm to obtain some attractive resource or capability from another member, the firm must have something of value to offer in exchange. The study's final outcome is a conceptual framework contributing to events planning and management, in order to improve their efficiency and effectiveness, and to optimize their benefits in the long run.

LITERATURE REVIEW

Concepts

Events generate strong economic and social benefits, and the events industry is being increasingly recognized as a professional entity worldwide (Bowdin et al., 2001). Events may be related to sport, culture, entertainment, business, or politics. According to the definitions provided by Getz (1997) events can be characterized by their size (e.g., number of visitors, level of media coverage), their economic impact on the host region, their duration and frequency, and the occasion (cultural event, sports event, business event, etc.). The size of an event is often positively related to its impact on the hosting society. One might classify events as special events, sporting events, cultural events, and business events. Special events can be defined as "a one-time or infrequently occurring event outside the normal program or activities of the sponsoring or organizing body" and "to the customer or guest. . . . as an opportunity for a leisure, social or cultural experience outside the normal range of choices or beyond everyday experiences" (Getz, 1997, p. 4). These events are usually viewed as a significant tourist asset for a host area, since the event directly attracts participants, while the resulting improved area profile also indirectly encourages general visitation. From the organizer's point of view, a special event is any one-time or infrequently occurring event outside their normal program of activities. Typically, academic research on event tourism embraces a number of core themes. These include: (a) events' impacts—economic, sociological, tangible, and intangible benefits or costs (Barker, Page, & Meyer, 2002; Burgan & Mules, 1992; May, 1995); (b) events' evaluation (Burgan & Mules, 2001; Dwyer, Forsyth, & Spurr, 2004); and (c) planning and management issues, including objectives, strategic plans, partnerships, networks, and collaboration (Bramwell, 1997; Getz, 1997; Gnoth & Anwar, 2000).

Impacts of Events

Academic literature (e.g., Bowdin et al., 2001; Gelan, 2003; Getz, 2008; Masterman, 2004) suggests that events might have both positive and negative impacts on stakeholders, local environment, and the economy and industry of the host area. Events engender potential benefits into the following fields.

LOCAL AND REGIONAL ECONOMY

Events have economic impacts in the fields of labor market (employment), investment and public finances policy (taxes and debt) by creating an income, "new money" injected into the local economy. Thrane (2002) suggests that inward investment and revenue generation contribute to the development and consolidation of facilities and programs that will benefit destination residents in the long run. The long-term industrial impacts of special and mega-events are mainly due to the development of an improved infrastructure, new tourist attractions, and a significant expansion of the hotel industry (Daniels, Norman, & Henry, 2004).

TOURISM

Tourism destination managers are increasingly looking at events as an important mechanism for enhancing tourism development in their regions. Events have the potential to attract visitors and their associated expenditure (Felsenstein & Fleischer, 2003) that stimulates local economic activity through linkages of tourism with other sectors of the economy (Dwyer, Forsyth, & Spurr, 2005). Events are being used to increase visitation (Morse, 2001), reduce the seasonality of tourist flow (Higham & Hinch, 2002), and foster destination development (Bramwell, 1997).

CITY AND DESTINATION MARKETING

Events have positive effect on image creation and notoriety for countries and destinations. Getz (1997) suggests that special events are powerful tools in targeting desired segments of tourism markets. Hosting special events enhances long-term awareness of the host destination in tourism markets. It is estimated that each of these outcomes depends, at least in part, on the attendance that events generate (Faulkner et al., 2000; Kim & Chalip, 2004). Consequently, from a marketing perspective, events have become an increasingly significant component of destination marketing strategies.

SOCIAL BENEFITS

Potential benefits go beyond tangible economic outcomes and include intangibles, such as image, notoriety, and community pride or identity (Fredline, Jago, & Deery, 2003; Wood, 2005). Residents are the ones who experience any social benefits such as the pride of hosting the event (Derrett, 2003). Events reinforce social and cultural identity by building strong ties within a community. Events also play an important role in creating trust, social cohesion and cohesiveness among community members (Gursoy, Kyungmi, & Uysal, 2004).

URBAN DEVELOPMENT AND REGENERATION

Special events linked with urban renewal programs are becoming increasingly important. For example, the Olympic Games have emerged as a significant catalyst of urban change and can act as a key instrument of urban policy for their host cities.

NEGATIVE IMPACTS AND COSTS

Although event benefits with respect to tourism promotional effects, community self-esteem, and business and employment opportunities are broadly appreciated, event costs are also acknowledged. A growing body of literature (e.g., Burgan & Mules, 2001; Getz, 1998) suggests that the cost of some events may outweigh the associated benefits. Social costs are associated with noise levels, traffic congestion, overcrowding and commercialization of festivals, and disruption of lifestyle. The negative economic impacts include the opportunity cost of taxpayers' money, distribution of costs and benefits among residents of host community, and social and economic costs because of displacement effects (Dwyer et al., 2005).

Impacts' Evaluation

As the number of conceptual and empirical studies on special events has been increasing rapidly, it can be seen that most of them either focus on the economic impact of events or on reasons and motivations for people to attend events (Dwyer et al., 2005; Higham & Hinch, 2002; Nicholson & Pearce, 2001). Moreover, a large body of literature is related to events evaluation (see among others, Burgan & Mules, 2001; Dwyer, Mellor, Mistilis, & Mules, 2000; Dwyer et al., 2004). Various approaches and methods have been suggested to evaluate events impacts, including among others: general economic models; a standardized approach to pre- and post-event evaluation; a combination between the welfare economics paradigm of cost–benefit analysis and the growth-based paradigm of economic impact; an assessment framework; and a multidimensional approach to motivations, satisfaction, decision-making, and expenditure trends; a holistic approach to monitoring sustainability, which integrates the economic view with ecological aspects and the investigation of impacts on the society. However accurate estimation of the size of the impacts on output in the region or country would be a necessary step in the overall evaluation. These estimates can be then used to measure the net benefit from the market transactions associated with the event.

Theories and Models for Event Planning and Management

Various theories and strategy models have been applied recently with respect to management of tourism organizations (Chon & Olsen, 2000; Fletcher & Cooper, 1996; Formica & Kothari, 2008; Sautter & Leisen, 1999), yet fewer are the theories with respect to event planning and management (Bramwell, 1997; Getz, 1997; Gnoth & Anwar, 2000). The most well-known models are based on the classical approach to strategy, according to which "strategy is an integrated set of policies and programs intended to achieve the vision and goals of the organization or destination" (Getz, 1997, p. 93). Building on this approach, a study by Gnoth and Anwar (2000) indicated the need for event-tourism strategy to take into account the interaction among target audiences, competitors, and organizational factors and advocated that the formulation of event-tourism strategy should be directed by top officials. Furthermore, literature on event management has acknowledged the importance of building relationships with other actors within the context of event tourism (e.g., Getz et al., 2007; Long, 2000). An important aspect of networks is that, "each partner is attractive to the other not only through the direct relationship and obvious trade of services, but through the unique micro-network of other already established relationships that it offers to its partner" (Erickson & Kushner, 1999, p. 350). A network analysis methodology applied by Mackellar (2006) indicated that interorganizational networks among tourism organizations, governmental authorities, and local industries can produce outcomes such as cooperation, resource sharing, innovation, and regional development. Along these lines, Stokes (2006) suggested that insights to network structures that shape events tourism strategies at the macrolevel are of benefit to marketers and policymakers. Finally, Stokes (2008) advocated that no single strategy perspective can reflect all activities that drive events tourism and thus alternative strategic approaches could provide deeper insights to strategies that would be more appropriate for subsets of activities.

Since tourism destinations often consider events as generators of economic activity, tourism, and awareness, the question arises: How can destinations plan and organize an efficient and competitive event? In search of an answer to this question, this study focuses on the value chain and network analysis approach. Whichever the objectives are to be reached, these might be accomplished by adopting appropriate approaches and methods in their management. This topic will be discussed in the next section.

A CONCEPTUAL FRAMEWORK FOR EFFICIENT EVENTS MANAGEMENT

From the previous discussion, it is obvious that there are two broad challenges associated with event management. First, there is a need to develop a conceptual framework for event tourism management that embraces the diversity of contexts and networks, while optimizing the developmental benefits in the longer term. Second, there is a need for appropriate marketing, a requirement to offer the most appropriate and accessible "bundle" of experiences to event tourists. The purpose of this section is to address these two broad, interlinked management challenges. Obviously, an event can influence the tourism sector in a destination in various ways. The point of view of the host area is the most crucial when planning and managing events. As for the marketing issue, it is stressed that destinations have become interchangeable and therefore need to implement appropriate strategies to respond to the dynamic environment within which they operate (Law, 2002). As a first step, the theoretical approach (i.e., value-chain, strategic management or network analysis) is briefly presented. In the second step, the methodological approach to formulate the suggested conceptual framework is explained.

Theoretical Approach

The theoretical approach is based on two pertinent approaches: the value-chain and strategic management or network analysis.

VALUE-CHAIN APPROACH OF EVENT DESTINATIONS

A tourism destination is a spatial unit encompassing a complex system of initiatives, plans and actions; and a diversity of actors, roles, and environmental factors that interact to determine its performance (Kaspar & Laesser, 1994). The quality of this system is of vital importance to destination's performance. According to Poon (2002) tourists generally perceive and evaluate

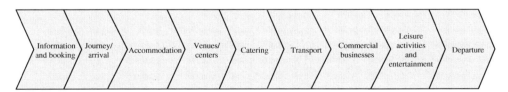

FIGURE 1 Value-chain of an event destination. (Color figure available online).
Source: Adapted from Porter (1998) and Poon (2002).

their visit as a whole package, an "experience," even though the various services are offered by different operators. In fact, their visit consists of a structured series of services and producers, which operate separately. The same holds true for event tourism. The value-chain of an event destination illustrates the number of various actors involved in offering all event-related services and products.

A destination's value-chain is a structured series of businesses, inter-actions, resources, and knowledge streams involved in the creation and delivery of value to the end-consumer. This creates the need for integration of supply chain activities, from determination of consumer needs through product development, production, and distribution. It is exactly because of this fragmentation that all actors taking part in the value-chain should deal with issues such as integration, collaboration, and networking of their activ-ities (Poon, 2002). Nowadays tourists desire and expect a series of services that allow multiple options and experiences. As it has been highlighted, analyses of economic impact and of event-related income show the rela-tionships and connections that exist among different economic sectors of a destination. The economic benefits of event tourism involve many actors in a destination (Dwyer et al., 2005). These enterprises offer a series of services: transportation, accommodation, venues, catering, entertainment, et cetera. The destination's value-chain is thus reflected in all its elements. Moreover, Ryan (2002) suggested that it is necessary to add value through involving local communities and stakeholders in an equitable process. This approach requires cooperation and networking between the destination's key components.

Strategic Management and Network Analysis

Events tourism is an established phenomenon described from the supply-side perspective as "the systematic development and marketing of events as tourism attractions" (Getz, 1997), a definition that, in itself, implies a strategic approach (Stokes, 2006). The strategic planning processes for events tourism is strongly advocated (Bramwell, 1997; Davidson, 2003; Getz, 2008; Gnoth & Anwar, 2000). It is estimated that such an approach results in numerous advantages: optimizes the use of human and natural resources, takes into account the needs of all stakeholders, encourages the building of connec-tions, identifying common concerns, capacity building, and coordination of effort; and has direct implications for the kinds of networks that could influ-ence events tourism. Events tourism strategies have been defined as "the strategic positions or approaches to events tourism development and mar-keting that are derived from prescriptive or descriptive strategy processes or an amalgam of them" (Stokes, 2004, p. 43).

The network analysis is a relational model of strategic management that helps to understand how events tourism strategies can be jointly determined by key stakeholders. Literature indicates that network analysis provides a framework for understanding how the pattern of relationships in a stakeholder environment can influence an organization's behavior. In the tourism context, where major attractions include special events, there are multiple sets of stakeholders, some within their own organized networks that influence strategy. Moreover, event management activities are based on resource interdependencies between partners; thus the network approach is particularly useful. For this reason, interorganizational relationships, including network structures, are gaining the attention of tourism researchers. The network approach that has been used by some authors in the field of tourism (Long, 2000; Pavlovich, 2003), and more recently with respect to event management (Larson, 2009; Mackellar, 2006; Stokes, 2004, 2006), allows researchers to examine the dynamics of inter-organizational relationships that lead to specific outcomes such as innovation and regional development.

A network analysis methodology applied by Mackellar (2006) demonstrated its use as a potential tool for researchers and managers in identifying and understanding inter-organizational relationships. Her study indicated that from the existing networks, it is possible to extend the value of events to intangible benefits such as business networking, regional development, social innovation, and improved destination attractiveness. Along these lines, Stokes (2006) suggested that insights to network structures that shape events tourism strategies at the macrolevel are of benefit to marketers and policy makers. She used the network model to investigate the interorganizational relationships that drive public sector strategy-making for events tourism in Australia and suggested that strategies of a reactive–proactive nature mostly guide events tourism development by Australia's corporatized event development agencies.

Formulating the Conceptual Framework

The proposed conceptual model aims at stressing the importance of developing and maintaining network relations and highlights the links between the various actors involved. It is an integrated conceptual approach that is based on the previously briefly presented theoretical approaches. A two-stage approach is implemented in order to formulate the conceptual framework for event management. Firstly, a comprehensive approach to events planning encompassing all fields (i.e., planning, product development, management, marketing, and monitoring or evaluation) and related goals is presented. This stage is needed in order to apprehend the whole scope of related parameters and expected outputs. It is also the foundation for setting up the suggested framework. In the second step, a conceptual framework is derived from the previous stage, which aims at (a) presenting the various fields, factors, networks, and interactions that may affect the development of event tourism in different contexts, and at (b) providing a logical and systematic process to be followed in managing events. In doing so, our understanding of the various factors that influence events is improved and the interorganizational relationships between events networks are highlighted. It is worth stressing that the two stages are interlinked. Such an approach is in line with suggestions formulated by the research literature. For example Venkatraman and Camillus (1984) have highlighted the different meanings and perspectives on the use of the concept of "fit" in strategic management. They proposed a conceptual scheme intended to address theoretical and managerial issues. One of these perspectives is the interorganizational strategy networks school, of which the main theme is strategy analysis at the collective level.

EVENTS OVERALL PLANNING

Any event, whatever its nature or size is, requires a strategic management approach and network analysis (Getz, 2007; Masterman, 2004). Challenges in hosting events include, among others, the following: (a) to elaborate and implement coherent policies, programs and action plans for events planning, management, and marketing; (b) to identify an opportunity for linking sports, culture, business, and leisure to tourism activity; and (c) tourism promotion and urban regeneration. In order for these challenges to be addressed, there is a need to adopt a strategic management approach. This approach means adopting and implementing the key principles of strategic management and marketing to event management contexts. Having as overall goal the optimization of tangible and intangible outputs, the crucial point is to have a comprehensive approach in all stages (i.e., pre-, during, and post-event) and fields (i.e., planning, management, marketing, monitoring, and evaluation). The framework proposed herein (see Table 1) constitutes a synthesis and integration of suggestions formulated by various authors, (mainly Allen, O'Toole, Harris, & O'Donnell, 2005; Bramwell, 1997; Dwyer et al., 2000; Getz, 1997; Getz & Fairley, 2002; Masterman, 2004; Morse, 2001).

A CONCEPTUAL FRAMEWORK FOR EFFICIENT EVENTS MANAGEMENT

The second stage consists of formulating a conceptual framework that contributes to efficient events management. One such framework is proposed in Figure 2. It has been argued that the context within which tourism occurs is a dynamic context and environment, that is, destinations undergo a constant process of economic, social, and cultural change, often in response to wider national and global influences (Law, 2002; Page & Hall, 2003; Sharpley & Roberts, 2005). The management of event tourism, although frequently a response to such change, must also evidently be able to embrace this dynamic context. This is the starting point that encompasses three dimensions (i.e., political, economic, and sociocultural environment)

TABLE 1 A Framework for Events' Overall Planning

Field and goal	Content/Parameters	Outputs
1. Planning: Planning and strategies are the foundation for decision-making.	Concern: Overall strategy (pre-event, during and post-event) necessary to reach objectives. Key elements of strategy: Analyze internal and external environment, develop a vision, and determine clear and precise objectives.	Objectives and strategies. Formulate a strategic plan. Sources of financing (e.g., grants, sponsorship, sponsor, sales, etc.). Pre-event marketing strategy. Build up partnership schemes.
2. Product/event development: Build up a portfolio of events.	Resources/attractions evaluation (infrastructures, etc.); through the planning approach, a destination attempts to build its tourism event-based product.	Type of event: Cultural, sporting, recreational/leisure, business. Events portfolio: Generating a lot of benefits, mainly contribution to create or enhance an event-based brand; theming strategy; offer a bundle of experiences.
3. Event management: Goal: Organize the event and elaborate appropriate action plans for implementation.	Concern: Management and performance. Management issues and operational strategies during the event. Policies, programs, and action plans.	Type of organizing body/partnerships in the management (new or existing; public, private, or mixed); actors involved and their roles. Legal and risk management issues: venue, leisure, sponsor, etc. Services management strategies: Access, communications, security and safety, health, information, special visitor services, and catering. Human resources management. Event logistics: ticketing, queuing, transport, waste, etc.
4. Marketing strategy: Objective: Commercial exploitation and enhance an image and continuous attractiveness.	An event's marketing plan. During and post-event. Image, target groups, and markets. Promotion and communications strategy.	Tourism promotion to stimulate and reinforce international visitation. Sponsorship: identifying sponsors, developing proposals, etc. Securing knowledge management for marketing purposes. A post-event marketing strategy: working with key market segments and developing research to monitor its efficiency. Marketing partnership schemes.
5. Monitoring and evaluation: Objectives: (a) To evaluate event's impacts and (b) To ensure and measure events' competitiveness and efficiency.	During and post-event phase. Concern: Benefices and costs on stakeholder and efficient use of resources. Evaluation: What, when, and why to evaluate events.	On-site monitoring, conflict resolution, and problem-solving. Assess stakeholder collaboration. Impact studies: attainment of goals/output achieved. Identifying future events: continuing use of infrastructure and knowledge through acquiring and hosting events. Restatement of goals, strategies, and program, if appropriate

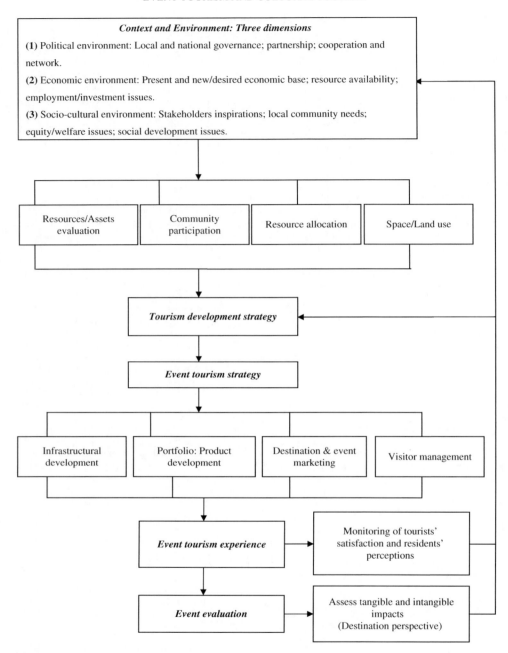

FIGURE 2 A conceptual framework for managing event tourism.
Source: Adapted from Page and Hall (2003) and Sharpley and Roberts (2005).

of the proposed framework. The political, economic, and sociocultural environment must be taken into account in order to identify appropriate management structures, networks, and interactions in developing event tourism, as well as opportunities or threats. Moreover, there are two needs to be satisfied (Law, 2002): (a) the need to consider tourism not in isolation but as a part of a holistic approach to economic and social policymaking and (b) the need to avoid either social exclusion or the lack of local community involvement in decision-making. These two needs are satisfied through the suggested model. With respect to this framework some key elements deserve to be stressed.

Context, environment, and strategy. This initial analysis is a necessary step to a strategic perspective. Once this analysis has been performed, attention can be paid to preparing a tourism development strategy. This strategy is the general framework that determines event tourism strategy.

Event tourism strategy. Embraces the supply of attractions and facilities, associated infrastructural developments and appropriate marketing plans, as well as visitor management strategies designed to optimize the visitor experience while minimizing the negative impacts on local population.

Community participation and consultation. It is vital that local inhabitants participate in large-scale events to secure broad-based support, and to simultaneously identify public concerns early on and take action to address these concerns. The issue is addressing the local population's perspective concerning opportunities, strengths, and visions, and also risks, weaknesses, and problems associated with the event. Simultaneously, local business and tourism enterprises must be involved. Another point is the allocation of financial resources, for example, which projects and on what basis (public, private, or mixed).

Implementation. Obviously, the necessary action plans are evolving through the strategy's implementation process. Appropriate action plans for each area should be carried out.

Event marketing strategy. It has been suggested (Allen et al., 2005) that an appropriate strategy would be to build up a portfolio of events, ranging from the occasional international or national mega-event to regular or one-time local events. This strategy could generate a series of beneficial outcomes (i.e., take advantage of an event by directly associating it to destination's image and increased awareness of the hosting destination).

Events evaluation and monitoring. The success of strategies and plans should be systematically monitored and assessed. An indicator system contributes to the assessment and measurement of events' efficiency. This system could be used for management purposes (i.e., to avoid negative impacts of future events) and for benchmarking (i.e., to assess impacts, processes or products in comparison to other competitors). Particular emphasis should be placed upon two parameters: (a) residents' attitudes and perceptions towards event tourism strategy and (b) attendees' satisfaction with the product they experience. It is important to focus on monitoring attendees' motivations and satisfaction. Understanding motives is an important ingredient in developing events that most fully meet the needs of participants. The phases of monitoring and evaluation, necessary steps within a strategic management approach, could lead to strategy and plan modifications, if necessary.

Obviously, the proposed conceptual framework simultaneously places emphasis upon two interlinked challenges: efficient management and appropriate marketing. However, it should be stressed that event tourism requires a case-study approach, as each destination is likely to adopt a unique combination of management and marketing policies according to local needs. This approach improves our knowledge and renders events more effective in achieving particular objectives. This framework suggests an integrated domain of fit by providing the whole scope of the elements to be aligned in order to ensure events destination—environment fit (Mackellar, 2006; Venkatraman & Camillus, 1984). Accordingly, it contributes in the improvement of event management's efficiency. The following issues are raised from the proposed exploration model: (a) The managerial use of this framework—the extent to which various elements can be controlled or influenced in order to improve efficiency; (b) the strategy formulation and implementation issue and their interactions (i.e., the process of arriving at the appropriate strategy); and (c) the measurement and assessment of efficiency—how efficiency (fit between strategy and structure) is to be measured. Such a framework could constitute the basis for designing an empirical methodology.

DISCUSSION AND CONCLUSIONS

In the future, professional events planning and management will become even more challenging due to the economic context and the increasing number of events taking place. In the filed of events management, the overall goal is to ensure efficiency (i.e., optimization in the use of resources) and effectiveness and competitiveness of events, understood as their ability to achieve quality (i.e., satisfaction of the actors or participants, attendees, and stakeholders). The literature review indicated that there are multiple actors, organizational structures, networks, and interactions involved in events management. This study has drawn attention to the need of adopting a network analysis and a value-chain approach to events. Furthermore, it emphasizes the importance of events as a component of destination's strategic management that could contribute to positive outcomes optimization. The most important success factor seems to be the required fit between the event itself and the destination, in terms of size, positioning, and dimensions.

The proposed framework aims to address the objective of improving events management efficiency. It highlights the various factors, organizations and their interactions that influence events management efficiency. It might be regarded as: (a) a conceptual instrument useful to address management challenges identified in this study and (b) a tool which contributes to the efficiency of event management strategies. It is intended to aid destination managers and tourism policymakers in adopting an integrated approach to events tourism, and researchers in implementing appropriate empirical work that would render this framework operational.

There are useful managerial implications to be drawn from the suggested framework. Decisions to host an event tend to rely on a hope that some positive impacts would be generated rather than on a conscious effort to increase the capabilities of the local economy to realize potential benefits. The implication is that destination managers who plan to host events should adopt and implement a strategic management approach and put a lot of effort in influencing network interactions. On the other hand, the marketing perspective has been incorporated into the framework. The challenge for event marketing is to identify the means to capitalize on motives and background in order to optimize event attendance. Furthermore, the suggested instrument contributes to promoting a more effective and profitable collaboration and cooperation among all actors who directly and indirectly participate in events tourism supply of a destination.

LIMITATIONS

However, the study has some limitations. First, it suggests an exploration model; consequently there is a need for further application and measurement. Second, it has to be empirically tested in order to control for its validity and reliability. Results from empirical studies could provide a basis for further development and refinement of the instrument. Third, further empirical work is needed to make it more operational with respect to the investigation of events networks dynamics and the development of appropriate strategies for event management. As it has been already stressed, a case-study approach to event management could improve our knowledge and render events more efficient and competitive. This is the most crucial issue for destinations that consider investing into the field of event tourism.

REFERENCES

Allen, J., O'Toole, W., Harris, R., & O'Donnell, A. (2005). Festival and special event management (3rd ed.). Queensland, Australia: John Wiley & Sons.

Barker, M., Page, S., & Meyer, D. (2002). Evaluating the impact of the 2002 America's Cup on Auckland, New Zealand. *Event Management*, 7(2), 79–92.

Bowdin, G., McDonnell, I., Allen, J., & O'Toole, W. (2001). *Events management*. Oxford, England: Butterworth-Heinemann.

Bramwell, B. (1997). Strategic planning before and after a mega-event. *Tourism Management*, *18*(3), 167–176. doi:10.1016/S0261-5177(96)00118-5

Burgan, B., & Mules, T. (1992). Economic impact of sporting events. *Annals of Tourism Research*, *19*, 700–710. doi:10.1016/0160-7383(92)90062-T

Burgan, B., & Mules, T. (2001). Reconciling cost-benefit and economic impact assessment for event tourism. *Tourism Economics*, *7*, 321–330.

Chon, K. S., & Olsen, M. (1990). Applying the strategic management process in the management of tourism organizations. *Tourism Management*, *11*, 206–213. doi:10.1016/0261-5177(90)90043-9

Daniels, M., Norman, W., & Henry, M. (2004). Estimating income effects of a sport tourism event. *Annals of Tourism Research*, *31*(1), 180–199. doi:10.1016/j.annals.2003.10.002

Davidson, R. (2003). Adding pleasure to business. *Journal of Convention and Event Tourism*, *5*(1), 29–38.

Derrett, R. (2003). Making sense of how festivals demonstrate a community's sense of place. *Event Management*, *8*(1), 49–58. doi:10.3727/152599503108751694

Dwyer, L., Forsyth, P., & Spurr, R. (2004). Evaluating tourism's economic effects: New and old approaches. *Tourism Management*, *25*, 307–317. doi:10.1016/S0261-5177(03)00131-6

Dwyer, L., Forsyth, P., & Spurr, R. (2005). Estimating the impacts of special events on the economy. *Journal of Travel Research*, *43*, 351–359. doi:10.1177/0047287505274648

Dwyer, L., Mellor, R., Mistilis, N., & Mules, T. (2000). A framework for assessing "tangible" and "intangible" impacts of events and conventions. *Event Management*, *6*(3), 175–189.

Erickson, G. S., & Kushner, R. J. (1999). Public event networks: An application of marketing theory to sporting events. *European Journal of Marketing*, *33*, 348–364. doi:10.1108/03090569910253189

Faulkner, B., Chalip, L., Brown, G., Jago, L., March, R., & Woodside, A. (2000). Monitoring the tourism impacts of the Sydney 2000 Olympics. *Event Management*, *6*, 231–246.

Felsenstein, D., & Fleischer, A. (2003). Local festivals and tourism promotion: The role of public assistance and visitor expenditure. *Journal of Travel Research*, *41*, 365–392. doi:10.1177/0047287503041004007

Fletcher, J., & Cooper, C. (1996). Tourism strategy planning. *Annals of Tourism Research*, *23*(1), 181–200. doi:10.1016/0160-7383(95)00057-7

Formica, S., & Kothari, T. (2008). Strategic destination planning: Analyzing the future of tourism. *Journal of Travel Research*, *46*, 355–367. doi:10.1177/0047287507312410

Fredline, L., Jago, L., & Deery, M. (2003). The development of a generic scale to measure the social impacts of events. *Event Management*, *8*(1), 23–37. doi:10.3727/152599503108751676

Gelan, A. (2003). The British Open; local economic impacts. *Annals of Tourism Research*, *30*, 406–425. doi:10.1016/S0160-7383(02)00098-1

Getz, D. (1997). *Event management and event tourism*. New York, NY: Cognizant Communications.

Getz, D. (2008). Event tourism: Definition, evolution, and research. *Tourism Management*, *29*, 403–428, doi:10.1016/j.tourman.2007.07.017

Getz, D., Andersson, T., & Larson, M. (2007). Festival stakeholder roles: Concepts and case studies. *Event Management*, *10*, 103–122. doi:10.3727/152599507780676689

Getz, D., & Fairley, S. (2002). Media management at sport events for destination promotion: Case studies and concepts. *Event Management*, *8*(3), 127–139. doi:10.3727/1525995031436926

Gnoth, J., & Anwar, S. A. (2000). New Zealand bets on event tourism. *Cornell Hotel and Restaurant Administration Quarterly*, *41*(4), 72–83. doi:10.1177/001088040004100417

Gursoy, D., Kyungmi, K., & Uysal, M. (2004). Perceived impacts of festivals and special events by organizers: An extension and validation. *Tourism Management*, *25*(2), 171–181. doi:10.1016/S0261-5177(03)00092-X.

Higham, J., & Hinch, T. (2002). Tourism, sport and seasons: The challenges and potentials of overcoming seasonality in the sport and tourism sectors. *Tourism Management*, *23*, 175–185. doi:10.1016/S0261-5177(01)00046-2

Kaspar, C., & Laesser, C. (1994). Systems approach. In S. F. Witt & L. Mountinho (Eds.), *Tourism marketing handbook* (pp. 110–134). Hertfordshire, England: Prentice-Hall.

Kim, N. S., & Chalip, L. (2004). Why travel to the FIFA World Cup? Effects of motives, background, interest, and constraints. *Tourism Management*, *25*, 695–707. doi:10.1016/j.tourman.2003.08.011

Larson, M. (2009). Joint event production in the jungle, the park, and the garden: Metaphors of event networks. *Tourism Management*, *30*, 393–399. doi:10.1016/j.tourman.2008.08.003

Law, C. (2002). *Urban tourism: The visitor economy and the growth of large cities* (2nd ed.). London, England: Continuum.

Long, P. (2000). After the event: Perspectives on organizational partnerships in the management of a themed festival year. *Event Management*, *6*(1), 45–59.

Mackellar, J. (2006). Conventions, festivals, and tourism: Exploring the network that binds. *Journal of Convention and Event Tourism*, *8*(2), 45–56. doi:10.1300/J452v08n02_03

Masterman, G. (2004). *Strategic sports event management. An international approach*. Oxford, England: Butterworth-Heinemann.

May, V. (1995). Environmental implications of the 1992 Winter Olympic Games. *Tourism Management*, *16*(4), 269–275. doi:10.1016/0261-5177(95)00016-H

Morse, J. (2001). The Sydney 2000 Olympic Games: How the Australian tourist commission leveraged the games for tourism. *Journal of Vacation Marketing*, *7*(2), 101–107. doi:10.1177/135676670100700201

Nicholson, R. E., & Pearce, D. G. (2001). Why do people attend events? A comparative analysis of visitor motivations at four south island events. *Journal of Travel Research*, *39*, 449–460. doi:10.1177/004728750103900412

Page, S., & Hall, C. M. (2003). *Managing urban tourism*. Harlow, England: Pearson Education.

Pavlovich, K. (2000). The evolution and transformation of a tourism destination network: The Waitomo caves, New Zealand. *Tourism Management*, *24*, 203–216, doi:10.1016/S0261-5177(02)00056-0

Poon, A. (2002). *Tourism, technology and competitive strategies* (3rd ed.). Oxon, England: CABI.

Porter, M. (1998). *On competition: A Harvard Business Review book*. Boston, MA: Harvard Business School Publishing.

Ryan, C. (2002). Equity, management, power sharing and sustainability—issues of the "new tourism." *Tourism Management*, *23*(1), 17–26. doi:10.1016/S0261-5177(01)00064-4

Sautter, E. T., & Leisen, B. (1999). Managing stakeholders, a tourism planning model. *Annals of Tourism Research*, *26*(2), 312–328. doi:10.1016/S0160-7383(98)00097-8

Sharpley, R., & Roberts, L. (2005). Managing urban tourism. In L. Pender & R. Sharpley (Eds.), *The Management of Tourism*. London: Sage.

Stokes, R. (2004). A framework for the analysis of events—tourism knowledge networks. *Journal of Hospitality and Tourism Management*, *11*(2), 108–121.

Stokes, R. (2006). Network-based strategy making for events tourism. *European Journal of Marketing*, *40*, 682–695. doi:10.1108/03090560610657895

Stokes, R. (2008). Tourism strategy making: Insights to the events tourism domain. *Tourism Management*, *29*, 252–262. doi:10.1016/j.tourman.2007.03014

Thrane, C. (2002). Jazz festival visitors and their expenditures: Linking spending patterns to musical interest. *Journal of Travel Research*, *40*, 281–286. doi:10.1177/0047287502040003006

Venkatraman, N., & Camillus, J. C. (1984). Exploring the concept of "fit" in strategic management. *Academy of Management Review*, *9*, 513–525. doi:10.2307/258291

Wood, E. (2005). Measuring the economic and social impacts of local authority events. *International Journal of Public Sector Management*, *18*(1), 37–53. doi:10.1108/09513550510576143

Yilmaz, Y., & Bititci, U. S. (2006). Performance measurement in tourism: A value chain model. *International Journal of Contemporary Hospitality Management*, *18*, 341–349. doi:10.1108/09596110610665348

Utilizing the VICE Model for the Sustainable Development of the Innibos Arts Festival

M. van NIEKERK and W. J. L. COETZEE

Department of Tourism Management, Tshwane University of Technology, Tshwane, South Africa

The purpose of the study is to ensure the continuous and sustainable growth of the Innibos Arts Festival in South Africa while balancing the needs and demands of the visitors to the festival, the tourism industry as a whole, and the surrounding community with a focus on the environment. Continuous growth of festivals in South Africa is ensured as government supports and promotes this as part of its strategy for economic development. However, the sustainability of the festivals has come under scrutiny as many of these festivals compete for similar tourism markets. Destination managers and developers all over the world, but specifically in New Zealand and the United Kingdom, have identified the visitors, industry, community, and environment (VICE) model as a critical success factor in the sustainable development of any tourism destination. Equitable interaction among the VICE must occur before the tourism destination will be sustainable. The VICE model was used to identify the profiles, demands, and needs of the visitors to the festival; the role and impact of the event on the industry and businesses; the impact on the Nelspruit community and environment (where the Innibos Arts Festival is held); and how these elements should synergize with a view to ensure sustainability. Self-completion questionnaires were used to determine the sustainability of the festival. A total of 2,584 visitor surveys, 206 business surveys, and 520 community surveys, which included questions on the environmental concept, were completed over the past 5 years (2004–2008). The results of the study indicated that the VICE model was successfully utilized in the study of the Innibos Arts Festival. It highlighted critical areas in the different categories of the VICE model that require attention and development. The successful management and development of these critical aspects would ensure the sustainability of the festival. It can therefore be concluded that the VICE model can be utilized to ensure the sustainability of festivals.

INTRODUCTION

The rapid growth of the tourism industry has caused a mêlée in the industry, as various tourism destinations are competing for their share in the global tourism market. The competitive nature of the tourism industry has raised the issue of sustainability, as destinations often compete for similar tourist markets. South Africa, for example, which is known for its wildlife, natural beauty, and cultural diversity, competes on the African continent for similar tourism markets with countries such as Kenya, Botswana, Zimbabwe, and Tanzania.

Continuous development and differentiation of the tourism product is therefore necessary to create a unique product that will position the destination more favorably against its opposition and to ensure the sustainability of the destination. Festivals and events such as the Innibos Arts Festival are often used as a new product offering that creates new demands and interests, according to Quinn (2006). Allen, McDonnell, and Harris (2002) confirmed this and stated that governments realize the benefits of events and festivals and promote these as part of their strategies for economic development, nation-building, and destination marketing.

The economic and social benefits of festivals and events have been thoroughly researched by various authors (Daniels & Norman, 2003; McHone & Rungeling, 2000; Crompton, Lee, & Shuster, 2001; Rogerson, 2007; Goldblatt, 2002; Allen et al., 2002). Quin (2006), however, stated that very few researchers have focused on the specific context of the sustainability of these events. When sustainability has featured, economic impact tends to be the central concern (O'Sullivan & Jackson, 2002) and little attention has been paid to whether these festivals can provide an effective vehicle for sustainable tourism. Bramwell and Lane (2008) argued that communities and a festival that are truly sustainable are those where the questions of social needs and welfare and economic opportunities are integrated into the particular environmental constraints.

The study therefore aims to utilize the visitors, industry, community, and environment (VICE) model—a model that is often used in sustainable destination development—to create a structure for the different stakeholders. The model can then be used to ensure the sustainability of the Innibos Arts

Festival and similar festivals. The research will present the needs, potential, and limitations of the demand and supply side, the positive and negative impacts of the festival on the local community and environment, as well as the important role that the Innibos Arts Festival has played in the development of new tourism products in the area.

The literature review will elucidate concepts of sustainability, festivals, and the VICE model, where after the methodology of the research study will follow. The study will then report on the findings of the research and will conclude with recommendations for ensuring the sustainability of the Innibos Arts Festival.

LITERATURE REVIEW

Festivals and events are now a worldwide tourism phenomenon (Prentice & Andersen, 2003; Getz, 1991; Grant & Paliwoda, 1998) and are central to our culture as perhaps never before (Allen et al., 2002). Goldblatt (2002) confirms this and states that festivals have shown tremendous growth as larger and smaller towns seek tourism dollars created by short-term events. Festivals are also used to stimulate tourism growth during off-season periods or to focus on domestic tourism markets. Goldblatt (2002) concludes that regardless of the motivations for the event, it provides a golden opportunity to celebrate culture while providing deep meaning for those who participate and attend.

Celebrating culture is the reason why arts festivals developed in South Africa. The Grahamstown National Arts Festival took place for the first time in 1974 and celebrated its 34th year of existence in 2008. According to Hauptfleisch (2006), the Grahamstown Festival can be seen as the grand-parent of modern South African festivals, which introduced the concept of multidisciplinary arts festivals to South Africa. He continues, "its origins, deriving from the 1820 Settlers' Foundation's original aim, namely to celebrate, (re-)establish, empower and maintain the cultural heritage of English-speaking South Africans in the face of the triple threat of Americanization, Afrikanerization and Africanization." The cultural aspect, on which the festivals were built, has ensured the success of the festivals over the years.

Hauptfleisch (2006) and Coetser (2002) suggest that the Afrikaans-language festivals started in the 1990s when the Afrikaans-speaking population (6 million out of 44 million people currently in South Africa) began to fear the extinction of their language and culture under the new South African dispensation and its expressed preference for English as the *lingua franca*.

As a result of this fear, the Klein Karoo National Arts Festival (KKNK) opened its doors in 1995, with the main aim to promote, encourage, and preserve arts and culture in Afrikaans. The Aardklop National Arts Festival followed in 1998 and the Gariep Arts Festival in 1999; the Matzikama Rittelfees and Word Festival followed in 2000, and the Volksblad Arts Festival in 2001; the Innibos Arts Festival and Suidooster Festival started in 2003; and the latest addition, the Cultivaria Arts Festival, in 2005. Hauptfleisch (2006, p. 186) states that the original impetus for these Afrikaans Arts Festivals was "the need to celebrate, (re-)establish, empower and maintain the cultural heritage of Afrikaans-speaking South Africans in the face of the language's diminished official status, from co-national language with English to one of eleven 'national languages.' " These festivals have managed to stimulate the creation of Afrikaans plays and writing and in themselves constitute events whose aim it is to celebrate the Afrikaner culture in all its diversity.

Since 1995, nine Afrikaans arts festivals originated in South Africa and, as they are competing for the same target market (Afrikaans-speaking people), the question of the sustainability of these festivals arises. One way of ensuring the sustainability of the festivals is to utilize the VICE model (Figure 1). It is a model that has been used by destination managers and planners all over the world, specifically in New Zealand and the United Kingdom, with the main aim of ensuring the sustainable development of destinations by looking at the following aspects: visitors, industry, community, and the environment.

According to Simmons (2004), a successful and sustainable tourism strategy identifies how to:

- Welcome, involve and satisfy visitors.
- Achieve a profitable and prosperous industry.
- Engage and benefit host communities.
- Protect and enhance the local environment.

The first aspect comprises visitors (demand). Visitors and the knowledge of visitors' psychology are extremely important in determining the

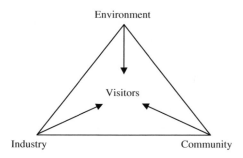

FIGURE 1 VICE model.
Source: Simmons (2004).

success and sustainability of tourism destinations (Del Bosque & Martin, 2008). Aspects such as attitudes, decision-making processes, experience, emotions, and satisfaction levels have to be taken into account in order to understand the psychology of the visitor to the festival. Nicholson and Pearce (2001) confirm this and state that there are three reasons for understanding the motivations of visitors for attending a festival. Firstly, it is the key to designing better products and services, as visitor satisfaction can be determined. Secondly, the visitors' decision-making processes can be understood, and thirdly, these factors will become more and more important as the number of Afrikaans Festivals increases and the diversity of these festivals leads to heightened competition. Figure 2 indicates the demand components and helps the festival planning committee to answer questions regarding who attends, why they attend, what services they utilize, how long they stay, their level of satisfaction with their visit, and the economic benefit that is generated in the local economy.

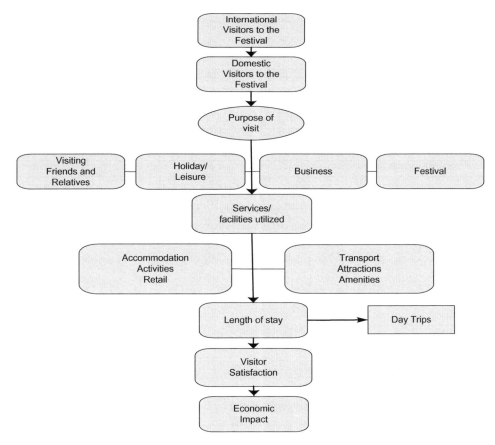

FIGURE 2 Visitor demand model for a festival.
Source: Simmons (2004).

If the Innibos Arts Festival wants to remain sustainable, it must pay attention to its visitors; it must know where they come from, involve them, and satisfy them, which in turn will ensure return visits to the festival.

Business and the tourism industry form the second aspect of the VICE model and can only be profitable and prosperous if money enters the local economy either through domestic or international visitors. Festivals ensure economic injections into the local economy and can turn around economic depreciation in off-season periods. Festivals create a unique opportunity for businesses in the local area to become involved and to benefit from the spin-offs of the festival. Researchers such as Allen et al. (2002) stated that when assessing the economic impact of a festival, there are two schools of thought that should be considered. The tourism industry, a commercial organization, or an entrepreneur is primarily concerned with the financial income and expenditure of the festival and, concurrently, whether or not the festival is likely to generate a profit for the business. The other school of thought is supported by a governmental point of view where the main focus is on the wider economical impact of the festival and its influence on the host community. For the Innibos Arts Festival to be sustainable, it is important to involve the tourism industry and local businesses in the preparations for the festival and to aim to ensure the economic viability of the industry. The economic impact of the festival can be measured by visitor numbers and visitor spending, as well as by direct surveys of business employment and financial ratios. Crompton, Lee, and Shuster (2002) explained the role of festivals in the community as shown in Figure 3. Residents will pay taxes to the local municipality, which uses a portion of these funds to subsidize the event, either by means of services or financial assistance. The Innibos Arts Festival will then attract nonresident visitors to Nelspruit who will spend money both inside and outside the festival facilities. The new money that is generated from these visitors creates jobs and income in the community for the residents, which completes the cycle.

The third aspect of the model is the community. The attitude of the community towards the festival should be fully investigated in the light of social structures, positive and negative impacts, as well as tourism development and investment opportunities. Community involvement and social impact of festivals are often researched (Sairinen & Kumpulainen, 2006; Kuvan & Akan, 2004; Williams & Lawson, 2001; Chen, 2001; Waitt, 2003; Delamere, 2001). Benefits that the festival can bring to the community include job and investment opportunities, improved public facilities, preservation of local culture, and the creation of local pride, while negative impacts of the festival can include crowding; traffic congestion; degradation of the environment; and higher costs, rates, and taxes (Quinn, 2006; Haley, Snaith, & Miller, 2005; Chen, 2000; Delamere, 2001). To ensure

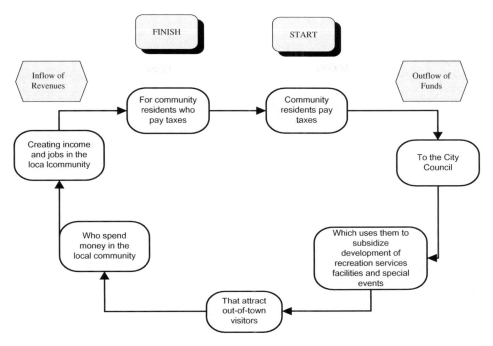

FIGURE 3 The conceptual rationale for undertaking economic impact studies.
Source: Crompton, Lee, and Schuster (2001).

sustainability, festivals must satisfy both community and visitor expectations. Effective community consultation is the key to sustainability of the festival as it ensures that the festival supports the economic and social goals of the area.

The environment can be identified as the last aspect in the VICE model. Bowdin, Allen, O'Toole, Harris, and McDonnell (2006) stated that the concern for sustainability of the environment during events and festivals is on the increase, and when discussing the environment, the built and natural environments should both be considered. Sustainable tourism has, for a very long time, focused on issues of environmental sustainability (Cottrell & Cutumisu, 2006) and festivals can have a significant impact on the environmental quality of the area temporarily, but also permanently. Aspects such as infrastructure requirements, water supply, electricity, the increase of water consumption in the area during the festival, solid waste services, and noise pollution should be investigated. Remediation undertaken after the festival should be noted, as well as precautions that should be put in place the following year with a view to help minimize environmental degrading. A structured approach to managing the impact of the festival on the natural assets is needed to ensure sustainability (Simmons, 2004).

METHODOLOGY

An explanatory study was conducted to utilize the VICE model for the sustainable development of the Innibos Arts Festival. The study was conducted from a positivist paradigm, where the world is guided by scientific rules that explain the behavior of phenomena through causal relationships (Jennings, 2001). An inductive approach was followed that allowed the researcher to pursue data collection within a theoretical framework, an approach that is dominant in the social sciences. The epistemological basis of the study placed the researcher in an objective and value-free position, where the researcher did not impact or have an influence on the results or findings of the research.

The target population of the study included all visitors to the Innibos Arts Festival for the past 5 years, a total of 314 000 people, businesses in Nelspruit (3,000) and the community of the city of Nelspruit (21,537). Nonrandom sampling by means of the purposive sampling approach was used to determine the sample for this study. The sample size calculator (Creative Research System, 2008) was used to determine the sample sizes. Table 1 indicates the sample sizes that were drawn from the visitors to the festival over the last 5 years.

Table 2 indicates the sample sizes that were drawn from the Nelspruit community during the time of the festival.

Table 3 indicates the sample sizes of the business survey conducted during the festival over the past 5 years.

TABLE 1 Sample Sizes of Visitors to the Festival

Year	2004 visitors	2005 visitors	2006 visitors	2007 visitors	2008 visitors
Population	22,000	45,000	60,000	87,000	100,000
Confident level	95%	95%	95%	95%	95%
Confident interval	6	5	4	5	4
Sample size	281	381	594	382	597
Completed	350	577	620	387	650
Total	+69	+196	+26	+5	+53

TABLE 2 Sample Sizes of the Nelspruit Community Survey

Year	2004 community	2005 community	2006 community	2007 community	2008 community
Population (census 2002)	21,537	21,537	21,537	21,537	21,537
Confident level	95%	95%	95%	95%	95%
Confident interval	9	20	9	12	7
Sample size	118	24	96	67	195
Completed	120	20	106	62	212
Total	+2	−4	+10	−5	+17

TABLE 3 Sample Sizes of the Business Survey

Year	2004 business	2005 business	2006 business	2007 business	2008 business
Population (No reliable figures available)	3,000	3,000	3,000	3,000	3,000
Confident level	95%	95%	95%	95%	95%
Confident interval	18	11	15	15	13
Sample size	29	77	42	42	56
Completed	29	77	45	0	55
Total	0	0	+3	−42	−1

The study made use of quantitative research methodologies. Self-completion questionnaires were completed over the 4-day period of the festival and were used to determine the sustainability of the festival. Over the past 5 years a total of 2,584 visitor surveys, 206 industry and business surveys, and 520 community surveys were conducted. In 2007, no business surveys were conducted due to human resource constraints. The environmental survey was only conducted in the fifth year of the festival. The Statistical Package for the Social Sciences (SPSS) 15 was used to analyze the data and to draw descriptive statistics and inferential statistics from the data.

RESULTS AND DISCUSSIONS

The results of the study are reported according to the components of the VICE model.

Visitors

Table 4 indicates the demographic information of visitors to the festival over the 5-year period. It can be seen that the distribution of gender was consistent over the 5-year period with a slight increase in female visitors during 2008. There was no real movement in the age groups of the visitors, although a slight increase is detected in the 36–45-year-old category. Table 4 also indicates a constant growth in the white population attending the festival; this also explains the growth in the language category "Afrikaans." The level of education and place of residence have remained similar over the past 5 years.

Table 5 indicates the travel patterns of visitors to the Innibos Arts Festival over the past 5 years. Attention should be given to their reasons for attending the festival, where a definitive increase can be detected in the category "Afrikaans festival." The festival is beginning to establish itself as an Afrikaans festival and not only a festival for sociable reasons. A slight

TABLE 4 Demographic Information

Demographics	2004 (%)	2005 (%)	2006 (%)	2007 (%)	2008 (%)
Gender					
Male	48	41	41	45	35
Female	52	59	59	55	65
Age groups					
18–25 years	32	32	28	38	24
26–35 years	22	24	22	20	21
36–45 years	18	17	21	24	26
46–60 years	19	19	24	15	24
60+ years	9	8	5	3	5
Race					
White	90	92	95	95	99
Other	10	8	5	5	1
Language					
Afrikaans	84	83	84	86	94
English	7	13	13	13	4
Other	9	4	3	1	2
Level of education					
No school qualification	6	4	10	3	1
Matric equivalent	41	40	43	33	40
Diploma/degree	30	31	29	42	34
Professional	8	10	9	7	12
Other (specify)	8	7	0	0	1
Postgraduate	7	8	9	15	12
Place of residence					
Mpumalanga	48	56	65	67	65
Gauteng	31	29	24	19	26
Other	21	15	11	14	9

increase in the "two days spent at festival" category and a decrease in the "four days spent at the festival" can be seen as a concern, although it can be explained by the place of residence of the visitors. Fewer people travel from Mpumalanga Province where the festival takes place and more people come from Gauteng Province, which is located 350 km from the festival location. Many of these visitors come to the festival over the weekend, which explains the increase in the "two days spent at the festival" category and a decrease in the "four days spent at the festival" category. Furthermore, it can be said that the slight increase in the use of guest houses or bed-and-breakfast establishments can be seen as a positive contribution to the tourism industry in Nelspruit.

The Innibos Art Festival is unique in that it can differentiate itself from other Afrikaans festivals in South Africa. The main festival ground is enclosed, which ensures accurate attendance figures through access control. This also allows for a more accurate economic impact study. Table 6 depicts the economic impact and contribution of the festival over the past five years. Although visitors increasingly tend to feel that entrance fees are too high, they still agree that it is value for money. The gross monthly income

TABLE 5 Travel Patterns of Visitors

Travel patterns	2004 (%)	2005 (%)	2006 (%)	2007 (%)	2008 (%)
Festival the only reason for visiting?					
Yes	52	43	40	32	38
No	23	25	21	18	24
Local	25	32	39	50	48
Reasons for attending the festival					
Quality productions	8	9	10	13	11
Variety of productions	11	11	12	11	11
Safety during the festival	4	6	6	8	4
The closest arts festival	11	10	11	11	11
Good ticket prices	4	5	5	6	1
Afrikaans festival	23	23	23	15	32
Different from other festivals	2	4	5	8	4
Sociable	17	24	25	25	21
Other	20	8	3	3	5
Days spent at the festival					
One day	12	17	17	13	15
Two days	15	17	18	13	22
Three days	13	18	20	18	19
Four days	60	48	45	56	43
Mode of transport					
Airplane	8	5	1	1	3
Own vehicle	89	92	95	96.5	94
Tour bus	1	2	2	2	1
Rented car	2	1	2	0.5	2
Type of accommodation					
Family and friends	42	37	28	24	24
Guest house or bed and breakfast	10	9	8	8	13
Hotel	6	6	7	4	5
Camping	12	7	7	3	4
Rented house	9	13	3	2	4
Other/local	21	28	47	59	50

and expenditure patterns of visitors are increasing, which ensure a higher economic impact in the area, as is evident in Table 6.

Another component in the visitor category is the satisfaction levels of the visitors. A satisfied customer will return to the festival. Table 7 indicates that 72% of visitors are repeat visitors and that a very high percentage of visitors will return to the festival. Visitors are also satisfied with the good variety that the festival program offers every year. Visitors are mostly satisfied or very satisfied with the festival with some room for improvement identified such as parking and toilet facilities.

Industry

The second aspect of the VICE model is the tourism industry and the prosperity that the festival brings to businesses in the area. Table 8 reports on the

TABLE 6 Economic Impacts and Contributions

Economic aspects	2004	2005	2006	2007	2008
Entrance fees					
Too high	34%	29%	32%	25%	30%
Value for money	50%	62%	59%	70%	66%
Too low	5%	3%	3%	1%	4%
Structured in another way	11%	6%	6%	4%	0%
Gross monthly income					
R0–R5,000	48%	43%	42%	44%	22%
R5,000–R10,000	23%	27%	23%	31%	41%
R15,000 more	29%	30%	35%	25%	37%
Expenditure patterns	(Average per person for the festival)				
Show tickets	R89.23	R159.69	R147.92	R84.12	
Accommodation	R168.28	R145.25	R148.36	R150.62	
Food and restaurants	R154.25	R192.66	R222.29	R164.27	
Transport	R69.12	R56.76	R66.69	R106.33	
Alcoholic drinks	R45.57	R154.29	R104.23	R210.92	
Nonalcoholic drinks	R38.23	R50.28	R52.68	R52.81	
Shopping at retail stores	R91.39	R103.06	R127.24	R96.74	
Tobacco products	R5.93	R35.24	R32.83	R17.71	
Souvenirs and gifts	R77.50	R74.16	R131.58	R109.39	
Parking	R2.33	R15.70	R15.02	R14.19	
Other	R23.53	R74.90	R0.00	R43.67	
Gate fees			R94.60	R45.00	
Average amount spent	R 765.38	R1,062.11	R1,048.84	R1,095.76	
Economic impact					
Visitor spending	R5,278,981	R8,438,325	R12,970,727	R18,017,800	
Organizer spending	R540,000	R220,000	R480,000	R830,000	
Exhibitor spending	R176,400	R302,500	R480,000	R500,000	
Total direct spending	R5,995,381	R9,785,825	R13,930,727	R19,347,800	
Multiplier	1.5	1.5	1.5	1.5	
Indirect impact	R2,997,691	R4,892,913	R6,965,363	R9,673,900	
Total impact	R8,993,172	R14,678,738	R20,896,090	R29,021,700	

Note. Exchange rate: US$1 = R7.75.

responses from the business sector. As previously mentioned, the industry survey was not conducted in 2007 due to human resources constraints. Table 8 shows that the festival has had a positive impact on businesses over the past 5 years. Losses reported to businesses due to the festival have been very low and most businesses increasingly employ part-time staff during the festival. The general feeling of businesses towards the festival is very positive and a decrease in leakages in the business sector is evident.

Community

The third aspect in the VICE model is the community aspect, which includes engagement and the benefits of the festival to the Nelspruit community.

TABLE 7 Visitor Satisfaction

Aspects for visitor satisfaction	2004 (%)	2005 (%)	2006 (%)	2007 (%)	2008 (%)
First time attendance					
Yes	–	–	–	–	28
No	–	–	–	–	72
Return visits					
Yes	88	94	98	99	97
No	12	6	2	1	3
The program					
Good variety	72	85	83	86	91
Not enough variety	18	10	11	12	6
Too explicit	4	2	2	1	2
Too conservative	6	3	4	1	1
Aspects	Very satisfied	Satisfied	Needs improvement	Did not use	
Art park	39	41	4	16	
Bosmall	35	43	6	15	
Food stalls	49	41	6	4	
Children's Entertainment	27	23	4	46	
Chill tent	32	23	5	40	
Toilets	28	44	23	5	
Security	54	37	5	4	
Information boards	43	41	12	4	
Open stages	60	29	5	6	
Entrance to festival	48	36	12	4	
Parking	34	37	24	5	

Table 9 presents the general community profile, which is very similar to the profile of the visitors. This similarity reduces the impact on the host community. Cultures, economic profiles, and education levels of visitors and the community of Nelspruit are very similar, which helps to keep tolerance levels high and irritation levels low. This is confirmed by the fact that very few of Nelspruit's community members leave Nelspruit during the festival.

Table 10 indicates that the community is increasingly taking ownership of and supporting the festival. A concern is the decrease in the "very positive about the festival" category to a "positive" feeling towards the festival. The community therefore still feels positive about the festival although the "wow" effect of the beginning years might be decreasing.

Table 11 shows how the local community currently experiences the sociocultural impact of the festival on the host community. It is evident that most of the positive impacts of the Innibos Arts Festival are also experienced by the community as positive, while they are not yet quite sure about the negative impacts of the festival. It is clear that the community had difficulty in evaluating the behavioral aspects of the festival-goers as many of them indicated "not sure" as a response.

TABLE 8 Impact of the Festival on the Industry

Impacts on industry	2004 (%)	2005 (%)	2006 (%)	2007 (%)	2008 (%)
Business located from festival grounds					
0–1 kilometer	100	65	50	–	88
1–5 kilometers	0	35	50	–	22
Impact of the festival on annual turnover					
Large increase	21	12	11	–	41
Increase	28	38	49	–	27
No increase	35	30	24	–	4
Decrease	10	14	13	–	2
Large decrease	6	6	3	–	0
Losses reported					
Yes	14	14	12	–	9
No	80	79	79	–	90
Not sure	6	7	9	–	1
Losses in terms of				–	
Theft	0	1	0	–	2
Breakage	0	1	0	–	2
Stock written off	7	3	3	–	4
Not applicable	93	96	97	–	86
Other	0	0	0	–	6
Losses compared to previous years					
More	7	4	4	–	4
Less	0	0	5	–	4
The same	0	5	12	–	15
Not applicable	93	91	89	–	77
Number of additional jobs created					
None	93	76	74	–	66
One to two	7	13	16	–	18
Two to three	0	0	0	–	9
Three to four	0	5	5	–	7
Five and more	0	6	5	–	7
Buying outside of Nelspruit (%)					
0–10	28	19	8	–	20
11–20	4	3	22	–	11
21–30	12	2	6	–	8
31–40	4	5	3	–	4
41–50	4	6	3	–	4
51–60	4	2	0	–	2
61–70	0	5	3	–	0
71–80	4	6	3	–	10
81–90	20	6	8	–	8
91–100	20	46	45	–	33
General attitude about Innibos					
Very positive	–	–	–	–	57
Positive	–	–	–	–	30
Neutral	–	–	–	–	13

TABLE 9 Community Profile

Community aspects	2004 (%)	2005 (%)	2006 (%)	2007 (%)	2008 (%)
Number of years in Nelspruit					
0–3 years	–	–	–	–	20
4–6 years	–	–	–	–	18
7 years and more	–	–	–	–	62
Gender					
Male	35	39	40	33	28
Female	65	61	60	67	72
Age groups					
18–25 years	13	6	20	8	28
26–35 years	29	39	30	17	22
36–45 years	32	44	28	39	22
46–60 years	22	11	17	30	22
60+ years	7	0	4	6	6
Race					
White	99	100	95	94	98
Other	1	0	5	6	2
Language					
Afrikaans	90	94	82	88	84
English	9	6	13	12	14
Other	1	0	5	0	2
Level of education					
No school qualification	5	0	5	3	3
Matric equivalent	25	22	49	25	48
Diploma/degree	48	67	30	48	32
Professional	0	0	0	0	16
Other (specify)	2	0	2	0	1
Post graduate	20	11	14	24	0
Gross monthly income					
R0–R5,000	49	50	38	27	30
R5,000–R10,000	37	33	47	44	41
R15,000 more	14	17	15	29	29
Do you leave Nelspruit during the festival?					
Yes	4	24	21	2	13
No	96	76	79	98	87

Environment

The last aspect in the VICE model is protection and enhancement of the environment. The impacts of the festival on the environment are indicated in Table 12. The community is of the opinion that the festival impacts positively on the environment and, although there are negative impacts, these are not significant.

IMPLEMENTATIONS AND CONCLUSIONS

The utilization of the VICE model in the case of the Innibos Arts Festival helped to identify critical areas in the various aspects of the model that,

TABLE 10 General Feelings Towards the Festival

Perception of event	2004 (%)	2005 (%)	2006 (%)	2007 (%)	2008 (%)
Did you attend the festival?					
Yes	34	41	64	71	83
Influence on quality of life					
Very positive	–	–	–	–	28
Positive	–	–	–	–	47
No influence	–	–	–	–	21
Negative	–	–	–	–	3
Very negative	–	–	–	–	1
Influence on quality of life in the community					
Very positive	–	–	–	–	35
Positive	–	–	–	–	53
No influence	–	–	–	–	9
Negative	–	–	–	–	3
Very negative	–	–	–	–	0
General perception of the festival					
Very positive	84	83	70	84	44
Positive	16	11	21	14	43
No influence	0	0	0	0	9
Negative	0	6	9	2	3
Very negative	0	0	0	0	1

if properly managed and developed, can ensure the sustainability of the festival.

- Visitors: The organizers of the festival currently have a well-defined profile of visitors to the festival as well as the changes in visitor profile that have occurred over the past 5 years. In general, the attitude, experiences, and satisfaction levels of visitors are high and they are motivated to return to the festival. There are no indications that the visitor numbers are declining and visitors are attending the festival mainly because it is an Afrikaans festival. The organizing committee should take these findings into consideration when planning future festivals.

- Industry: The *I* in the VICE model indicated that businesses and the tourism industry have a positive attitude towards the festival. The profitability and economic impact of the festival have increased and businesses are reaping the benefit of the positive impacts of the festival. When some businesses indicated in the earlier years of the festival that the event was taking away their business, the organizing committee spread shows all over the city to maximize the benefits to the whole industry. This reactive measurement has ensured the continuous support of the industry towards the festival.

- Community: The *C* in the VICE model indicated that the community has taken ownership of the festival. The demographic profile of the

TABLE 11 Sociocultural Effects of the Festival

Sociocultural	Agree (%)	Not sure (%)	Do not agree (%)
The festival:			
offers the opportunity to participate in interesting activities.	86	9	5
offers a new form of entertainment.	86	9	5
gives the opportunity to feel proud about Nelspruit.	84	12	4
offers the opportunity to meet new people.	79	14	7
ensures interaction between the host community and festival goers.	74	21	5
promotes good norms and values.	55	34	11
causes licentious behavior among people.	36	40	24
causes an increase in criminal activities.	30	33	37
causes a decline in social and moral norms.	33	26	42
causes a decline in the availability of facilities.	32	23	45
causes stress and disorganization in the lives of members of the community.	28	25	47
offers the host community the opportunity to take part in the organization of the festival.	54	29	17
offers the opportunity to promote the local culture.	76	12	12
successfully manages the abuse of liquor.	42	32	26

TABLE 12 Environmental (Built and Natural) Impacts

Environment (built and natural)	Agree	Not sure	Do not agree
The festival ensures the maintenance of facilities and the conservation of the environment.	59	28	13
The number of festival-goers to the area increases.	77	15	8
The main festival grounds and the areas around it are improved.	71	21	8
Public transportation during the festival increases.	66	27	7
Noise levels increase during the festival.	65	23	12
Litter increases around the festival grounds.	55	30	14
The environment (built and natural) is damaged during the festival.	43	29	28
The availability of parking decreases during the festival.	62	23	15
Traffic congestion increases.	68	22	10
There are too many people in Nelspruit during the festival.	51	17	32
It is becoming more difficult to find a quiet area in the city.	49	19	32

community is similar to that of the visitors, which reduces the sociocultural impact on the host community. The common aspects are culture, building pride, and sustaining Afrikaans as language in South Africa. The attitudes and perceptions of the community are positive and they understand the benefits of the festival such as infrastructure improvement and job creation.

- Environment: The *E* in the VICE model was specified as the built and the natural environment. Although the environment takes strain with the increased number of people to the festival, the effects on the environment are not long-lasting. The community is of the opinion that the festival ensures the development and maintenance of the environment. The organizing committee understands the impact of the festival on the environment and invests money in the improvement and rehabilitation of the environment before, during, and after the festival.

The aspects of the VICE model are therefore in a healthy condition and if the situation can be maintained, the Innibos Arts Festival will be sustainable for the foreseeable future.

LIMITATIONS

The VICE model is not yet known in the world and more studies should be done to determine the effectiveness of the model in determining sustainability of festivals. The environmental side of the model can be done in a more comprehensive way to ensure sustainability of the environment.

REFERENCES

Allen, J., O'Toole, W., McDonnell, I., & Harris, R. (2002). *Festival and special event management*. Sydney, Australia: John Wiley & Sons.

Bowdin, G., Allen, J., O'Toole, W., Harris, R., & McDonnell, I. (2006). *Events management* (2nd ed.). London, England: Elsevier.

Bramwell, B., & Lane, B. (2008). Priorities in sustainable tourism research. *Journal Of Sustainable Tourism, 16*(1), 1–4.

Chen, J. S. (2001). Assessing and visualizing tourism impacts from urban residents' perspectives. *Journal of Hospitality and Tourism Research, 25*, 235–250.

Coetser, J. (2002). *The South African War: Occasion and event in Afrikaans theatre*. Retrieved from http://www.childlit.org.za/KonfBoerCoetser.html

Cottrell, S. P., & Cutumisu, N. (2006). Sustainable tourism development strategy in WWF Pan Parks: Case of a Swedish and Romanian national park. *Scandinavian Journal of Hospitality and Tourism, 6*, 150–167.

Creative Research Systems. (2008). *Sample size calculator*. Retrieved from http://www.surveysystem.com/sscalc.htm

Crompton, J. L., Lee, S., & Shuster, T. J. (2001). A guide for undertaking economic impact studies: The Springfest example. *Journal of Travel Research*, *40*, 79–87.

Daniels, M. J., & Norman, W. C. (2003). Estimating the economic impacts of seven regular sport tourism events. *Journal of Sport Tourism*, *8*, 214–222.

Delamere, T. (2001). Development of a scale to measure resident attitudes toward the social impacts of community festivals, Part II: Verification of the scale. *Event Management*, *7*, 25–38.

Del Bosque, I. R., & Martin, H. S. (2008). Tourist satisfaction: A cognitive-affective model. *Annals of Tourism Research*, *35*, 551–573.

Getz, D. (1991). *Festivals, special events and tourism*. New York, NY: Van Nostrand Reinhold.

Grant, D., & Paliwoda, S. (1998). Segmenting Alberta arts and festival consumers. *Festival Management and Event Tourism*, *5*, 207–220.

Goldblatt, J. (2002). *Special events*. Sydney, Australia: John Wiley & Sons.

Haley, A. J., Snaith, T., & Miller, G. (2005). The social impacts of tourism: A case study of Bath, UK. *Annals of Tourism Research*, *32*, 647–668.

Hauptfleisch, T. (2006). Identity: Festivals in South Africa and the search for cultural identity. *New Theatre Quarterly*, *22*, 181–198.

Jennings, G. (2001). *Tourism research*. Sydney, Australia: John Wiley & Sons.

Kuvank, Y., & Akan, P. (2005). Residents' attitudes toward general and forest-related impacts of tourism: The case of Belek, Antalya. *Tourism Management*, *26*, 691–706.

McHone, W. W., & Rungeling, B. (2000). Practical issues in measuring the impact of a cultural tourist event in a major tourist destination. *Journal of Travel Research*, *38*, 300–302.

Nicholson, R. E., & Pearce, D. G. (2001). Why do people attend events: A comparative analysis of visitor motivations at Four South Island events. *Journal of Travel Research*, *39*, 449–460.

O'Sullivan, D., & Jackson, M. (2002). Festival tourism: A contributor to sustainable local economic development. *Journal of Sustainable Tourism*, *10*, 325–342.

Prentice, R., & Andersen, V. (2003). Festival as creative destination. *Annals of Tourism Research*, *30*(1), 7–30.

Quinn, B. (2006). Problematising "festival tourism": Arts festivals and sustainable development in Ireland. *Journal of Sustainable Tourism*, *14*, 288–305.

Rogerson, C. M. (2007). Tourism routes as vehicles for local economic development in South Africa: The example of the Magaliesberg Meander. *Urban Forum*, *18*, 49–68.

Sairinen, R., & Kumpulainen, S. (2006). Assessing social impacts in urban water front regeneration. *Environmental Impact Assessment Review*, *26*, 120–135.

Simmons, D. (2004). *Editor. Tourism planning toolkit for local government*. Retrieved from http://www.tourism.govt.nz/Our-Work/Local-Government-/Tourism-Planning-Toolkit

Waitt, G. (2003). Social impacts of the Sydney Olympics. *Annals of Tourism Research*, *30*(1), 194–215.

Williams, J., & Lawson, R. (2001). Community issues and resident opinions of tourism. *Annals of Tourism Research*, *28*, 269–290.

Destination Image and Events: A Structural Model for the Algarve Case

JÚLIO MENDES, PATRÍCIA OOM DO VALLE,
and MANUELA GUERREIRO

Research Centre for Spatial and Organizational Dynamics (CIEO) and Department of Economics, University of Algarve, Faro, Portugal

Algarve is Portugal's top tourism destination. In looking to develop the traditional sun and beach tourism, the Portuguese government launched the Allgarve program in 2007 with the aim of positioning the region as a premier tourism destination, promoting the cultural industry as a modern and competitive component of the regional economy. Using partial least squares modelling (PLS), the study explores the relationship between the image projected by Allgarve and the image of Algarve as a tourism destination. Results show that the program has had a positive and reasonably strong influence on the destination image. In terms of affective elements, findings show that these were not easily perceived by tourists, as anticipated by the Allgarve program. An important outcome of this study is to contribute towards better management of future editions of the Allgarve program.

INTRODUCTION

Growing concern in society has led to the need to develop integrated marketing strategies in tourist destinations and to strategically manage the image of these destinations through action plans that result in effective destination image processing.

Imprinting images and expectations on the part of both visitors and local residents is often characterised by symbols and visual icons (e.g., logotypes, colors, names, graphic design elements, etc.) together with other informational elements relevant to the target consumer such as residents, companies, current, and potential visitors. However, other groups, beyond the control of those responsible for destination management, may also be reached.

The Algarve region, located in the southernmost part of Portugal, represents an important tourism destination for the country and promoted largely as a sun and sea destination, with advertisement campaigns that focus nearly exclusively on this tourism offer. Although this has remained relatively unchanged since the 1960s, a new campaign called "Re-energize Algarve" has looked to convey a modern and dynamic attractiveness of the region since 2004. The composite nature of Algarve as a tourist destination provides tourists with a unique and unforgettable experience. "Re-energize Yourself" was presented as campaign headline which sought to appeal to a wide range of experiences in one place. Algarve is presented as a destination offering beach, culture and tradition, and golf as well as an emerging destination and host for international conventions (MyBrand, 2007).

The need to distinguish Algarve from other competing tourist destinations, particularly those located in the Mediterranean, has led government authorities to invest in the definition and implementation of a new repositioning strategy for the region. A cultural, artistic, and sports events program of international stature was launched in 2007. The annual program aims to reposition the destination image and attract more and higher spending tourists. *Allgarve,* the brand name attributed to the program, seeks to represent a distinct identity and communicate an image of the destination in an attempt to bring added dimension and value to tourists (MyBrand, 2007).

Although destination image has been one of the most explored fields in the tourism industry, the effects of event and destination images has yet to be adequately addressed. Based on a set of attributes resulting from the promotional campaigns on Algarve, this article analyzes the creation and management of a distinctive and appealing perception, or image, of the destination and discusses the strategy adopted, whilst seeking to contribute to a better understanding of the way in which the image of a program of events influences the image of a tourist destination as a whole.

LITERATURE REVIEW

A destination is generally built around a central product providing it with an identity and an image. The tourist initiates the travel decision process by choosing a destination (e.g., town, city, region, country, or continent) mainly based on its core product (e.g., sun and beach, heritage, events, etc.). The central products are essentially related to the type of geographic and social structure in question (e.g., urban, rural, or coastal).

Destination images influence the decision-making process and the choice of where to travel (Baloglu, 1997), as well as the level of satisfaction that the tourist feels when the expectations based on a preconceived image and the reality of the destination are compared (Chon, 1990). Woodside and Lysonski (1989) concluded that destinations with strong, positive images are more readily contemplated in the choice process that surrounds the decision to travel. Chi and Qu (2008, p. 625) considered that destination image "is an antecedent of satisfaction" and that satisfaction "has a positive influence on destination loyalty."

In terms of the tourism destination context, destination image refers to "an individual's mental representation of knowledge, feelings, and global impressions about a destination" (Baloglu & McCleary, 1999, p. 870). Echtner and Ritchie (1991, p. 8) defined destination image as "the holistic impression made by the destination." It consists of "functional characteristics, concerning more tangible aspects of the destination, and psychological characteristics, concerning the more intangible aspects."

Although Castro, Armario, and Ruiz (2007, p. 177) regarded image as a "tricky concept that is difficult to define," several proposals can be found in the literature. The concept of image corresponds to a "mental or visual impression of a place, a product or an experience" (Milman & Pizam, 1995, p. 21). It is a dynamic construct that results from a set of beliefs, ideas and impressions that an individual has of a destination (Kotler, Asplund, Rein, & Heider, 1999). An image is the set of selective representations and perceptions that are related to the frameworks of reference of individuals (Mayo & Jarvis, 1981). According to Gertner and Kotler (2004), image may be defined as "the sum of beliefs, ideas and impressions that people have of that place." It is a "personal perception" and "different people can hold quite different images of the same place" (Gertner & Kotler, 2004, p. 51).

Destination image, in turn, is the basis of international positioning. As Echtner and Ritchie (1991, p. 2) noted, "in order to be successfully promoted in the targeted markets, a destination must be favourably differentiated from its competition, or positively positioned, in the minds of the consumers." Positioning involves "creating the appropriate image of the product in the minds of the consumers in the targeted markets" (Echtner & Ritchie, 1993, p. 3).

The strategy for the development of the brand and the image of the destination should begin with a clear identity based on trait-based characteristics. This presupposes an initial phase of self-diagnosis so as to identify what is truly original and unique in a given destination. The tendency of the last few years has been for destination managers to concern themselves exclusively with the way in which their destinations are perceived, through impact evaluation studies. In fact, nowadays destinations are essentially positioned according to perceived images tourists develop in competing markets (Baloglu & Mangaloglu, 2001), and also based on identifiable attributes.

It is therefore necessary to invest in positive tourist destination images in order to gain a more prominent position in the marketplace. Echtner and Ritchie (1993, p. 37) argued that for a destination to be successful it must be "favourably differentiated from its competition, or positively positioned, in the minds of the consumers." It is important to assess the existing image of tourism destinations in order determine how far tourists' perceptions are from the intentional positioning, which may result in new adoption of reposition strategies. This is relevant approach when there is a discrepancy between the actual and desirable image of the tourism destination.

Destinations, according to Alford (1998, p. 53) constitute a "selling [of] tourist experiences" and as such may represent opportunities for tourism destinations to position themselves as unique.

Although, in the literature, destination image is one of the most explored fields in tourism research, studies aimed at understanding the multidimensional nature and the formation process of images of tourism destinations are relatively scarce (Gallarza, Saura, & García, 2002; Beerli & Martín, 2004). The complexity and subjectivity that characterizes the image concept in the case of a tourism destination, results in different adopted approaches (Stepchenkova & Morrison, 2008; Baloglu & McCleary, 1999). The destination image construct is commonly regarded as being the con-sequence of two components: the cognitive or perceptual component, representing the "knowledge and beliefs about a destination;" and the affective component, representing the "feelings about the destination" (Stepchenkova & Morrison, 2008, p. 549; Baloglu & McCleary, 1999, p. 870).

The cognitive structure of destination image and the relationship between the cognitive and affective nature of destination image are con-sidered in several studies. However, "theoretical and empirical research on the influence of psychological factors on destination image has been limited" (Martin & Rodríguez del Bosque, 2008, p. 264).

The cognitive component of the image is related to the "evaluation of the known attributes or their comprehension in an intellectual way" (Scott, 1965 cited in Gartner, 1993, p. 193). It corresponds to a set of external stim-uli, or facts. The overall image of the destination thus arises from a process of formation that combines perceptual or cognitive and affective evalua-tions (Baloglu & McCleary, 1999). For Gartner (1993), sources of information are the main contributing agents in the formation of perceptions and eval-uations. Prebensen (2007) argued that tourist experience and information about tourism destinations are of great relevance in the context of the image formation process.

In terms of the cognitive component, based on the knowledge and beliefs about a destination, and the affective component, defined by the feelings about a destination, the image of a tourism destination encompasses behavioral, or conative, component related to "how travellers act toward a destination" (Stepchenkova & Morrison, 2008, p. 549). According to Pike and Ryan (2004, cited in Stepchenkova & Morrison, 2008, p. 549) conative component can be interpreted as "a propensity to visit a destination within a certain time frame." According to Stepchenkova and Morrison (2008) the cognitive and the affective components of the tourism destination image influence the behavioral component.

Baloglu and McCleary (1999) proposed a model according to which the image is formed through stimulation factors (associated with external incentives, information sources, and previous experience) and personal factors (related to social—mainly age, education, and marital status; and psychological characteristics of individuals—values, motivations, and personality). In this process, factors such as perception or cognition related to knowledge of the objective attributes of the destination intervene, as well as affective evaluation that arises from the feelings and associations that each individual develops about the destination.

Diverse sources of information and cultural and psychological factors are, according to Stern and Krakover (1993), factors that influence the formation process of the overall image that individuals have of a destination. Knowledge of the factors that influence the image formation process among different segments of (actual and potential) tourists allows managers to define eventual strategies for repositioning the brand, for promoting the various attributes of the place more effectively, and for accentuating the differentiating features in the face of competition. Building and managing an appropriate destination image are critical to effective positioning and marketing of a tourism destination (Echtner & Ritchie, 1993, p. 3).

Woodside and Lysonski (1989) have noted that marketing variables and other information sources may influence the cognitive image component but not the affective perceptions that lead to the choice of tourism holiday destinations.

Although individuals can clearly have an image of a destination without ever having visited the region *a priori* (perceptions), or without ever having been exposed to commercial sources of promotion (Echtner & Ritchie, 1991), several studies show that tourists tend to obtain information on alternative destinations. Thus, promotion strategies for tourism destination brands and the organization of mega-events represent a decisive role in image construction and contribute as well to a destination's popularity.

In some cases, events and mega-events are planned with the clear aim of contributing to the repositioning of the image of a destination, distinguishing it from competing markets through the association of new attributes. In such cases, destinations employ imagery in order to produce tangible results such as culture and impressing on variety, activity, and sophistication (Getz, 1997). Due to the fact that events generally attract the attention of the media and are thus often a good way of obtaining publicity, they constitute an important stimulus factor in the image formation process of a destination.

In this context, events help to project and communicate the positioning of the brand, produced by curiosity and the possibility of gained experience, and believed to intervene in the image formation process. Getz (1991) considers that scenes from events generate a genuine image of the region, which should then impact positively on the decision-making process of holiday destinations. The impact of events on destination image reinforces competitiveness and, when considered within the brand positioning strategy framework, represents a component of the destination product mix.

Large events, while multiplying on a global scale, contribute to some homogeneity in terms of the means by which locations contribute to image formation. They convey and reinforce the positioning of tourism destinations as desired places to live, work and visit. It is in this context that destination brand management should be equated with the organization of (cultural and/or other) events, constituting a mix element whose main role is to increase the attraction of destinations in terms of awareness and image. Events can constitute an interesting opportunity for destinations to communicate to a receptive audience (Nobili, 2005).

Although brand management and the positioning of destinations have become increasingly more popular among academics with events developed within location marketing strategies steadily rising, regional impact and assessment studies are still somewhat scarce and the relationship between special events and positioning strategies and brand management (Nobili, 2005).

A positive relation between the image of a country and the events it organizes is shown in several studies (Ahmed, 1991; Nebenzahl & Jaffe, 1991; Ritchie & Smith, 1991). For Ahmed (1991), mega-events help above all to broaden the reputation of the destination and, eventually, to correct a negative image.

Participation in events during a stay in a tourist destination allows the visitor to take part in unforgettable experiences. Tourism is, in itself, an industry that trades products—nature, events, culture, and history—and presents them to the visitor as unique, memorable experiences (Craik, 1995). Experiences constitute a new facet of services, especially when living in an era of transition, from economy of services to economy of experiences (Pine & Gilmore, 1999). Visitors seek fantastic experiences when embarking on trips (Boniface, 1996). When purchasing an experience, one is paying to spend one's time enjoying memorable events in a memorable place (Pine & Gilmore, 1999).

Similarly, we can argue that visiting a tourism destination is, in itself, an experience that is certain to be memorable. However, the value chain that circumvents the supply of tourism products can be maximised if the destination represents a chance for visitors to carry out a gratifying experience with access to the local cultural scene. Visitors look to feel part of the environment and as such expect simple, readily easy experiences that fulfil their objectives. Events allow visitors to participate as actors in the experience (Boniface & Fowler, 1996; Kotler et al., 1999; Pine & Gilmore, 1999). Although the experience of participating in an event is limited to the moment in which it is lived, its value remains as a memory and contributes to the process of destination image formation.

SETTING

Algarve, a region whose principal economic activity is sun and sea tourism (though currently undergoing a process of strategic diversification), is the cradle of Portuguese tourism which first attracted tourists in search of a good climate and the beach in the 1960s. There has since been a steady demand increase for sun and sea, a product that the region specialized in during the 1970s and 1980s.

Although sun and sea represent the main motivating reason for visiting Algarve, studies show that the region offers new market opportunities. Besides entertainment, there is another interesting facet which appeals to tourists; namely, historical, cultural, and architectural heritage. This may represent a potential form of attracting more tourists, and in this way encouraging an increase in the average length of stay and daily expenditure.

Algarve is currently investing in a diversified range of products regarded as strategically important and includes golf (aimed at complementing the sun and sea product and reducing seasonality in the region), sports (through nautical events and new, marinas, port facilities), international conferences and initiatives (to reduce seasonality and enabling accommodation units to maintain a reasonable occupancy rate throughout the year), culture-oriented tourism, health tourism, and nature tourism.

Since the onset of tourism in the region, Algarve has been promoted as a tourist destination brand name. Until the 1990s, Algarve as a brand was positioned as a sun and sea destination.

However, over the last decade effort has been made to develop a brand name for the region, which has provoked a fragmented projection of the destination's concept and identity. The notion of an all-in-one destination is prominent although this may have implications on Algarve's image and positioning.

At the beginning of the current decade, the Algarve Regional Tourism Board (RTA) and the Ministry of Economics (through Investimento Comércio e Tourism Portugal [ICEP]) developed a branding strategy for Algarve as a tourist destination, which involved focusing primarily on promoting the brand name in the mass media of main source markets. The promotional campaign aimed to disseminate four anchor products: the region itself as a tourist destination, golf, sports, and conferences and events. Based on the new "re-energize" concept for Algarve, the brand relied essentially on the region's physical attributes such as nature, sun and sea, culture and tradition, entertainment, and sports activities (nautical sports and golf).

More recently, in 2007, the Portuguese government launched a program of events that was given the brand name Allgarve. The program covers three summer periods (2007–2009) and had an initial budget of 6 million euros for the first 2 years. Allgarve operates as an umbrella brand name for the promotion of events and integrated the general Algarve brand. The objective was to create a unique brand that did not compete with the region's more familiar brand. Besides sun and sea, campaigns looked to promote other products that would differentiate it from other destinations.

With the slogan "Lifetime Experiences," Allgarve is a program of events centred on culture, sports, and entertainment whose strategic objective is to reposition the Algarve as a sophisticated and glamorous tourist destination (MyBrand, 2005). The range of events on offer includes music concerts in a variety of venues such as historic sites, golf courses and parks, the cantata Carmina Burana at the Teatro das Figuras, contemporary art exhibitions, jazz sessions, international golf tournaments, and sailing competitions. Most large-scale events have a high level of media impact, which is one of the main generating sources of brand recognition. Word-of-mouth is another significant form. Main markets for the region include: Portugal, Spain, the UK, Germany, and France. The name Allgarve was chosen to express the multifaceted character of the Algarve as a tourist destination, aimed at both national and international tourists.

The three main strategic objectives of the Allgarve program can be summarized as follows: to create significant differentiation in regard to other international sun, sea, and golf destinations; to create new opportunities for enjoyment for current tourists; and to increase tourism figures in general.

The literature review indicates that the participation in events can influence the process of destination image formation. Thus, the research hypothesis of this study is as follows: the image of the Allgarve campaign has a positive effect on the destination image. In other words, those who have a positive image of the campaign are more likely to present a more positive image of the region.

METHODOLOGY

Questionnaire and Data

This study uses data from a questionnaire applied to foreign tourists visiting the Algarve region during the 2008 summer months. The questionnaire consisted of four sections: Section I looked to measure the image of Algarve; Section II sought information about the Allgarve campaign (knowledge, image, and participation); Section III evaluated destination loyalty (willingness to recommend and willingness to return); and Section IV collected information on respondent's demographic profile (gender, age, nationality, marital status, educational qualifications, and employment situation).

This study employs statistical methods with the aim of assessing the causal relationship between the questions of Sections I and II. Destination image is the construct measured using 14 destination-image items included in Section I. These items were graded on a 5-point Likert-type scale (1 = *completely disagree;* 5 = *completely agree*) and establish that Algarve is: sun and beach, golf, tradition, nature, gastronomy, fun, culture, art, nautical sports, a safe region, a familiar region, a inexpensive holiday destination, a fashionable destination, and a quiet destination.

The Allgarve image represents the construct measured using the three questions selected for Section II: (a) To what extent do you agree with the name (Allgarve) for the campaign? (1 = *completely disagree;* 5 = *completely agree*); (b) To what extent do you agree that the campaign Allgarve contributes to a positive differentiation of the Algarve region in relation to other international alternatives? (1 = *completely disagree;* 5 = *completely agree*); and (c) To what extent have these holidays met your expectations based on the campaign? (1 = *far from meeting my expectations;* 5 = *exceeded all my expectations*). For the sake of simplicity, these questions will be referred to in the structural model as Allgarve Image 1, Allgarve Image 2, and Allgarve Image 3, respectively.

The questionnaire was carried out at Faro International Airport and completed by tourists waiting for their departure flight. The sample of tourists was selected using a systematic sampling procedure. A total of 282 questionnaires were obtained. Table 1 shows some demographic features of the sample. Respondents were almost equally distributed by gender (47.5% are male), belonged mainly to the age category 30–44 years (26.1%) or older than 45 (49.6%) and had secondary (42.7%) or college education (54.1%). The majority were English (56.4%) and married (58.7%). The average age of respondents was 47 with a standard deviation of 15 years.

Data Analysis Methods

In order to address the purpose of this research, two multivariate methods were applied. Firstly, an exploratory factor analysis (The variables analyzed in the factor analyses were the 14 items used to evaluate the Algarve image. In order to assess the adequacy of this approach, the Kaiser-Meyer-Olkin of measure sampling adequacy and the Bartlett's test of sphericity were performed. The number of factors to be extracted was determined by evaluating the eigenvalue scores, the scree plot, and the factor loadings. For the extraction method, a principal components analysis and a varimax rotation were carried out, using SPSS 15.0.

Secondly, a structural equation modelling (SEM) procedure was used to study the relationship between the constructs destination image and the

TABLE 1 Characteristics of the Sample

Variables	Distribution of answers (%)
Gender	
Female	45
Male	55
Age	
15–29	27.2
30–44	34.9
45+	37.9
Nationality	
English	64.8
Scottish	22.4
Irish	9.6
German	3.2
Marital status	
Married	70.5
Single	23.3
Divorced	4.7
Widowed	1.6
Educational qualifications	
Secondary	44.2
College	55.8
Employment situation	
Active worker	53.5
Domestic worker	2
Student	5.9
Retried	38.6

Note. Age: mean = 39.4, standard deviation = 13.69.

Allgarve image and, therefore, to test the research hypothesis of this study. This model was estimated and tested by applying partial least squares regression (PLS), using SmartPLS 2.0 (Ringle, Wendle, &Will, 2005). PLS regression is a recent technique (Chin, 1995, 1998; Chin, Marcolin, & Newsted, 2003) that allows estimation of models with latent variables even when data does not present a multivariate normal distribution. This technique is particularly adequate for small samples. Due to the limited nature of the sample size and nonconforming multivariate normal distribution, PLS was preferred over the traditional covariance-based structural equation modeling technique.

Similarly to the covariance-based models or Lisrel models, the PLS regression analysis enables the simultaneous estimation of the structural model (that shows the relations among the latent variables) and the the measurement model (that depicts the relation between each latent variable and the corresponding observed variables or indicators). In this study, the latent variables were destination image and Allgarve image. In the measurement model, the latent variable destination image was measured by the three factors obtained from the factor analysis. Regarding the latent variable, Allgarve image, the indicators were the responses to the thres aforementioned questions; that is, Allgarve Image 1, Allgarve Image 2, and Allgarve image 3.

The PLS regression allows us to test the measurement model and the structural model. The reliability of the measurement model is analysed by observing, for each latent variable, the average variance extracted (AVE), composite reliability, Cronbach's alpha coefficient, and communality. AVE is a measure of the percentage error variance in a measure that should exceed a 0.5 threshold (Dillon & Goldstein, 1984). Composite reliability indicates to what extent a latent variable is adequately described by its observed variables and should exceed 0.7 (Chin, 1998). Cronbach's alpha is a well-known index of internal consistency and gives an indication of how well a range of observed variables explains a latent variable. According to DeVellis (2003), the Cronbach's alpha should be greater than 0.5 for proper reliability and consistency. Lastly, communality measures the ability of an observed variable to explain the corresponding latent variable and should be greater than 0.5 (Chin, 1998).

The measurement model should further be examined in terms of convergent validity and discriminant validity (Enskog, 2006). Convergent validity evaluates to what degree the indicators of a latent variable actually measure such a latent construct. There is evidence of convergent validity if the factor loadings are greater than 0.7 and if the observed variables load stronger on the corresponding latent variables than on the remaining ones (Trochim, 2006). Discriminant validity assesses whether the latent variables are in fact measuring different concepts. Chin (1998) points out that there is discriminant validity if the squared root of the AVE for each latent variable is larger than their correlation with the other latent variables.

The structural model depicts the relations among the latent variables. To test the structural model, it is important to observe the path coefficients for the hypothesized relationships between the latent constructs. A path coefficient needs to be evaluated in terms of its sign, magnitude and significance level. One of the attractive features of PLS path analysis is the fact that it does not rely on any distributional assumptions. Thereby, the significance levels that rest on the normal theory cannot be used. This implies that the information on the variability of parameter estimates and, thus, their significance, must be generated using resampling procedures (Theme, Kreis, & Hildebrandt, 2006). SmartPLS applies bootstrapping as a resampling method in order to derive valid standard errors and t values. In addition, the coefficient of determination, R^2, should be computed to evaluate the structural model and it is calculated by squaring the path coefficient between two latent variables.

RESULTS

Exploratory Factor Analysis

An EFA was performed to determine the underlying dimensions of Algarve image by analysing patterns of correlations among the 14 image items. A principal components analysis was used for extraction purposes and a varimax rotation was applied. A KMO index of 0.894 was achieved, exceeding the threshold value for a suitable factor analysis of 0.6 (Tabachnick & Fidell, 2007). On the other hand, Bartlett's test of sphericity was significant ($p = 0.000$). A range of criteria were employed to identify the number of factors to be retained, such as the eigenvalues, the scree plot, and the factor loadings. A three-factor solution was retained accounting for around 60% of the total variance. The three factors have an eigenvalue greater than 1 and the loadings of the three-factor solution present a clear and interpretable solution. Observing the items with higher loading within each factor, the three factors were named Culture and Nature Destination, Safe and Inexpensive Destination, and Beach and Sports Destination. These factors and each item loading are reported in Table 2. Additionally, a reliability analysis was performed. The Cronbach's alpha coefficients for each factor indicate a reasonable degree of internal consistency.

The remaining columns of Table 2 show responses provided for Categories 4 (agree) and 5 (completely agree) in terms of each image item and also the corresponding mean and standard deviation. The items with greater values in these categories, which are those with higher mean, are Algarve is sun and beach (88.83%), Algarve is a familiar region (82.22%) and Algarve is a safe region (81.92%). On the contrary, the items with lower values in these categories are Algarve is art (50.19%), Algarve is nautical sports (64.29%) and Algarve is a inexpensive destination (64.96%).

From the three most representative attributes of the Algarve image as a tourist destination, we verified a pre-eminent position of the affective component that could indicate an emotional relation with the destination. On the other hand, Algarve is art and Algarve is nautical sports are among the perceived attributes least representative, and constitute two of the most important repositioning strategies for the region.

PLS Regression Analysis

The purpose of using PLS regression in this study was twofold. Firstly, it was performed in order to analyse the relationship between the latent variables, destination image, and the *Allgarve* image (the structural model) and, thus, to test the proposed research hypothesis. Secondly, it was carried out to verify how well the indicators for the latent variables were reliable and valid measures of such latent concepts (the measurement model). In the

TABLE 2 Algarve Image Items and Factors from Factor Analysis

Image items and factors	Loading	% Agree + Comp. Agree	M	SD
Culture and nature destination (Alpha = 0.7869; explained variance = 43.22%)				
Algarve is culture[a]	0.771	71.06	3.86	0.913
Algarve is tradition[a]	0.761	73.96	3.87	0.933
Algarve is nature[b]	0.723	80.30	3.95	0.858
Algarve is gastronomy[b]	0.706	68.89	3.84	0.976
Algarve is art[a]	0.655	50.19	3.56	0.964
Algarve is fun[a]	0.528	83.64	4.13	0.789
Safe and inexpensive destination (Alpha = 0.776; explained variance = 8.78%)				
Algarve is a fashionable destination[a]	0.725	64.55	3.74	0.918
Algarve is a quiet destination[a]	0.685	78.06	3.94	0.911
Algarve is an inexpensive destination[a]	0.679	64.96	3.73	1.024
Algarve is a safe region[a]	0.583	81.92	4.08	0.884
Algarve is a familiar region[a]	0.578	82.22	4.07	0.842
Beach and sports destination (Alpha = 0.683; explained variance = 7.68%)				
Algarve is golf[b]	0.860	74.73	3.90	0.961
Algarve is sun and beach[b]	0.719	88.83	4.17	0.863
Algarve is nautical sports[b]	0.532	64.29	3.76	0.884

[a]Affective image. [b]Cognitive image.

PLS model, the indicators of destination image comprised the three factors obtained from factor analysis while the indicators of Allgarve image were represented by the aforementioned three questions, Allgarve Image 1, Allgarve Image 2, and Allgarve Image 3.

Table 3 shows the results from the reliability analysis of the measurement model. As can be seen, all the results exceed the aforementioned thresholds. Both AVE's are clearly greater than 0.5, the composite reliability exceeds 0.7 by a comfortable margin, and the Cronbach's alphas and the communalities are larger than 0.5.

TABLE 3 Reliability Analysis of the Measurement Model

Latent variables	Average variance extracted (AVE)	Composite reliability	Cronbach alpha	Communality
Destination image	0.857	0.947	0.917	0.857
Allgarve image	0.872	0.953	0.927	0.872

TABLE 4 Convergent Analysis of the Measurement Model

Observed variables	Destination image	Allgarve image
Culture and nature destination (Dest_im1)	0.945	0.733
Safe and inexpensive destination (Dest_im2)	0.931	0.662
Beaches and sports destination (Dest_im3)	0.924	0.695
Allgarve Image 1 (All_im1)	0.630	0.917
Allgarve Image 2 (All_im2)	0.668	0.936
Allgarve Image 3 (All_im3)	0.765	0.924

Next, the model was tested in terms of convergent validity and discriminant validity. In assessing convergent validity, factor loadings and cross loadings were observed (Table 4). Findings show that all observed variables load high on their corresponding latent variable with a value greater than 0.9. Furthermore, each indicator loads higher on their latent variable than on the other. This analysis provides evidence of a good correlation between each observed variable and the corresponding construct.

In considering discriminate validity, it is important to analyze to what extent the two constructs diverge from each other. In this regard, we observed the intercorrelation between the two latent variables provided as an output of the PLS regression. This value was 0.7479, which was lower than the square roots of the AVE's (0.926 e 0.934). According to Heeler and Ray (1972), this finding suggests discriminant validity of the measurement model.

To assess the structural model, the path coefficient values, their statistical significance and the coefficient of determination, R^2, were observed. Figure 1 depicts the structural model with the estimated path coefficients on the model itself. The R^2 for the dependent latent variable was 0.56. Table 5, in turn, shows the results from the bootstrapping in terms of the t statistic. All the t values are very high which implies that the path coefficients are statistically significant ($p = 0.000$). These findings are indicative of good measurement and structural models.

However, the most important finding is that the path coefficient that links the two latent constructs is high (0.7479) and statistically significant.

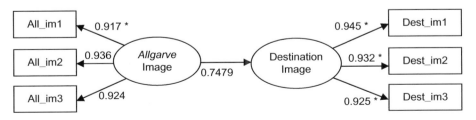

FIGURE 1 Results from the Proposed Structural Model.
*Significant at the 0.01 level.

TABLE 5 Outer Model t-Statistics (Bootstrapping)

Variables	Destination image	Allgarve image
Culture and nature destination (Dest_im1)	85.14*	
Safe and inexpensive destination (Dest_im2)	53.97*	
Beaches and sports destination (Dest_im3)	46.82*	
Allgarve image 1 (All_im1)		40.80*
Allgarve image 2 (All_im2)		56.40*
Allgarve image 3 (All_im3)		63.26*
Allgarve Image → Destination Image	22.91*	

*p-value = 0.000.

This result implies that the image of the Allgarve campaign has had a positive and reasonably strong effect on the destination image, which supports the research hypothesis. In other words, those who have a positive image of the campaign are more likely to present a more positive image of the region, concerning the following three factors: beach and sports, culture and environment, and security and cost.

DISCUSSION

As the Regional Tourism Board recognizes, Algarve is traditionally known internationally as a sun and sea destination. This is backed by main generating source markets and has been the basis of considerable marketing efforts that have sought a more competitive position without affecting its established product. Given the popular conceptions associated to the destination and difficulties in differentiating the region from other competing markets, a culture and events program was launched with the aim of repositioning the image of the destination. An events program directed at tourists normally assumes two important objectives: an increase in the number of visitors during the period when the events take place and greater regional exposure through publicity and media coverage. Both are decisive in (re)building of the destination image.

The challenge is managing two distinct brands and two different campaign strategies, so that the destination benefits and repositioning efforts are effective. It is fundamental to note that images are not static and that personal images can therefore not only be influenced, but can be altered.

For agencies in charge of promoting destinations using images that are suitable for its markets, through marketing mix for instance, it is crucial that they know which factors influence image formation. The results from the PLS regression show that there is a positive relation between the image of the Allgarve program and the image of the destination as a whole. This provides important strategic directions for the Algarve Tourism Board to improve the destination's competitiveness.

Tourism promotion for the Algarve has traditionally focused on physical (or cognitive) attributes of the destination—beaches, golf courses, the natural environment—and the image formed by foreign tourists, and verified in Table 2 through the pattern of responses to the 14 image items.

Besides the physical attributes, however, the new promotion trends increasingly appeal to the tourist's emotion, such as culture, confidence, safety, friendliness, quality, et cetera. The Allgarve program and the image it aims to deliver to its target groups are based on lifestyle, glamour, and a cosmopolitan atmosphere. On the other hand, the results of this study indicate that some of these values have not yet been perceived by tourists, nor have they been totally integrated into the image of the destination, in particular those preferring culture (art and fashion, for example, as can be seen in Table 2). A plausible explanation for this is that the program is still relatively new and change of image has not yet taken effect.

CONCLUSIONS AND LIMITATIONS

The results obtained allow us to conclude that the direction taken in terms of repositioning the image of the Algarve destination is reaching tourists who enjoy visiting the Algarve. These tourists have provided positive feedback on the Allgarve program and establish a link between the two types of image, which is favorable to the repositioning of the destination.

The results of the estimation of the model show that the program of events is contributing to improving the organic image of the tourist destination, which corresponds to the objectives defined at the start of the campaign. This observation supports those of other authors who have found that events are catalysing phenomena for attracting and satisfying visitors, and, as such, they are an important vehicle for the formation of destination image. Since the image of a tourist destination is an ongoing development process, we can safely assume that there is a structural correspondence between values, ideas and symbols delivered by both the campaigns.

Moreover, as the image of the Allgarve campaign has had a positive and reasonably strong effect on the destination image, we expect a synergetic effect to develop, resulting in positive word of mouth from visitors.

This study does, however, have some limitations that should be considered. Firstly, in terms of the sample size, it should be noted that a convenience sample such as the one used does not allow us to make conclusive generalizations. Through this exploratory study, we hope to have provided directions for future research on a topic that is so strategically important for tourist destinations.

Secondly, by using the airport for data collection, we ruled out the possibility of including tourists who arrived in the region by road or rail. In the case of Algarve, the Spanish border, for example, is equally an important entry point to have been considered.

Thirdly, respondents did not include domestic tourists. Although general consensus points to this market segment as that holding most negative perception about Allgarve, more specifically because the label appeals more the the international market than the national market. This may result from a misunderstanding on the nature of the program.

This study attempts to gain some insight on the progress of the program, that is, the image of the Algarve that tourists are taking home with them. It would be interesting to carry out a comparative study on the evolution of images that visitors have of both the destination and the campaign itself.

REFERENCES

Ahmed, Z. (1991, February). Marketing your community–correcting a negative image. *The Cornell H. R. A. Quarterly*, 24–27.

Alford, P. (1998). Positioning the destination product: Can regional tourist boards learn from private sector practice? *Journal of Travel and Tourism Marketing*, 7(2), 53–68.

Baloglu, S. (1997). The relationship between destinations images and socio-demographic and trip characteristics of international travellers. *Journal of Vacation Marketing*, *3*, 221–233.

Baloglu, S., & Mangaloglu, M. (2001). Tourism destinations images of Turkey, Egypt, Greece and Italy as perceived by U.S.-based tour operators and travel agents. *Tourism Management*, *21*(1), 1–9.

Baloglu, S., & McCleary, M. (1999). Tourism destination images of Turkey, Egypt, Greece and Italy as Perceived by U.S.-based tour operators and travel agents. *Tourism Management*, *22*, 1–9.

Beerli, A., & Martín, J. D. (2004). Factors influencing destination image. *Annals of Tourism Research*, *31*, 657–681.

Boniface, P., & Fowler, P. J. (1996). *Heritage and tourism in the global village*. London, England: Routledge.

Castro, C. B., Armario, E. M., & Ruiz, D. M. (2007). The influence of market heterogeneity on the relationship between a destination's image and tourists' future behaviour. *Tourism Management*, *28*, 175–187.

Chi, C. G., & Qu, H. (2008). Examining the structural relationships of destination image, tourist satisfaction and destination loyalty: An integrated approach. *Tourism Management*, *29*, 624–636.

Chin, W. W. (1995). Partial least squares is to Lisrel as principal components analysis is to common factor analysis. *Technology Studies*, *2*, 315–319.

Chin, W. W. (1998). The partial least squares approach for structural equation modeling. In G. A. Marcoulides (Ed.), *Modern methods for business research*. Hillsdale, NJ: Lawrence Erlbaum Associates.

Chin, W. W., Marcolin B. L., & Newsted, P. R. (2003). A partial least squares latent variable modeling approach for measuring interaction effects: Results from a

Monte Carlo simulation study and an electronic-mail emotion/adoption study. *Information Systems Research*, *14*, 189–217.

Chon, K. (1990). The role of destination image: A review and discussion. *Revenue of Tourism*, *2*, 2–9.

Craik, J. (1995). Are there cultural limits to tourism? *Journal of Sustainable Tourism*, *3*(2), 87–98.

DeVellis, R. F. (2003). *Scale development: Theory and application*. London, England: Sage.

Dillon, W. R., & Goldstein, M. (1984). *Multivariate analysis: Methods and applications*. New York, NY: Wiley.

Echtner, C. M., & Ritchie, J. R. B. (1991). The meaning and measurement of destination image. *Journal of Tourism Studies*, *2*(2), 2–12.

Echtner, C. M., & Ritchie, J. R. B. (1993, Spring). The measurement of destination image: An empirical assessment. *Journal of Travel Research*, *31*, 3–13.

Enskog, U. (2006). *Process awareness and use at Ericsson AB* (Unpublished master's thesis). IT University of Göteborg, Sweden.

Gallarza, M. G., Saura, I. G., & Garcia, H. C. (2002). Destination image: Toward a conceptual framework. *Annals of Tourism Research*, *29*(1), 56–78.

Gartner, W. C. (1993). Image formation process. *Communication and Channel Systems in Tourism Marketing*, *2*, 191–215.

Gertner, D., & Kotler, P. (2004). How can a place correct a negative image? *Place Branding*, *1*(1), 50–57.

Getz, D. (1991) *Festivals, special events and tourism*. New York, NY: Cognizant Communications.

Getz, D. (1997). *Event management & event tourism*. New York, NY: Cognizant Communication.

Kotler, P., Asplund, C., Rein, I., & Heider, D. (1999). *Marketing places Europe—attracting investments, industries, residents and visitors to European cities, communities, regions and nations*. London, England: Prentice Hall.

Martin, H. S., & Rodríguez del Bosque, I. A. (2008). Exploring the cognitive–affective nature of destination image and the role of psychological factors in its formation. *Tourism Management*, *29*, 263–277.

Mayo, E. J., & Jarvis, L. P. (1981). *The psychology of leisure travel*. Boston, MA: CBI.

Milman, A., & Pizam, A. (1995). The role of awareness and familiarity with a destination: The Central Florida case. *Journal of Travel Research*, *33*(3), 21–27.

MyBrand. (2005). http://www.mybrandconsultants.com/public/media/projects/39.pdf

Nebenzahl, I. D., & Jaffe, E. D. (1991). The effectiveness of sponsored events in promoting a country's image. *International Journal of Advertising*, *10*, 223–237.

Nobili, V. (2005). The role of European capital of culture events within Genoa's and Liverpool's branding and positioning efforts. *Place Branding*, *1*, 316–328.

Pine, B. J., & Gilmore, J. H. (1999). *The experience economy—work is theatre & every business a stage*. Boston, MA: Harvard Business School Press.

Prebensen, N. K. (2007). Exploring tourists' images of a distant destination. *Tourism Management*, *28*, 747–756.

Ringle, C. M., Wendle, S., & Will, A. (2005). *SmartPLS—version 2.0*. Hamburg, Germany: University of Hamburg.

Ritchie, J. R., & Smith, B. (1991). The impact of mega-events on host region awareness: A longitudinal study. *Journal of Travel Research*, *30*(1), 3–10.

Stepchenkova, S., & Morrison, A. M. (2008). Russia's destination image among american pleasure travelers: Revisiting Echtner and Ritchie. *Tourism Management*, *29*, 548–560.

Stern, E., & Krakover, S. (1993). The formation of a composite urban image. *Geographical Analysis*, *25*(2), 130–146.

Tabachnick, B. G., & Fidell, L. S. (2007). *Using multivariate statistics* (5th ed.). Boston, MA: Pearson Education.

Theme, D., Kreis, H., & Hildebrandt, L. (2006). *PLS path modeling: A software review*. (SFB 649 Discussion Paper No. 2006-084). Retrieved from http://sfb649.wiwi.hu-berlin.de/papers/pdf/SFB649DP2006-084.pdf

Trochim, W. M. (2006). *Research methods knowledge base*. Retrieved from http://www.socialresearchmethods.net/kb/pmconval.php

Woodside, A. G., & Lysonski, S. (1989). A general model of traveller destination choice. *Journal of Travel Research*, *27*(4), 8–14.

Cultural Event as a Territorial Marketing Tool: The Case of the Ravello Festival on the Italian Amalfi Coast

MARIA I. SIMEON and P. BUONINCONTRI

Institute for Service Industry Research, National Research Council, Naples, Italy

In a destination management approach, territorial marketing policies to make a territory attractive are increasingly establishing on the supply of cultural events. These cultural initiatives are able to strengthen the local identity and to enhance the distinctive resources, both tangible and intangible, of an area. This article analyzes the event Ravello Festival as a tool of territorial marketing to increase the competitiveness of the Amalfi Coast and Ravello, becoming a distinctive symbol of the territory. The article first focuses on Ravello Festival, examining its history, management, and supply system. Ravello as tourist destination product in which Ravello Festival and the local resources are considered the fundamental elements is subsequently examined. Finally, the article considers the Ravello Festival's strengths, highlighting their coherence with the development strategy of Ravello. In conclusion, the strategic role of Ravello Festival is emphasized, as a quality event able to promote Ravello as City of Music in the world.

INTRODUCTION

At the present time, the competitive environment is becoming increasingly uncertain, dynamic, and turbulent in the tourism market characterized by new origin and destination areas. This new situation is due to a growing globalization and an increasing demand complexity. In this scenario, territories have focused on several marketing strategies to improve their image, differentiate themselves from competitors, and attract resources and visitors (Tamma, 2000): the local tourism development mostly depends on the capacity of a destination to differentiate its products from those of competitors and strategically focus on its distinctive resources so as to gain and enhance its competitive advantage (Pechlaner, Fischer, & Hammann, 2006; Schianetz, Kavanagh, & Lockington, 2007).

These important competitive goals can be achieved if the territories develop supply systems in a *destination management* perspective, using *territorial marketing* tools.

Destination management is a management method based on the awareness of how important the benefits of an integrated supply system are, and how they can be defined through a "number of activities and attraction factors which, located in a specific space, are able to provide an integrated supply which enhances local resources and culture" (Martini, 2005, p. 95). The objective is to generate tourist flows and satisfy the economic needs of local actors through synergies and cooperation between all the subjects involved in the governance and development of this supply system (Howie, 2003). The destination management model is strictly linked to the definition of *destination*: "a place towards which people travel and where they choose to stay for a while in order to experience certain features or attractions of some sort" (Leiper, 1995). Cooper, Fletcher, Gilbert, Shepherd, and Wanhill (1998) define destinations as the focus of facilities and services designed to meet the needs of the tourists. Buhalis (2000) describes the destination as a combination of all products, services, and experiences provided locally in order to maximize benefits for all stakeholders.

The foremost element is the experience made by tourists who, by selecting and combining the most suitable elements for their vacation, define the destination (Pechlaner, 1999).

The concept of tourist destination as a system implies not only to many products and services, but also a multiplicity of interacting local actors playing different roles and contributing to create the overall experience lived by tourists within a specific area (Manente & Cerato, 2000): the basilar principle of the destination management is, in fact, to consider the relationship between the local actors as a fundamental part of a destination.

Destination management includes all the strategic, organizational, and operational decisions to manage the creation and also the promotion of a territorial supply system.

There is a strong link between destination management and territorial marketing, the fundamental tool for the promotion and strengthen of local development: through territorial marketing the policy makers develop strategies to attract resources and visitors and, exploiting the typical local resources, try to achieve a competitive advantage to ensure a sustainable and constant development (Van den Berg, Van der Borg, & Van de Meer, 1998; Golfetto & Podesta, 2000).

Territorial marketing can be defined as a set of collective actions applied to attract new economic and productive activities into a specific area or territory, to encourage the growth of local business and to promote a positive image. The success of territorial marketing comes from its ability to discover the needs of actual and potential tourists and to develop incisive actions to satisfy them. In this way, the destination becomes more attractive, and therefore more competitive.

The various territorial marketing policies can be based on the enhancement of existing endogenous resources, on exogenous resources, and/or on innovative projects. The fundamental issue about the territorial development is not only the capacity of the destination to attract new resources, but the capacity to internally generate the conditions of transformation and exploitation of its internal assets (Ritchie & Crouch, 1993).

Territorial marketing provides great attention to the communication and promotion of the territorial supply system, through the creation of Web sites, advertising, the establishment of a tourism brand, and the realization of important events. In particular, event-based tourism has a strong impact on an area and on its appeal (AIEST, 1987); an event can have a significant effect on the image of the place hosting it, both for residents and for temporary citizens, determining for these latter a greater propensity to return in future (Buhalis, 2000).

Event-based tourism—or tourism focused on the creation of events—is now one of the most important development strategies used by territorial marketing. The events, in fact, influence the image of the locality where they are made and, therefore, can be considered as fundamental elements of differentiation, especially if based on distinctive and unique local resources (Ferrari & Resciniti, 2007).

Starting from these considerations, this article analyzes the Ravello Festival as a territorial marketing tool able to increase the competitiveness of the Amalfi Coast and to become a clear symbol of the town of Ravello, Italy. Ravello is a quiet town of 2,500 inhabitants 350 meters above sea level founded in the 6th century AD and, because of the beauty of its artwork, along with its fine villas, streets, and gardens, it is one of the biggest attractions on the Amalfi Coast.

The article first examines the history, management and supply system of the Ravello Festival.

Ravello as a tourist destination product (TDP) is subsequently examined. The competitive advantage of Ravello as TDP is based on the uniqueness of its resources, which puts the area into a natural monopoly situation. Moreover, it is based on the Ravello Festival as the main tool of territorial marketing. The Ravello Festival strengths are finally examined, highlighting their coherence with the development strategy of the area of Ravello.

In the conclusion, the strategic role of the Ravello Festival is emphasized, as a quality event able to promote Ravello as "city of music" in the world, to improve the local identity, and to strengthen the attractiveness of the Amalfi Coast.

RAVELLO FESTIVAL HISTORY, MISSION, AND MANAGEMENT

Ravello Festival is a very ancient musical festival, begun in 1953, but its current structure was experimented with for the first time in 1994 and finally established with the launch of the *Fondazione Ravello* (Ravello Foundation) in 2002; until that year it was a symphonic festival that lasted 4 weeks. The Fondazione Ravello provided a fresh imprint to the festival; its objectives are the promotion of the Ravello Festival, the enhancement of historical and artistic assets, and the coordination of cultural events in Ravello. The foundation has contributed to make Ravello one of the finest centers of refined culture operating in Italy.

The foundation has also created *Ravello Relais*, a network of national and international personalities with the aim to protect the culture and identity of Ravello. The network operates providing suggestions and proposals for the territorial development.

Table 1 lists the last six Ravello Festival editions (2003–2008), and shows the evolution and features of the festival:

- *Theme*: The Ravello Festival theme changes every year to renew the event. Previous themes were Power (2003), Dream (2004), Contrast (2005), Game (2006), Passion (2007), and Diversity (2008). The themes are presented every year in several ways and are developed in several forms—music, scientific and literary reflection, dance, cinema, design, and visual arts. Diversity, for example, has been considered in its positive sense as fruitful coexistence and pacific comparison between different entities, and in its negative connotation as refusal of equality, fairness, tolerance, and inclusion.
- *Duration*: The festival has had an increasingly extended duration and aims to be 365 days long in the next edition. The 2008 edition was the first to last 127 days, allowing the festival to be considered the largest event of 2008 in Europe.
- *Sections and Events*: Another improvement of the festival has been the increasing number of sections and events every year. From four sections—symphonic music, cinema, photography, and chamber music—and 104 events in 2003, the 2008 edition has realized nine sections—symphonic music, chamber music, cinemusic, visual arts, training, trends, science and literature, special events, and dance—along with 190 events. Ravello

TABLE 1 Ravello Festival 2003–2008

Year	2003	2004	2005	2006	2007	2008
Theme	Power	Dream	Contrast	Game	Passion	Diversity
Duration	6/29–10/23	6/27–9/22	7/1–9/18	6/30–9/17	6/29–9/8	6/27–10/31
No. sections	4	8	8	8	8	9
No. events	104	100	100	100	100	190
No. visitors	16.202	36.618	37.428	46.009	63.858	79.706
Budget €	2.000.000	2.500.000	2.300.000	2.500.000	2.300.000	2.500.000
Incomes €[a]	—	—	160.539,32	200.185,72	300.386,40	360.453,65
Special guests	Zaffrelli; Royal Philharmonic Orchestra	Barra; Campanella; Luca di Montezemolo	Pehlivanian; Battistelli	Janacek Philharmonic Orchestra; Onorato	Galimberti; Biondi; Bolle	Glenn; Caine; L. Einaudi; Mertens

[a]The data does not consider incomes from workshops, meetings and exhibitions.

Source: Azienda Autonoma Soggiorno e Turismo, 2005a, Azienda Autonoma Soggiorno e Turismo, 2005b, Azienda Autonoma Soggiorno e Turismo, 2005c, De Ciuceis, 2006, http://www.ravellofestival.com

Festival 2008 also proposed several new night concerts and a series of exhibitions and seminars focusing on design; there were also 16 symphonic music concerts and two exhibitions of contemporary art; and October was devoted to meetings and exhibitions on design and new trends.

- *Visitors, Budget, and Income*: The Ravello Festival growth generated a positive increase in the budget, the number of visitors, and, consequently, in the income: the total visitors of the 2008 edition were 79,706. Among them, a great number has been of foreign nationality. In the same year, the income resulting only from the performances—not including workshops, meetings, and exhibitions—was €360,453.65.

The Ravello Festival has always had a very clear mission: to present visitors with the typical Ravello model of life based on reflection, creative moments, exchange, and ethics. This mission is made possible by the consistency between what the visitors want and what Ravello can offer them; Ravello allows the audience to enjoy a unique atmosphere with the serenity of its countryside, a mild climate, powerful cultural monuments, and the politeness of its citizens.

The values of quiet, cultural growth and welcome are shared by the local community, and ratified in the *Carta di Ravello*, adopted in 1992 by the Municipality.

Based on these principles, the festival intends to achieve the following goals:

- *Cultural and Artistic*: The Ravello Festival offers excellent music performances, enhancing simultaneously all the cultural resources of the area.
- *Tourism and Territorial Marketing*: The Ravello Festival wants to be the main tool to promote all the area and strengthen local identity.

To achieve these objectives, in accordance with the structural features of the town of Ravello, the festival has developed a clear niche strategy:

1. The maximum number of visitors has been defined, considering the little capacity of Ravello;
2. The supply has been planned: number and type of hotels; number and type of events to attract the target goal; and
3. Actions have been defined to constantly maintain the supply appropriate to the desired visitors' needs.

Considering the mission, goals, and strategy, the Ravello Festival desired target consists of cultural tourists, along with lovers of classical music and beautiful landscapes. The target of the Ravello Festival is composed of highly cultured tourists wishing to visit Ravello for its beautiful landscape, mild climate, monuments, welcoming atmosphere, and an excellent classical music event.

The Ravello Festival has therefore adopted a consistent territorial marketing strategy, which has helped to attract more visitors and cultural tourists, increasing the direct and indirect economic benefits of the whole site. The most important visitors have a good spending capacity and the hotels in the area have a high utilization rate.

The economic dimension of the Ravello Festival is relevant, and continues to grow continuously. For the 2007 edition there were some 63,093 paying spectators. Most were Italian, but there were also a good number of foreign visitors, especially German, British, American, French, and Spanish, as the Amalfi Coast is known and appreciated worldwide.

The festival is popular with Ravello residents, too: for example, in 2004 only 88 Ravello citizens attended the festival, while in 2005 this figure rose to 738.

The attention to the quality of the event is also noticeable in the breakdown of costs (Figure 1); in 2004, almost half the costs covered artistic expenses (49%), the other major expenditure items were advertising (19%), organization and development costs (16%), general costs (7%), travel and accommodation for artists (6%), and merchandising (3%) (Fondazione Monte dei Paschi di Siena, 2004).

The Ravello Festival available budget for 2007 was €1,994,000. The main sources of funding are Monte dei Paschi di Siena, Region and Municipality. The 2008 edition has required the involvement of 850 artists and 150 operators with a budget of €2,500,000, of which 62% was provided by private funding and 38% by public policies of the region and municipality.

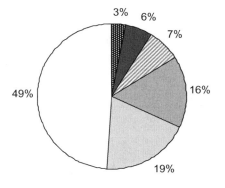

FIGURE 1 Main items of expenditure, 2004.
Source: Adapted from Porzio (2008).

The sponsors of the Ravello Festival, which increase every year, are totally consistent with the spirit of the event so as to promote the image of exclusivity, luxury, and high quality. Companies and brands that collaborate with the festival present a very strong link with Ravello traditions and are representative of the "Made in Italy" brand known around the world.

RAVELLO FESTIVAL SUPPLY SYSTEM

From a marketing approach, it's possible to analyze the Ravello Festival through two perspectives:

1. In an operative point of view, the Ravello Festival can be considered as a supply system that consists of several activities, products, and services to satisfy the visitors' needs. In setting marketing strategies it is very useful to analyze a festival through its supply system; it is interesting to consider all factors that can make the Ravello Festival a rich and satisfying event for everyone, even if the motivations to participate are many and varied for each visitor.
2. In an analytical point of view, the Ravello Festival can be studied through the main marketing tools developed in the supply system and those activated in the several moments of meeting with its audience. The behavior of consumption in the different phases of exchange between demand and supply are very important to examine because the event has to define different marketing tools to attract, satisfy, and make loyal the actual and potential visitors.

Considering the Ravello Festival supply system, it can be defined a "set of aesthetic and cultural factors of attraction—perceived as a complex experience—able to meet the specific needs of visitors and which can be on different levels" (Colbert, 2000, p. 36).

In particular, it's possible to identify three levels: *core activities, enriched activities,* and *collateral activities* (Figure 2) that offer a unique and high quality experience, stimulating the cognitive, emotional, and social processes.

The festival, in fact, not only provides a service of musical entertainment, but also offers many additional services that contribute to the creation of benefits for the visitors of Ravello and its event.

The core activity is about the benefits that make the event unique compared with other festivals. The Ravello Festival core activities are the classical music concerts set in a particular location of the town, and the other performances organized during the festival, from dance to visual arts, and so on. The main location of the event is a large and inimitable overhanging stage built on Villa Rufolo's Belvedere.

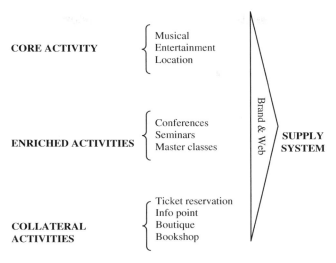

FIGURE 2 The Ravello Festival supply system.
Source: Adapted from Argano, Bollo, Dalla Sega, and Vivalda (2005).

Enriched activities concern the mix of products and services not directly linked to the event mission, but which help to attract more visitors; as well as musical concerts the Ravello Festival also includes seminars, symposiums, and master classes.

Collateral activities include all those services that, though not essential, improve the overall quality of experience. A collateral asset consists of information, reservation, and ticketing services; another collateral service offered by the Ravello Festival is the possibility to buy promotional gifts at the bookshop and clothing with the festival logo at the boutique. The festival presents also an e-shop where is possible to buy the merchandising material made by several famous Italian companies—Tramontano, Conte of Florence, Museo della Carta Amalfi—to underline the "Made in Italy" quality and the festival link with the local traditions.

Though the core activity may be the primary factor in the moment of decision-making as regards attending the event, the enriched and collateral activities can also play a large part: enriched activities can interest new users that can then move closer to the core of the festival; the collateral services too, if well defined, can add value to the customer, helping to consolidate and create a loyal public.

The success of territorial marketing strategies based on the achievement of a cultural event supply system is strongly linked to the ability to engage visitors by offering the possibility to participate in experiences that can satisfy their needs and desires, in a consistent manner with their expectations (Collodi, Crisci, & Moretti, 2005).

The Role of Brand and Web Site in the Ravello Festival Supply System

A fundamental role in all the Ravello Festival supply system is played by the brand and the Web site, two important marketing tools used to spread a positive image of the Ravello Festival and to attract new potential visitors.

The brand is the medium to communicate the long tradition of the event, its values, and originality. In general, the brand strategies applied to an event make possible to position the event in the minds of visitors in a strong positive and unique manner, and to communicate the value proposition to the target.

The main benefits of a brand event are (Clarke, 2000):

1. The brand guides the tourist's choice in a high involvement purchasing process, both emotionally and economically; and
2. Branding strategies facilitate transmission of intangible factors difficult to transfer to consumers.

Three dimensions that define the identity of the Ravello Festival brand may be described (Risitano, 2006):

1. Personality, which refers to emotional, symbolic, and experiential elements of the event. To show these items to the public an impressive human-character was created, an angel without wings with violin in hand flying over the town of Ravello (Figure 3);
2. Name, given by the association between the name of the place, Ravello, and the type of event, the festival. The choice of the name *Ravello Festival* allows the user to quickly develop strong, unique and distinctive associations, and emphasizes the strength of local identity; and
3. Logos and symbols—visual elements that allow the user to create brand awareness and communicate the event value proposition in a distinctive

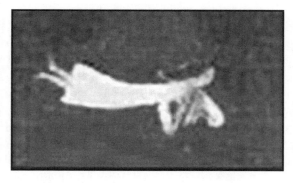

FIGURE 3 The Ravello Festival personality: An angel without wings.
Source: http://www.ravellofestival.com

FIGURE 4 The Ravello Festival logo.
Source: http://www.ravellofestival.com

way (Figure 4). Since 2003, the Ravello Festival symbol is the angel without wings, though each year it has been reviewed and adapted to the theme edition.

Another marketing tool to create value for Ravello Festival users is the Web site, available in Italian and English. It instantly involves the visitors in the Spirit of Ravello and the spirit of the event: on the Web site homepage appears the angel without wings flying over Ravello as well as photos of the festival location (Figure 5).

FIGURE 5 The Ravello Festival website.
Source: http://www.ravellofestival.com

FIGURE 6 The Ravello Festival website: newsletter.
Source: http://www.ravellofestival.com

The Web site is an extremely important instrument to communicate with real and potential visitors of the town (Guarino, 2003): through the Ravello Festival web site customers gain information, book or buy tickets online, receive the newsletter, and interact with the festival organizers even when they are back in their country.

The Marketing Tools Activated Before, During, and After the Festival

The second perspective to analyze the Ravello Festival in a territorial marketing approach is considering the main instruments used in the different moments of meeting between the event and its audience: (a) interactions with the audience before they enter Ravello; (b) moments of meetings with visitors on the area; and (c) interactions with audience after the festival has ended.

Knowledge of the behavior of consumption is, in fact, particularly interesting because it allows identifying the stages and the main elements that lead to the realization of customer satisfaction (Bramwell, 1997).

In the first moment, consumers still are in their territory and feel the need to participate in a classical music event. It is a very important moment because the potential client starts to consider various activities: evaluation of alternatives, seeking information, and ticket purchase. The marketing and communication actions must ensure that the festival falls within the set of possible choices of the client: Ravello Festival should be promoted as an event able to satisfy the consumer needs, both Italian and foreign.

The promotion of Ravello Festival occurs through several instruments:

- Press office: Ravello Festival has two press offices—national and international—in order to carry out precise and targeted communication. The National Press Office organized three conferences in 2008 (Naples, Rome, and Salerno), and organized the promotion of the event in magazines, newspapers, TV, and radio; the International Press Office took care of the festival promotion on international media.
- As for communication online, Ravello Festival has a Web site, but also sponsorships on other Web sites (www.fondazioneravello.com, www.comune.ravello.it, www.ravellotime.it, etc.).

Before the performances start, Ravello Festival considers also the following elements to attract visitors (Rigatti Luchini & Mason, 2008):

- The reputation of the area. Ravello is one of the most beautiful towns on the Amalfi Coast, and the festival uses the fame of this coast for its promotion;
- The image of the event. The organizers have developed a distinctive brand, adjusted each year to the theme of the event, to spread a positive image of the festival. Another important activity is the reservation and purchase of tickets through several ways—online, phone, box office, or text message.

In this first contact with customers, communication on the price, via e-mail or telephone, is also important: accurate activity relating to ticket booking and price communication ensures that the customer is problem-free and completely satisfied with the Ravello Festival supply system. It has determined a growth in the number of visitors: from 2005 to 2007, they are increased by 40%, with a significant presence of foreign tourists.

The second moment concerns the form of participation at the event and the communication and promotion of the festival directly on the site where it is located. Customers need to be satisfied even when they are already in Ravello and are participating in the Ravello Festival performances.

The principal objective is the maximum evaluation of the customer experience (Pine & Gilmore, 2000). The main variables that can influence the perception of the event quality and the customer experience are the environmental and weather conditions of Ravello. Most of the Ravello Festival concerts are performed in open spaces, and this links the success of the festival to Ravello weather conditions; to avoid this problem from the next year the Ravello Festival is expected to take place in the auditorium of the famous Brazilian architect Oscar Niemeyer.

During the festival, it is also essential to consider (Cuadrado & Mollá, 2002):

- How the visitor is welcomed in the area. Ravello Festival has organized a box office to issue booked tickets and information on seating;
- The way of listening to the visitor, providing information and solving problems. Ravello Festival audience can contact the box office to request and obtain information;
- Transparency in pricing. The calendar of events contains all details as regards performances prices and available discounts.

The third moment concerns the phase of interaction with event consumers that begins when the festival ends and lasts until the next festival; to create a link with the customers that hopefully leads to a return visit in the future. This phase is a difficult one since in this moment the visitor will consider whether the festival has satisfied their needs or not; visitor satisfaction influences their choice to return the following year to Ravello and to promote the festival among relatives and friends (Shankar, Elliot, & Goviding, 2001).

In this phase it is vital that throughout the year the visitor realizes that the festival can satisfy their needs, and that over time the festival has been continuously renewed and improved. Ravello Festival considers fundamental this aspect and has defined several activities and conferences to communicate the festival news. The main tool for building a lasting and positive relationship with the customer after the performances is the Internet, and e-mail in particular (Martini, 2008). E-mail allows visitors to communicate with the festival organizers: it is possible to listen to users at any time, to pick up signs of dissatisfaction or satisfaction, complaints, and advice or encouragement.

Ravello Festival also provides the opportunity to subscribe to a mailing list in order to receive information on the festival. This tool makes possible to learn more about the Ravello Festival target and to understand target needs, through registration information, name, surname, nationality, and city of residence.

The moment of interaction after the festival should also encourage the visitors to spread a positive image of the festival by word-of-mouth, and to increase the number of participants the following year (Carú & Cova, 2006). The sale of promotional gifts related to the event is another important tool for promoting a positive image of the Ravello Festival. The festival has a bookshop selling posters, brochures, books, and CDs, and a boutique that sells clothing and fashion accessories with the Ravello Festival logo. In this way the user can make purchases, which lengthen the festival experience and strengthen the feeling of being part of an easily recognizable community of cultured subjects.

RAVELLO TOURIST DESTINATION PRODUCT

Ravello Festival, thanks to its fame and quality, plays an important role in the tourist destinations of the Amalfi Coast and Ravello. But it is crucial emphasize that the festival is not the only attractor of the area: it is a fundamental part of Ravello's TDP, consisting, on the one hand, of distinctive resources like landscape, natural beauty, tradition, history, art, and cultural heritage, and on the other of infrastructure and services like hotels, restaurants, and information points (Simeon, 2007).

In a destination management perspective, in fact, Ravello aims to become a more strongly integrated TDP, correlating all its resources and defining a system that consists of core services, additional needed services, and additional differentiated services (Figure 7).

The core service is given by the mix of experience the customer wants to live at the destination and is the main reason for the trip. At this level three elements may be considered: (a) culture (important historical sites in Ravello, such as its villas); (b) landscape and nature; and (c) events (Ravello

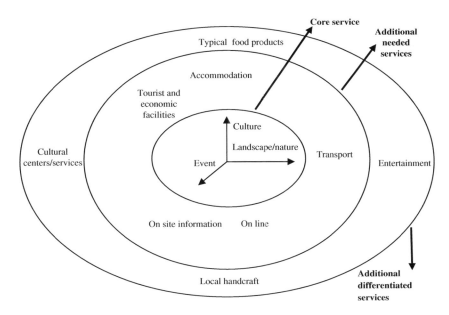

FIGURE 7 Ravello tourist destination product.
Source: Adapted from Cantone, Risitano, and Testa (2005).

Festival). Ravello Festival is, in fact, inextricably linked to the history of Ravello and is therefore a basic service for the visitors.

The additional needed services are those that facilitate access to and use of the basic services: accommodations, on-site and online information services, transport, and car parks.

Additional differentiated services are those that make the destination unique when compared to its competitors, satisfying customer needs in an original way. In the territory of Ravello, local crafts (hand-decorated pottery); typical food products (wine, mozzarella and cheeses, *limoncello* lemon liqueur), and cultural services are all well developed. In addition there are several important cultural centers, such as the Lisa Mascolo school for culture manager training; the European University Centre for Cultural Heritage, extremely active in organizing training courses and conferences related to culture; and the school of musical refinement.

Ravello has, therefore, cultural, historical, and landscape resources that are very competitive and original.

The resources of a tourist destination can lead to three types of rents (Peteraf, 1993, Keller, 2000):

1. Ricardian rents: Typical of tourist destinations that implement volume strategies;
2. Paretian rents: Distributed among the holders of the resource and the tourist destination; and
3. Schumpeterian rents: Derived from the ability to innovate the TDP and to exploit the lower price elasticity of current and potential demand.

The Ravello competitive advantage is based on Schumpeterian rents; Ravello cannot pursue strategies of volume, but must undertake a niche strategy. It is, in fact, not possible to accommodate a large number of tourists or increase the accommodation capacity of Ravello, due to physiological limits of the territory.

This analysis is based on the studies of Peteraf (1993) about the cornerstones of competitive advantage in a resource-based view, and considers that the relationship between the resources of a territory and the competitive advantage derives from a proper enhancement of the tangible and intangible local assets. Peteraf presents four conditions:

1. *Resource heterogeneity*, based on the uniqueness of tourist destination resources: Ravello has rare resources linked to its history, traditions, and culture that allow the town to position itself in a monopoly condition;
2. *Ex post limits to competition*, necessary to sustain the rents and due to the hard reproduction or replacement of distinctive resources. Ravello bases its competitive advantage mainly on its intangible resources and these are very hard to reproduce in other areas;

3. *Imperfect resource mobility* that ensures the bound between resources and the TDP; it's not possible to transfer the Ravello tangible assets in another area reproducing also the intangible ties with the local culture and traditions; and

4. *Ex ante limits to competitions*, considering that not all the tourist destinations are able or want to compete to achieve the same resources. In the case of Ravello, this territory pursues enhancement policies based on tangible and intangible resources that are unique and not reproducible and on the Ravello Festival, strongly linked to these resources. The other territories couldn't reproduce this successful formula.

To conclude, Ravello as TDP establishes its competitive advantage on the uniqueness of its resources, which puts the area into a natural monopoly situation, and on the realization of a major event, the Ravello Festival. The event is an important lever for territorial marketing (Gertz, 1991) and has a significant influence on the image of the town of Ravello into the visitor's mind (Gwinner, 1997); at the same time it represents the system of values in which the community recognizes itself (Leoni, 2006). To be successful, in fact, the event must be coherent with the area's identity and has to propagate the spirit of the place, understood as the result of the territory's history and the evolution over time of the area's tangible and intangible resources (Ostillio & Trailo, 2000; Caroli, 1999).

The event, therefore, has to create a strong link with the unique and distinctive local assets (Ferrari & Veltri, 2007): Ravello Festival may hypothetically be reproduced in other places, but would not be possible to rebuild the ties with Ravello's traditions and culture, which remain strongly linked to the surrounding area.

RAVELLO FESTIVAL STRENGTHS AND RAVELLO STRATEGY OF INTEGRATED TERRITORIAL DEVELOPMENT

The Ravello Festival is the main territorial marketing tool for the Amalfi Coast and can be considered the driving force for the implementation of the Ravello strategy of integrated territorial development. Ravello, in fact, wants to be a TDP in which the competitive factor is represented by the high integration between all the distinctive resources.

The festival success is based on three strengths perfectly consistent with the event mission and the strategy of the territory.

The first strength is the strong integration of the Ravello Festival with the territory of Ravello and the local community. The festival was built starting from the *genius loci* of Ravello and in total harmony with the identity of the place and the spirit of the citizens. This allowed the perfect fusion of the festival mission with the local community objectives: the success of the event is the main cause of the economic and tourist success of Ravello. The Ravello Festival is not an instrument to damage the atmosphere of the town, but its principal territorial marketing tool. This strong integration allows improving the image of Ravello through the exploitation of the local resources.

The second strength resides in the history of Ravello Festival—extremely long as it is the second oldest musical event in Italy—and in its originality, which continues to endure over time thanks to the annual renewal and extension of the supply, so it's possible a visitors fidelization and the improvement of Ravello's tourism sector (Amato, 2006).

The third strength is connected to the organizers' ability to actually turn the Ravello structural problem in terms of accommodation capacity—few facilities—into a strong point for the festival; the Ravello Festival is, in fact, a niche event of the highest level, and the small number of facilities does not make it accessible to mass tourism.

It's moreover important to highlight that to remain competitive over time, the Ravello Festival cannot rest on the success it has achieved, but must constantly adapt its supply system to changes in the environment and customer needs, exploiting the local distinctive assets (Viceconte, 2004).

Ravello qualifies itself as an excellent TDP characterized by resources and cultural tourist services of quality. In accordance with the Ravello Festival strategic actions, the town is focusing on a niche strategy and on an integrated development of the local resources.

These strategic goals want to improve the culture and economy of the territory affirming Ravello in the world as a "city of music," promoting the high-quality tourism market and improving job opportunities in the cultural industry. It wants to achieve this goal by extending the Ravello Festival to 365 days a year and increasing tourism during periods of low demand. The town wants to attract visitors and tourists all year long; cultural tourists during the summer, with the realization of Ravello Festival, and congressional tourists in the winter. The cultural tourists are attracted also in the winter by extending the Ravello Festival supply across all 12 months of the year by 2010. These objectives are supported by the realization of the auditorium by the famous architect Oscar Niemeyer, completed at the end of January 2009. The idea to create an indoor space for the music in Ravello came about in 2002 to ensure a year-long program for the Ravello Festival. The building is not very expensive and fits perfectly into the landscape and atmosphere of Ravello.

The auditorium will become a great attractor for Ravello tourism and is expected to host conferences, seminars, conventions, and cultural events, developing the economy of the area 365 days a year and giving continuous employment to locals, especially to young people. The auditorium, in fact, will enable the development of many collateral activities at the festival, helping to make the event a symbol of the city and to enhance all the area.

The strategy of integrated local development is supported by public policies, such as the local development plan, PIT (integrated territorial project) "Ravello City of Music" (2003), which received European funding of some 10 million euros and involves the province, region, municipality and other important local institutions as the Fondazione Ravello. The PIT guideline is to stimulate a quality cultural supply, based on passion for music, territorial enhancement, and the desire to maintain links with tradition.

To support integrated territorial development, the PIT is also providing strategic actions in the fields of:

- Infrastructure: Logistics operations, new parking, improved lighting, construction of an urban plan;
- Training: Recovery of local traditions and crafts, training of experts in to exploit Ravello's resources and promote the image of Ravello worldwide; and
- Financing: To finance tourism business, restaurants and hotels.

CONCLUSIONS

The importance of the Ravello Festival for the whole community is such that Ravello is known throughout the Amalfi Coast and beyond as the city of music. A similar recognition highlights the ability of the festival to be a cultural event and symbol of the territory of Ravello, and the main instrument of territorial marketing. The Ravello Festival is realized to entertain guests with music, cinema, dance, and art, and is the principal attractor for strengthening the growth and competitiveness of the area that hosts it. In this way the festival (Krantz & Schäzl, 1997; Montanari, 2002):

- contributes to the image of the territory;
- may be considered a genuine element of differentiation based on local traditions and culture and a distinctive point to promote the local tourist brand;
- is strongly integrated with the territory and the local community, thanks to the strong tie with territorial resources;
- defines the competitive positioning of the territory of Ravello; and
- helps to develop the local employment, mobilizing internal potential.

Ravello Festival is, in fact, characterized by high quality, authenticity, and complete integration with the community of Ravello and its traditions, and is perfectly consistent with the local Genius Loci and Spirit of Ravello.

To conclude, is possible to affirm Ravello Festival is a successful example of event-based tourism. In recent years several changes were introduced to the Ravello Festival management and organization to achieve these goals and to increase the impact on the competitive advantage of Ravello and the Amalfi Coast. Despite that, the festival still remains bound to its mission and original objectives. It is a quality cultural event, which is part of the heritage of the local community, attracts loyal audience over time—but also new visitors—and is able to evoke an exclusive image, emphasized by the location, the coherence with the Spirit of Ravello, and the integration with the territorial resources.

REFERENCES

AIEST. (1987). *The role and impact of mega-events and attractions on regional and national tourism development*. St. Gall, Switzerland: AIEST Edition.

Amato, R. (2006). *A Roma l'omaggio a Tchaikovsky. Ravello celebra Wagner e il gioco, interview with Domenico De Masi*. Retrieved from www.repubblica.it

Argano, L., Bollo, A., Dalla Sega, P., & Vivalda, C. (2005). *Gli eventi culturali. Ideazione, progettazione, marketing, comunicazione*. Milan, Italy: Franco Angeli.

Azienda Autonoma Soggiorno e Turismo. (2005a). Il festival dei grandi numeri. *RavelloTime, 1*, 136.

Azienda Autonoma Soggiorno e Turismo. (2005b). Il festival dei grandi numeri. *RavelloTime, 1*, 137.

Azienda Autonoma Soggiorno e Turismo. (2005c). Il festival dei grandi numeri. *RavelloTime, 1*, 140.

Bos, H. (1994). The importance of mega-events in the development of tourism demand. *Festival Management & Event Tourism, 2*(1), 55–58.

Bramwell, B. (1997). Strategic planning before and after a mega-event. *Tourism Management, 18*, 167–176.

Buhalis, D. (2000). Marketing the competitive destination of the future. *Tourism Management, 21*, 97–116.

Cantone, L., Risitano, M., & Testa, P. (2005, July). *Heterogeneity of contextual resources and destination branding management: The Campi Flegrei Case*. Sinergie-Cueim Heterogeneity, Diversification and Performance Conference 2005. Cosenza, Italy.

Caroli, M. G. (1999). *Il marketing territorial*. Milan, Italy: Franco Angeli.

Carù, A., & Cova, B. (2008). L'immersione del consumatore in un contesto esperienziale: La narrazione introspettiva come modalità di ricerca. In U. Collesei & J. C. Andreani (Ed.), *Proceedings of the Fifth International Congress on Marketing Trends* (pp. 10–12). Venice, Italy.

Clarke, J. (2000). Tourism brands: An exploratory study of the brands box model. *Journal of Vacation Marketing, 6*, 329–345.

Colbert, F. (2000). *Il marketing delle arti e della cultura*. Milan, Italy: Etas.

Collodi, D., Crisci, F., & Moretti, A. (2005, January). *Consumer behaviour nei prodotti artistici: Una prospettiva di ricerca*. Paper presented at the Fourth International Congress on Marketing Trends in Europe. Paris, France.

Cooper, C., Fletcher, J., Gilbert, D., Shepherd, R., & Wanhill, S. (1998). *Tourism: Principles and practices* (2nd ed.). London, England: Addison-Wesley.

Cuadrado, M., & Mollà, A. (2002) Una segmentazione dei consumatori di performing arts basata sui bisogni degli spettatori. Retrieved from www.fizz.it

De Ciuceis, P. (2006). RavelloFestival 2006. *Porto & Diporto*, 28–33.

Ferrari, S., & Resciniti, R. (2007). La gestione degli eventi turistico-culturali nella prospettiva esperienziale. *Annali della Facoltà di Economia di Benevento, 12*, 257–284.

Ferrari, S., & Veltri, A. R. (2007). L'approccio esperienziale ai beni culturali come strumento di differenziazione dell'offerta turistica. Retrieved from www.fizz.it

Fondazione Monte Dei Paschi Di Siena. (2004). *Final budget*. Available at http://www.fondazionemps.it

Getz, D. (1991). *Festivals, special events and tourism*. New York, NY: Van Nostrand Reinhold.

Golfetto, F., & Podestà, S. (2000). *La nuova concorrenza. Contesti di interazione, strumenti di azione, approcci di analisi*. Milan, Italy: Egea.

Guarino, A. (2003). *La comunicazione di un Festival: Il Milano Film Festival*. Retrieved from www.fizz.it

Gwinner, K. (1997). A model of image creation and image transfer in event sponsorship. *International Marketing Review, 14*, 145–158.

Howie, F. (2003). *Managing the tourist destination*. London, England: Continuum.

Keller, P. (2000). Globalization and tourism. In W. Gartner & D. W. Line (Eds.), *Trends in outdoor recreation, leisure and tourism* (pp. 287–297). New York, NY: CABI.

Krantz, M., & Schätzl, L. (1997). Marketing the city. In C. Jensen-Butler, A. Shachar, & J. van Weesep (Eds.), *European cities in competition*. Aldershot, England: Avebur.

Leiper, N. (1995). *Tourism management*. Melbourne, Australia: RMIT Press.

Leoni, P. (2006, October). *Introduction*. Paper presented at the Conference Events and social cohesion in the communities. How to measure the value of an event, the construction of the key performance indicators. Rimini, Italy.

Manente, M., & Cerato, M. (1999, March). *Destination management. Understanding destination as a system*. Proceedings of the International Conference From destination marketing to destination marketing and management, Venice.

Manente, M., & Cerato, M. (2000). Destination management per creare valore. In H. Pechlaner, K. Weiermair, & C. Laesser (Eds.), *Destination management. Fondamenti di marketing e gestione delle destinazioni turistiche* (pp. 55–71). Milan, Italy: Touring University Press.

Martini, U. (2005). *Management dei sistemi territoriali*. Torino, Italy: Giappichelli Editore.

Martini, U. (2008). *L'impatto di Internet sulla struttura del mercato turistico leisure*. Retrieved from www.economia.unitn.it

Montanari, A. (2002). Grandi eventi, Marketing urbano e realizzazione di nuovi spazi turistici. *Bollettino sulla società geografica italiana, 7*(4), 757–782.

Ostillio, M. C., & Trailo, G. (2000). *Management dei sistemi informativi di marketing. Competenze, fiducia e tecnologia in evoluzione*. Milan, Italy: Egea.

Pechlaner, H. (1999). Alpine destination management and marketing in Italy. *Turistica*, 7(2/3), 38–47.

Pechlaner, H., Fischer, E., & Hammann, E. M. (2006). Leadership and innovation processes—development of products and services based on core competencies. *Journal of Quality Assurance in Hospitality and Tourism*, 6(3/4), 31–57.

Peteraf, M. A. (1993). The cornerstones of competitive advantage: a resource-based view. *Strategic Management Journal*, 14(3), 179–191.

Pine, B. J., & Gilmore, J. H. (2000). *L'economia delle esperienze*. Milan, Italy: Etas.

Porzio, A. (2008). *Event based tourism e strategie di marketing territoriale per lo sviluppo integrato del territorio. La città di Ravello e il suo Festival*. Retrieved from www.fizz.it

Ramello, G. (2000). Festival musicali ed esternalità. *Sviluppo Economico*, 4(2), 101–114.

Rigatti Luchini, S., & Mason, M. (2008). Qualità, soddisfazione e intenzioni comportamentali nel marketing degli eventi: Il caso dell'asparago friulano. In U. Collesei & J. C. Andreani (Eds.), *Proceedings of the Fifth International Congress on Marketing Trends* (pp. 10–12). Venice, Italy.

Risitano, M. (2006, May). *The role of destination branding in the tourism stakeholders system. The Campi Flegrei case*. IV International Doctoral Tourism and Leisure Colloquium, Barcelona, Spain.

Ritchie, B., & Crouch, G. (1993, October). *Competitiveness in international tourism: A framework for understanding and analysis*. Annual Congress of the International Association of Scientific Experts in Tourism, Baliloche, Argentina.

Schianetz, K., Kavanagh, L., & Lockington, D. (2007). The learning tourism destination: The potential of a learning organization approach for improving the sustainability of tourism destinations. *Tourism Management*, 28, 1485–1496.

Shankar, A., Elliot, R., & Goulding, C. (2001). Understanding consumption: Contributions from a narrative perspective. *Journal of Marketing Management*, 17, 429–453.

Simeon, M. I. (2007). Patrimonio culturale e valorizzazione turistica nel Mezzogiorno d'Italia. In I. Zilli (Ed.), *Il turismo tra teoria e prassi* (pp. 183–205). Naples, Italy: ESI.

Tamma, M. (2000). Aspetti strategici del destination management. In H. Pechlaner, K. Weiermair, & C. Laesser (Eds.), *Destination management. Fondamenti di marketing e gestione delle destinazioni turistiche* (pp. 31–54). Milan, Italy: Touring University Press.

Van den Berg, L., Van der Borg, J., & Van de Meer, J. (1998). *Urban tourism*. Aldershot, England: Ashgate.

Viceconte, E. (2004). *L'esperienza del luogo e del tempo* (Working Paper). Naples, Italy: Stoa. Available at http://eprints.stoa.it/180

"Touristic Fun": Motivational Factors for Visiting Legoland Windsor Theme Park

ALI BAKIR

*Faculty of Design, Media and Management, Bucks New University,
High Wycombe Campus, Buckinghamshire, England*

SUZANNE G. BAXTER

Thorpe Park, Surrey, England

*This study revealed the motivation constructs for visiting Legoland
Windsor tourist attraction. Data was collected from visiting families using semistructured interviews and nonparticipant observations. Grounded theory was employed and the construct of "fun"
that emerged as the main motivator for families to visit was deconstructed into its push–pull parts using traditional and revised
push–pull frameworks, and contrasted to the travel career ladder model. The study offered an insight into the notion of fun
as a motivator for families to visit a theme park. More importantly, by deconstructing the notion of fun associated with family
theme park, a touristic setting, this study offered a significant contribution to knowledge; it provided a theorization of the concept,
"touristic fun," previously undertheorized. It also contributed to
the literature on motivation, particularly, to visiting family theme
parks. The study has also several implications for the development,
management, and marketing of attractions of this type.*

Although the basic components of the various motivation concepts and
models revolve around needs and motives, behavior or activity, and goals
or satisfactions (Harrill & Potts, 2002), nevertheless, the literature on motivational constructs remains problematic. In exploring this literature, Murphy

and Alexander (2000) raised a number of issues, mainly over: the general definition and theoretical clarity of motivational constructs; the accessibility or relative consciousness of motivational beliefs; the interdependent or independent nature of the relations between different motivational constructs; and the stability of motivation over time, domains, and contexts. Furthermore, the methodological approach adopted in motivational studies and visitor motivation is heavily weighed towards the positivist, quantitative approach, whose limited interpretative power does not allow the development of full understanding of the area studied. The tourism literature offers competing and somewhat conflicting accounts of motivation, its constituent elements, and their interrelationships. Whilst there is rich literature on motivation, little has been written on what motivates families to visit family theme parks. The aim of this article is to contribute to addressing the shortcoming in the literature by revealing the motivation constructs of families for visiting Legoland Windsor tourist attraction.

TOURISM MOTIVATION: CONCEPTS AND MODELS

Ross (1998), among others, emphasized the relevance that motivation has to tourism, and the 1990s saw a huge surge in research, theories, and models of motivation and tourism. Parinello (1993) stated "the importance of motivation in tourism is quite obvious; it acts as a trigger that sets off all the events involved in travel" (p. 233). However, Pearce (1993) commented: "Research into why individuals travel has been hampered by the lack of a universally agreed . . . conceptualization of the tourist motivation construct" (p. 114). Pearce pointed out that there are so many motivational factors, postulated by different studies and theories, that there is no one model or idea that encompasses the motives for travel. Thus identifying the possible motivators has become a minefield, particularly as it has also been difficult to study the constructs independently due to the heterogeneity of tourism products (Swarbrooke & Horner, 2003).

The drives and needs view of psychological motivation is widely held in the tourism literature. In suggesting a functional approach, Fodness (1994) wrote: "The reason people give for their leisure travel behavior represents the psychological functions (the needs) the vacation serves (satisfies) for the individual" (p. 560). This is supported by Davidoff (1994) who claimed that incentives, emotions, and cognitions combine with homeostatic mechanisms to create drives; people may become accustomed to getting certain extrinsic and intrinsic rewards out of a particular act, and, therefore, the expectation or anticipation of something based on previous experiences can act as a motivator.

Iso-Ahola's (1982) claim that motives are cognitive representations of future states is not dissimilar to the expectancy–valence theory of motivation.

It also draws support from many authors, including Witt and Wright (1992), who suggested that behavior is related to expected goals and outcomes that can be achieved through an activity like tourism. The optimum arousal theory that has begun to saturate the literature points to the problem with the notion of tension reduction. It suggests that if we have too much stimulation we withdraw and seek relaxation and if we have too little stimulation we seek out stimulating experiences.

One of the first studies into tourist motivation is that of Dann (1977) centering on, what he coined, the "push and pull" factors; those which motivate people to leave home and those attributes of the destination which attract people. Based on data obtained from a sample of tourists visiting Barbados, he suggested that the push factors were anomie and ego-enhancement (the need for social recognition which people do not obtain from their reference groups). The view that once you have these push factors the pull factors begin to allure you is supported by Crompton (1979), who identified the following sociopsychological push motives: escape from a perceived mundane environment, exploration and evaluation of self, relaxation, prestige, regression to a childhood state, enhancement of kinship relationships (family bonding), facilitation of social interaction, novelty, and education. Factors such as prestige, escape from routine, making new friends, and relaxing are also found in McIntosh (1977). In response, Dann (1981) advanced seven approaches to understanding tourism motivation: anomie, destination pull factors, motivation as fantasy, motivation as a classified purpose, motivational typologies, and motivation and tourist experiences. Dann thus recognized that in order to understand motivation for travel, a multidisciplinary approach is required, encompassing insights from the fields of psychology, sociology, tourism, and marketing or consumer behavior.

One of the other major theories of tourist motivation is the travel career put forward by Pearce (1988), which suggested that motivations are fluid and dynamic and change with age, life-cycle stage, past experiences, and the influence of others. The idea of time and experience playing a role in motivation supports Dann's (1981) view that motives are both psychological and sociological and that there can be push and pull factors involved. Pearce (1988) devised the notion of the travel career ladder from testing different demographic segments at Australian theme parks, finding that different segments placed different levels of importance on various needs (for example 13–16-year-olds placed higher level of importance on thrills compared to family groups). Pearce's travel career ladder—the ascending five categories of needs: relaxation, stimulation, relationship, self-esteem, and fulfillment, is another multivariate hierarchical model; moving up the travel ladder as opposed to moving up Maslow's (1954) pyramid of needs. In advancing the travel career ladder model, Pearce seems to have overlooked his travel career concept of tourist motivation where he suggested that these motivations are fluid and dynamic. Ryan (1997) picked up this anomaly by criticizing Pearce's model as oversimplistic; he asserted that it would be more useful to apply the model and how the needs change with family life cycle and tourist experiences. Being a consumer behaviorist, Ryan accentuated the more profound appreciation of society and culture as a motivation to travel and experience attractions. He also suggested that tourists and visitors aim to experience new things but actually find themselves part of an anonymous, amorphous mass; although they arrive with preconceptions, expectations and motivations, these can be confirmed or disproved by the experience and this shapes their future motivations.

THEME PARKS: VISITORS' MOTIVATION

Motivational factors as applied to tourism decision-making literature have somewhat been focused on choosing destinations and types of holidays (e.g., Reisinger & Turner, 2002; Sirakaya & Woodside, 2005). Although there has been a number of empirical studies on travel motives as applied to "visitor attractions" visitation (e.g., Leask, Fyall, & Garrod, 2002; Swarbrooke, 2002), there seems to be little research into motives for visiting family theme parks. In a survey of 38 theme parks in the United States and Australia, Pearce and Moscardo (1985) found that although theme parks form a major development in contemporary leisure and recreation, psychologists have offered little to research in these areas. They also stated that current research practices on theme parks lack conceptual focus, methodological rigor, and analytical sophistication. Kao, Huang, and Wu (2008) explored the effects of what they called "theatrical" elements of theme parks (including attractiveness of scripts, charm of setting, planning of activities, and consistency of theme) on consumers' experiential quality (e.g., immersion, surprise, participation, and fun). Basing their research on Asian theme parks, Wong and Cheung (1999) found weak to moderately strong relationships between motivations for theme park visits by visitors and their demographics and lifestyle patterns. As a result, they urge management of these parks to focus on satisfying lower-level needs, such as stimulation, by developing and marketing an adventure theme comparable with Western theme parks.

However, of direct relevance to this study, is research undertaken by Johns and Gyimothy (2002, 2003) at Legoland Billund in Denmark. Johns and Gyimothy (2002) used grounded theory to investigate customer perceptions and satisfaction; they found that the park catered well for children's needs, but left adults with a feeling that they were "babysitting." Johns and Gyimothy (2003) looked at push and pull factors and the difference between adults and children. They discovered that the push factors for adults were prestige, regression, family relationships, and to a lesser extent novelty; whereas for children the main push factor was social interaction. The pull factors for adults were intrinsic satisfaction (at having pleased their children), whereas the pull factors for children where much more varied and poignant (arousal or stimulation, intrinsic satisfaction, and involvement). Some other idiosyncratic factors came up for both adults and children. For example, nostalgia and pilgrimage were major factors for adults since most of them had visited Legoland Billund as a child themselves, and it is also seen by some to be truly Danish and a must see attraction because of the history of Lego.

In the next section, the article discusses the methodological approach of the study of motivation to visit Windsor family theme park.

THE RESEARCH APPROACH: STRAUSS' GROUNDED THEORY

There are many types of research designs that could be used to examine the motives, both in the positivist and interpretative paradigms. Sekaran (2003) suggested three types of research design; exploratory, descriptive, and causal (sometimes called correlation). However, as this research seeks to have insight into people's thoughts and behaviors in a unique setting, the qualitative or exploratory paradigm was used. Babbie (1998) argued that exploratory research is ideal for uncovering important categories and meanings that the participants hold. Sekaran (2003) added that exploratory research is specifically suitable for examining new areas where little is known about the phenomenon under study. However, with all research designs there are limitations and the semi-structured interview is no exception: samples are small and not representative of the population, the data is not always replicable for comparisons, the researcher's presence or demeanor may influence participants and cause bias, and respondents can misunderstand what is being asked in open ended questions.

This article used Legoland Windsor as an "instrumental" case study (Creswell, 2002), whose primary purpose is to advance our understanding and provide an insight into family motives for visiting a theme park. The sample was drawn from visiting families to Legoland Windsor; the sampling method was thus purposive, allowing us to "think critically about the parameters of the population we are studying and choose our sample case carefully on this basis" (Silverman, 2005, p. 129). Silverman stated that sampling in qualitative research is neither statistical nor purely personal but it is theoretically grounded. Purposive and theoretical sampling (first coined by Glaser & Strauss, 1967) are often treated as synonyms and the only difference is when the purpose behind purposive sampling is not explicit. In both samples the ability to generalize is obviously compromised but it is widely recognized that in qualitative research, theoretical propositions are more valuable than having data that are generalizeable (Bryman, 1988). Informal, semistructured interviews were conducted and field notes compiled to help understand what motivates families to visit. Nonparticipant observations were also conducted to ascertain the behavior the families displayed on their visit. This triangulation allowed for different data to be explored simultaneously in the same context and setting, increasing the reliability of the findings. By adopting these two methods of data collection an insight also emerged into both the push and pull motives, which also illuminated the families' interaction within the theme park environment. A nonparticipant observation pilot study was conducted which revealed that families experienced everything together as a family whilst having fun or the adults watched the children having fun. As the nonparticipant observations were made in a public place, there was no ethical dilemma to worry about.

Strauss' version of grounded theory was employed (Strauss & Corbin, 1990). Strauss and Corbin stated that there is a continuous interplay between analysis and data collection as it is systematically gathered and analyzed throughout the process. This is done by using a series of steps including coding and memoing leading to emergent themes. Grounded theory allows categories or themes to emerge; then these categories are saturated with appropriate cases, and eventually the cases are developed into a more general analytic framework (the emergent core theme or category) that can be applied and tested in other settings.

There is a heated debate over the process of grounded theory research, particularly between Glaser and Strauss, its two originators (see Glaser, 1994). In this study, Straus' version was adopted, and therefore it is important to outline the process that was used. Here, the theory is developed from a corpus of data (observations, field notes, and data from informal semistructured interviews). It is assumed that the variables interact in complex ways and that unpacking them to generate theory is as important as the theory itself. The idea is to draw out the implicit into an explicit theory or explanation of the phenomenon. The basic method is to read and re-read the data systematically and to label and integrate the labels into higher-level categories following Strauss and Corbin's (1990) coding scheme, briefly outlined next. It is not the aim of this article to critique grounded theory or any version of it; rather the aim is to use it to enhance our understanding of motivation to visit a family theme park. For a detailed application of the coding scheme and a critique of its capacity for prediction, change, and control, see Bakir and Bakir (2006a, 2006b); for a wider critique of grounded theory, particularly its reflexivity, see Hall and Callery (2001).

The first level of coding is referred to as "open coding," where the aim is to find the building blocks of the data, the nouns and verbs of the conceptual world being described. The key questions are, "What is being referenced here?" and "What does this mean to the participant?" The second level of coding is "axial coding," where the open codes that seem connected are grouped together forming intermediate explanations or theories using the "coding paradigm," explained in the axial coding in the next section. The ultimate, or third level of coding is "selective coding," the process of fitting the axial codes together to allow one category to subsume them and emerge as the core category. This core category then becomes the storyline that everything else feeds into—the main driver or phenomenon. It is this subsuming property of Strauss' version, both in axial and selective coding, that makes it most suitable method of analysis for this study, as it will show how the emerging core category of visitor motivation can be deconstructed, revealing its constituent parts. Memoing (field notes, code notes, and theoretical notes) are made in each step of the process.

In generating a grounded theory about the motivation of families to visit Legoland Windsor, we have left pointers to allow other researchers to audit our work by following our reasoning; looking at the provided figures, quotations, notes, and emerging concepts.

The limitations or anticipated issues connected with the context and setting of Legoland are that visitors are on a family day out and might not want to stop and talk about why they came here. To try and counteract this, families were approached whilst queuing so as not to take up too much time (they will be waiting anyway and the research questions will be taking up otherwise wasted queuing time). Another challenge was the fact that the data collecting researcher has worked at Legoland Windsor for 5 years and introduced herself as an employee to the participants. This may cause bias, and the analysis may be tainted by the researcher's previous knowledge of the park and its guests. This was averted by getting another researcher to check the data for interrater reliability. Families were interviewed throughout the summer and autumn of 2007 on different days (in term time, holidays, wet days and sunny days, busy and quiet days) in order to eliminate the date of visit as a factor. Five observations were made and 24 interviews were conducted before "theoretical saturation" (Strauss & Corbin, 1990) was obtained, where further interviews did not produce new knowledge. It is important to reiterate that being able to generalize the emerging grounded theory was not the key concern as the main aim of this exploratory research was to unpack the constructs involved in family motives to visit Legoland Windsor to inform further research. Adults and children were approached in their family groups and comments made by the adults were differentiated from children's comments in the collection of field notes. It is also important to stress that, on ethical grounds; children were not approached or spoken to without their parents consent and presence.

VISITORS' MOTIVATION: DEVELOPING A GROUNDED THEORY

As mentioned in the methodology section, this study adopted Strauss' version of grounded theory, where data from observations and interviews were first labeled through open coding, the resulting codes were linked together and grouped into main categories or themes through axial coding, and these categories were then subsumed by one core category through selective coding, providing an explanation of the motivation for families visiting Legoland Windsor theme park. These coding processes are explained in the following subsections.

Labeling the Data: Open Coding

The coding process of grounded theory is an ongoing process that takes place alongside data collection. After every interview and observation, field notes were taken and analyzed and open coded before moving on to the next interview. The main thing that people were observed to be doing was queuing but the actual behaviors that were present were talking as a family, looking at the map, and planning the day or the rest of the day, what to do next; the children were "excited" while the adults were "smiling" and "laughing," and seemed pleased that their children were "happy." The open codes that thus emerged from the five observation sessions are shown in Table 1.

In analyzing the data from interviews, the most striking thing about the codes that emerged is that almost all the interviewed families (22 out of 24) mentioned fun as a motivator to visit: "it's fun for the children, we want them to experience new things," and "we expected something fun and a little bit different." The code, fun, was thus one of the main drivers for visitation. Fun was talked about a lot and it was also apparent in the behavior and emotion that were observed. The children seemed to have fun and this made the parents happy. Another code, "a treat," sums up this idea; the adults often said it was as a treat, whether it was for the summer holidays, a birthday, or for any other reason, the parents seemed to want to please their children: "We like to please our children, plain and simple, when they're happy we're happy." Whilst the notion of having fun is a very obvious finding, what constitutes fun at Legoland will be unpacked. It is interesting to note that 20 of the families that were interviewed said they first heard about Legoland Windsor from friends or family—"word-of-mouth" and "recommendation," strongly suggesting that past visitors enjoyed their experience at Legoland Windsor.

Legoland Windsor has interactive rides that families can take part in. They are themed around Lego product ranges and in the vast majority of

TABLE 1 Open Coding of Observations

Code label	Number of observations present
Excitement	2
Smiling, laughing, and happy	1
Talking together	1
Queuing	4
Looking at the map and planning the day	2
Dad helping/teaching	2

these rides a visitor can take on different roles like a helicopter pilot, dragon slayer, fire-fighter, or driver. Sixteen families mentioned "interactive rides" as one of the motivating factors to visit. This is closely linked with fun, which we will explain further in the axial coding section. It is also worth noting that 16 family respondents mentioned that the "quality" of Lego products led them to believe that Legoland would also be of a superior quality. The idea of perceived quality is important in tourism where most products like theme park visitation are intangible and cannot be experienced until the actual visit. The assumption that a Legoland park would be of high quality based on the experience of high quality Lego toy products gives visitors confidence in their choice to visit. Six respondents also mentioned that they had visited Legoland Billund as children and remember how fun and good it was and so this motivated them to give their children the same kind of experience. This fits with Johns and Gyimothy's (2002, 2003) "nostalgia" notion that some of their interviewees alluded to.

Describing the uniqueness of Legoland Windsor compared to other theme parks, respondents retorted: "The Lego, the miniature village in Lego and seeing the model makers. All parks have rides but this is different," and "the Lego elements—the models. The rides are made to look like Lego and you can take on roles that you might when playing with Lego at home." Many respondents (16 families) talked about the "Lego theming" or the models. A quarter of the respondents stated that the staff was one of the best things about Legoland: "Making the day fun," and "helping the children to have fun," allowing the category fun-enabling staff to emerge. Some respondents (8 families) seemed to assume before their visit that the park was "aimed at children" and gave this as a motivating factor to visit but when they got to the park they started talking about how "clean and safe" the place was, and this motivated them to want to revisit and "recommend" it to other people with children as a good day out for families (20 responding families had been recommended by other friends and family who had visited before).

For repeat visitors and annual pass holders the motivation seemed to come from having a slightly different experience to normal, for example, the new ride, Vikings River Splash (opened in August 2007), or a "special event": "The concert is something different to normal—it's aimed at kids. . . . but we now focus on the special events like today," "we've come today because of the acts at the Legoland live concert." "Experiencing Lego in different ways" seems to be an important aspect of repeat visitation:

> The children love Barney and Lazy Town and watch them at home so coming to see them live is kind of like Legoland is for Lego—they play with it at home and then come to Legoland to experience it in different ways—the events and the park is an extension of play and entertainment that children already have at home.

Thus if day visitors were motivated by fun participating in interactive activities of Lego-themed attractions that have been highly recommended by friends, then repeat visitation or becoming annual pass holders seemed to be also about having "reliable fun"; and through experiencing Lego in different ways and seeing something different or something out of the ordinary—special event:

> We've come here today (October half-term) to have fun, we've heard a lot about the fireworks from friends. We've booked a whole mini-break around this weekend and although we've been before with the twins we now think our youngest (age 3) is old enough to appreciate it now.

Marketing activity could drive motivation to visit; six interviewed families touched on the "new ride" opening in the summer as a driver to visit and the same number mentioned the "television advert" as a factor: "The children have wanted to come all year, they asked every time they saw the advert and this is the first opportunity we've had to visit." Sixteen responding families said the children made the choice to visit and only four said that the adults made the choice. This is in contrast to a previous brand tracking activity (2 years ago) with regard to Legoland television advertising where it showed that there was an even split. This may suggest that the new advert content and format appeal more to children who motivate and coerce the parents to visit. As for the new ride, it is a well-known fact in the theme park industry that new rides will always draw in big crowds. In theme parks aimed at adults the goal is to put in the biggest, tallest, fastest rides in order to attract visitors and compete with other parks. However, in children's theme parks, such as Legoland, the goal of the marketing activity is to offer the children an opportunity to experience Lego in different ways; it is to do with theming with Lego products (e.g., this year's Lego Vikings) and creating a ride that has not only a storyline and theming based on that but also that is aimed at families and is fun, reliable fun for all.

The school holidays significantly affect attendance numbers at the park. In the summer holidays and half-terms the park will be very busy, especially if the weather is good. This seemed to split the interviewees up in terms of motivation. Fourteen families mentioned the school holidays. Some people mentioned that they had tried to avoid the school holidays as it would be too busy and they were only motivated to come in quieter times such as weekdays and term times. Other people said they chose to visit in the summer holidays or October half-term because, "the children are on holiday and it's a nice thing to do for the holidays," "we are treating the children to a day out because it was the school holidays." One family even suggested that they had brought their four year old to the park in late August because, "he was starting school for the first time next week and this was a final treat before starting school." In this way the school holidays play different roles when it comes to motivation to visit. Interestingly though, 20 families mentioned queues as the thing they liked least about the park or why they "had planned their day when at the park around queues." "Queue avoidance" seemed to be a very pertinent topic and was more highlighted the busier the park was. Interestingly, however, in recommending the visit to others, people avoid the queuing issue or how busy the park and the rides get; all respondents said that they would recommend the park to friends and family. This suggests that queuing does affect enjoyment on the day but it does not effect the motivation to visit and recommending the park to others. This was also the same for expense; some visitors mentioned that they had come in on promotional vouchers or internet discounts and that this motivated them to visit at different times of the year, that they were not advised by friends that it is expensive and they would not mention that in their recommendation to others either. A summary of the open codes which emerged from the interviews is shown in Table 2.

Making Connections and Grouping the Open Codes: Axial Coding

Axially coded categories are groups of open codes that seem interconnected. They are essentially mini or intermediate explanations or theories that bridge the gap between open coding and selective coding. Here the open codes have been slotted into an axial framework, the "coding paradigm" (Strauss &

TABLE 2 Open Coding of Data from Interviews.

Code label	Number of interviews present
Word-of-mouth/recommendation	20
Quality/legacy of LEGO products	16
Fun, reliable fun	22
Interactive rides	16
A treat	10
Adults visited LEGOLAND Billund as a child, nostalgia	6
Brand loyalty to LEGO	14
Special event, different, unique; experiencing LEGO in a different way	8
Clean and safe	8
Fun-enabling staff	6
Aimed at children	8
LEGO theming/models	16
School holidays	14
TV advert	6
New ride	6
Avoidance of queues	20
Expense	6
Internet	4
Promotions	2
Birthday	2
Educational	2

Corbin, 1990), which consists of six related groups of concepts: the phe-nomenon (what it is), the causal conditions (what makes the phenomenon occur), the context (background variables), intervening conditions (moder-ating and mediating variables), action strategies (goal-orientated activities), and the consequences (what happens as a result of this phenomenon and conditions—intended or unintended). Grouping the codes in this axial framework allows us to understand how the codes interact with one another and separate those out into what are the motivational factors and what are the contributing factors. It also shows how the emerging intermediate categories can be deconstructed into the codes they subsumed.

Grouping the open codes that emerged from the observations and inter-views resulted in two interrelated phenomena (intermediate categories): fun and excitement. The causal conditions for these phenomena were: interac-tive rides, quality or legacy of Lego, visited Legoland Billund as a child, special events, experiencing Lego in a different way, reliability of fun, and Lego theming or models. Brand loyalty, television promotion campaigns, and word-of-mouth recommendation were the context within which these phe-nomena occurred. The action strategies included: looking at the map, talk-ing, laughing, dads teaching or coaching the children in new things, treating the children, participating in activities aimed at children, and trying a new ride. The intervening conditions included: the onset of school holidays, clean and safe environment, and fun-enabling staff. Some of the obvious conse-quences were queuing and expense. The axial coding is shown in Table 3.

The Core Motivation Driver: Selective Coding

Strauss and Corbin (1990) considered that paying attention to processes is vital. They were concerned with describing and coding everything that is dynamic, changing, moving, or occurring over time in the research setting. The process of moving from axial coding to selective coding or deriving the core category is probably the most important in the generation of the theory. It should provide an explanation of the phenomenon under study, in this case the motivation to visit Legoland. Based on the data that has been coded and analyzed, a major category appears to be the excitement of the children. The children were laughing, doing things like jumping up and down and running off when they saw interesting things, dragging adults, asking to go on things, and looking in general at some attractions and models. Excitement fed into most of the other behaviors present in the five conducted obser-vations. Not dissimilar to excitement, what emerged as the main driver for motivation to visit was fun. It is also apparent that the theme of fun has the conceptual capacity to encapsulate the concept of excitement, suggesting that all the other codes are subsumed under this theme in different ways; the core category or storyline is, therefore, fun.

TABLE 3 Axial Coding: Grouping the Open Codes Using the Coding Paradigm

Axial framework	Relevant open codes
Phenomenon (intermediate categories)	Fun
	Excitement
Causal conditions	Interactive rides
	Quality/legacy of LEGO
	Visited LEGOLAND Billund as a child
	Special events
	Experiencing LEGO in a different way
	Reliability of fun
	LEGO theming/models
Context	Brand loyalty
	TV advert
	Word-of-mouth recommendation
Intervening conditions	School holidays
	Clean and safe environment
	Fun-enabling staff
Action strategies	Treating the children
	Participating in activities aimed at children
	Trying new ride
	Looking at the map
	Talking, laughing
	Dads teaching/coaching the children in new things
	Jumping up and down and running off when seeing interesting things
	Dragging adults, asking to go on things, spending
	Looking at some attractions and models.
Consequences	Queues
	Expense

In the next section, the notion of fun, which has emerged from this study as a motivating factor for visiting Legoland theme park, will be elaborated and further deconstructed, using the push/pull framework and the travel career ladder notion.

DISCUSSION AND CONCLUSION: "TOURISTIC FUN"

The debate over tourists' motivational factors seems to hinder research into developing a conceptual motivational construct (Pearce, 1993). As a result there is no widely accepted theoretical model of motivation in tourism; in fact there are several problematic motivational models as we saw in the introduction. This study adds to the debate by offering the idea of fun, the emerging core theme, as the main motivating factor to visit a family theme park like Legoland; the sense of fun, family fun, perceived reliable fun, fun activities, and fun-enabling staff.

Many of the motivational constructs that have emerged in this study are similar to Johns and Gyimothy's (2002, 2003) idea of pleasing the children. This idea was common amongst the adults interviewed in this study.

When asked "who chose to visit?," the majority of families said, the children. It is a well-known fact in this industry that children are targeted in Legoland's advertising. Legoland has developed a "Heroes Wanted" advertising and branding campaign over the last couple of years which is very much aimed at children taking on roles at the park, as well as in their family groups. Burman (1992) posits that children have not only become markets for consumption; they have themselves been commodified to signify the class position and lifestyle of their parents. This highlights the notion that parents not only want to please their children but also want to be seen by others to be taking their children to high profile, expensive places like Legoland; in this way it also acts as a status enhancer. Perhaps this postulation can partly explain the findings in this study of why so many of the visiting families came to the park based on personal recommendations from friends and family and why all those interviewed said they would recommend the park as a clean and safe environment and fun.

The factors that have emerged as motivators from the data can be deconstructed into both push and pull factors (see Figure 1). Dann (1981) mentioned anomie and ego-enhancement as push factors and Crompton (1979) developed these factors further. Using Crompton's push constructs,

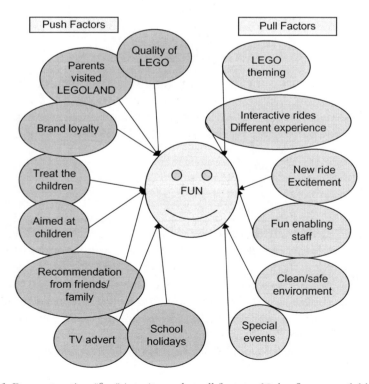

FIGURE 1 Deconstructing "fun" into its push–pull factors. (Color figure available online).

this exploratory study found that the most prominent push factors described by Legoland Windsor's visitors were novelty (a unique, new experience), regression (to act child like), nostalgia (remembering visiting when they were younger), and family relationships (spending time together and bonding). Crompton's construct of education for the children was not talked about as widely in this study of Legoland Windsor.

Using the pull factors of Unger and Kernan (1983), this study found that a major pull factor is creating a state of arousal or excitement in the children but not for the adults whose role seemed to be to please their children. In terms of intrinsic satisfaction, many of the respondents in this study mentioned fun—to feel happy and excited. Although children were not interviewed separately in this study, as we saw in the results, the vast majority of the adults interviewed (22 out of 24) stated that fun was a motivating factor to visit. This study seemed also to elicit Unger and Kernan's construct of "involvement," interaction with the rides. The interviewed families spoke about how interesting it was to take part in the rides rather than just go on them and how this differed from other theme parks.

It is evident that most of the push factors that emerged in this study were similar to Johns and Gyimothy's (2002, 2003). However, this does not seem to be the case with many of the pull factors. This may be partially explained by the fact that unlike Johns and Gyimothy's, in this study children were not interviewed separately and, therefore, the ideas of their motivation were given through their parents. Perhaps, interviewing children at Legoland Windsor about why they specifically wanted to visit may prove insightful; a limitation of this research.

Pearce (1988) devised the notion of the travel career ladder from testing different demographic segments at Australian Theme Parks, finding that different segments placed different levels of importance on various needs (for example 13–16-year-olds placed greater importance on thrills compared to family groups). Pearce's five categories of needs (relaxation, stimulation, relationship, self-esteem, and fulfillment) are a multivariate model supporting the humanistic idea of the hierarchy of needs advanced by Maslow (1954) in that we move up the ladder or hierarchy. In this study only two of Pearce's categories, "fulfillment" and "stimulation," seem to have emerged. This may suggest that Pearce's classification could have been idiosyncratic to the Australian theme parks he studied. Equally, it should be acknowledged that the study presented here is not only based on one theme park, but also on one market segment, family visitors, and thus the two emerged categories might be the result of the design of the current study. More prominent in this study was the intrinsic fulfillment of fun, which through its deconstructed codes (see Table 3 and Figure 1) seems to lend support to Ryan's (1997) claim that family life-cycle and tourist experiences shape the motivation for visitation.

In summary then it appears that the motivation to visit Legoland Windsor for the first time is a mixture of being recommended by friends and family, the children playing with Lego and the adults trusting the brand name of Lego and it's legacy, as well as the perceived sense of fun that the family will have together on the interactive rides and in this unique setting full of Lego models. It appears that the adults partake in this visit because their children want or ask to, and they want to treat them, but also that they want to be seen treating them for whatever extrinsic or intrinsic motivation that might provide. It is also suggested that repeat visitation usually occurs when the visitors have both enjoyed the experience or when something new and exciting is offered, such as annual pass discounts and special events. Above all, though, the core theme of fun encapsulates all of these motives and motivating factors. Visitors expect to, want to, and do have fun at Legoland Windsor, despite the expense, despite the queues (at least on the whole), and they spend time as a family. This exploratory study provides an insight into, and better understanding of, the motives involved in making a decision to visit Legoland Windsor. Fun has emerged as a prime motivator in visiting this family theme park. Walter (1991) is perhaps the only author who in the course of drawing distinctions between fun, enjoyment and leisure, developed a view on the social meaning of fun. He found fun as an experiential process within leisure: "an active social structuring in direct face-to-face interaction, wherein the individual is externally . . . engaged to create a social-human bond" (p. 133) with others. Walter did not, however, attempt to unpack the social meaning of fun, and in the absence of other studies, the concept of fun in a tourism or leisure setting remains largely under theorized. It could be argued that in finding fun as the prime motivator for visiting a family theme park, this study reaffirms a commonsensical notion and thus offers a small contribution to knowledge. However, arriving at the idea of fun, through grounded theory to describe visitors' motivation to a family theme park, has deconstructed this type of fun by revealing all the constructs that it encompassed and emerged from. The notion of fun was also deconstructed using the push–pull framework, as shown in Figure 1.

As the notion of touristic fun has not been seriously theorized, this study adds to the tourism literature by contributing to the theorization of fun in a family theme park—a touristic setting, thus partially plugging this theoretical gap. The study also contributes to the literature on motivation and visitor attractions; particularly, the literature on motives as applied to family theme parks. It will also inform the marketing strategies of Legoland Windsor and their future advertising, promotion, and sales communication efforts. It is hoped that this exploratory study will inspire further, much needed, research, particularly, in the under theorized area of fun in tourism contexts, and to expand on the constructs which emerged in this study and investigate if they apply more widely to other visitor attractions.

REFERENCES

Babbie, E. R. (1998). *The practice of social research.* Belmont, CA: Wadsworth.

Bakir, A., & Bakir, V. (2006a). A critique of the capacity of Strauss' grounded theory for prediction, change, and control in organizational strategy via a grounded theorization of leisure and cultural strategy. *The Qualitative Report, 11,* 687–718. Retrieved from www.nova.edu/ssss/QR/QR11-4/bakir.pdf

Bakir, A., & Bakir, V. (2006b). Unpacking complexity, pinning down the "elusiveness" of strategy: A grounded theory study in leisure and cultural organizations. *Qualitative Research in Organizations and Management: An International Journal, 1*(3), 152–172.

Bryman, A. (1988). *Quantity and quality in social research.* London, England: Unwin Hyman.

Burman, E. (1992). Feminism and discourse in developmental psychology: Power, subjectivity, and interpretation. *Feminism & Psychology, 2*(1), 45–60.

Creswell, J. W. (2002). Educational research: Planning, conducting, and evaluating quantitative and qualitative research. Upper Saddle River, NJ: Merrill-Pearson Education.

Crompton, J. (1979). Why people go on a pleasure vacation. *Annals of Tourism Research, 6*(4), 408–424.

Dann, G. (1977). Anomie, ego-enhancement and tourism. *Annals of Tourism Research, 4* (4),184–194.

Dann, G. (1981). Tourism motivation, an appraisal. *Annals of Tourism Research, 8*(2), 155–169.

Davidoff, L. L. (1994). *Introduction to psychology.* New York: McGraw-Hill.

Fodness, D. (1994). Measuring tourist motivation. *Annals of Tourism Research, 21*(3), 555–580.

Glaser, B. G. (1994). *Basics of grounded theory analysis; emergence vs. forcing.* Mill Valley, CA: Sociology Press.

Glaser, B. G., & Strauss, A. L. (1967). *The discovery of grounded theory.* Chicago, IL: Aldine.

Hall, W. A., & Callery, P. (2001). Pearls, pith, and provocation. Enhancing the rigor of grounded theory: Incorporating reflexivity and relationality. *Qualitative Health Research, 11,* 257–272.

Harrill, R., & Potts, T. (2002). Social psychological theories of tourist motivation: Exploration, debate, and transition. *Tourism Analysis, 7,* 105–114.

Iso-Ahola, E. S. (1982). Toward a social psychological theory of tourism motivation: A rejoinder. *Annals of Tourism Research, 6,* 257–264.

Johns, N., & Gyimothy, S. (2002). Mythologies of a theme park: An icon of modern family life. *Journal of Vacation Marketing, 8*(4), 320–331.

Johns, N., & Gyimothy, S. (2003). Post-modern family tourism at LEGOLAND. *Scandinavian Journal of Hospitality and Tourism, 3*(1), 3–23.

Kao, Y., Huang, L., & Wu, C. (2008). Effects of theatrical elements on experiential quality and loyalty intentions for theme parks. *Asia Pacific Journal of Tourism Research, 13,* 163–174.

Leask, A., Fyall, A., & Garrod, B. (2002). Heritage visitor attractions: Managing revenue in the new millennium. *International Journal of Heritage Studies*, *8*, 247–265.

Maslow, A. (1954). Motivation and personality. New York, NY: Harper and Row.

McIntosh, R. W. (1977). Tourism: Principles, practices, philosophies. New York, NY: Wiley and Sons.

Murphy, P. K., & Alexander, P. A. (2000). A motivated exploration of motivation terminology. *Contemporary Educational Psychology*, *25*, 3–53.

Parinello, G. R. (1993). Motivation and anticipation in post industrial tourism. *Annals of Tourism Research*, *20*(2), 233–249.

Pearce, P. L. (1988). *The Ulysses factor: Evaluating visitors in tourist settings*. New York, NY: Springer-Verlag.

Pearce, P. L. (1993). Fundamentals of tourist motivation. In D. G. Pearce & R. W. Butler (Eds.), *Tourism research: Critiques and challenges* (pp. 113–134). London, England: Routledge.

Pearce, P. L., & Moscardo, G. (1985). Tourist theme parks: Research practices and possibilities. *Australian Psychologist*, *20*, 303–312.

Reisinger, Y., & Turner, L. W. (2002). Cultural differences between Asian tourist markets and Australian hosts: Part 2. *Journal of Travel Research*, *40*, 385–395.

Ross, G. F. (1998). *The psychology of tourism*. Victoria, Australia: Hospitality Press.

Ryan, C. (1997). The tourist experience: A new introduction. London, England: Cassell.

Sekaran, U. (2003). *Research methods for business*. New York: Wiley & Sons.

Silverman, D. (2005). *Doing qualitative research*. London, England: Sage.

Sirakaya, E., & Woodside, A. G. (2005). Building and testing theories of decision making by travellers. *Tourism Management*, *26*, 815–832.

Strauss, A., & Corbin, J. (1990). *Basics of qualitative research: Grounded theory procedures and techniques*. London: Sage.

Swarbrooke, J. (2002). *The development and management of visitor attractions*. Oxford, England: Butterworth-Heinemann.

Swarbrooke, J., & Horner, S. (2001). *Consumer behavior in tourism*. Oxford, England: Butterworth-Heinemann.

Unger, L. S., & Kernan, J. B. (1983). On the meaning of leisure: An investigation of some determinants of the subjective experience. *Journal of Consumer Research*, *9*, 381–392.

Walter, P. (1991). Distinctions of fun, enjoyment and leisure. *Leisure Studies*, *10*, 133–148.

Witt, C. A., & Wright, P. L. (1992). Tourist motivation: Life after Maslow. In P. Johnson & B. Thomas (Eds.), *Choice and demand in tourism* (pp. 33–55). London, England: Mansell.

Wong, K. K. F., & Cheung, P. W. Y. (1999). Strategic theming in theme park marketing. *Journal of Vacation Marketing*, *5*, 319–332.

Turkey as a Heritage Tourism Destination: The Role of Knowledge

MARIA D. ALVAREZ and MERAL KORZAY

Department of Tourism Administration, Boğaziçi University, Istanbul, Turkey

The study aims to determine whether the knowledge and aware-ness related to the culture, history, and ancient civilizations of a destination might be instrumental in creating a more positive image for the place. The research is carried out in the context of Turkey, a country that has been affected in the past by its image as a cheap mass-tourism destination, and which is currently attempt-ing to position itself as a heritage tourism destination. To increase the effectiveness of positioning efforts, destinations need to under-stand the factors that may help construct a more positive image of the place. The study also examines the sources of informa-tion used, and investigates which sources are related to a greater knowledge and more positive perceptions regarding the destina-tion. Implications for the marketing and promotion of Turkey as a heritage tourism destination are derived.

INTRODUCTION

Destination image has become a popular area of investigation among tourism researchers, as it has been found to influence choice, tourist sat-isfaction, and postpurchase behavior (Bigné, Sánchez, & Sánchez, 2001; Chon, 1990; Ritchie & Crouch, 2003; Um & Crompton, 1990; Woodside & Lysonski, 1989). In particular, several articles have been concerned with the image of Turkey as a tourism destination (e.g., Alvarez & Korzay, 2008; Baloglu, 2001; Sirakaya, Uysal, & Yoshioka, 2003; Sönmez & Sirakaya, 2002;

Tasci, Gartner, & Cavusgil, 2007) due to the predominantly negative effect of historical and geopolitical factors on the image of this country (Boria, 2006; Sönmez & Sirakaya, 2002). According to investigations on the image of Turkey, this country suffers from a distorted image (Sönmez & Sirakaya, 2002) or a negative brand bias (Tasci et al., 2007). However, a more positive image of this destination is obtained as a result of visitation (Dülger, Girişken, Yıldız, & Yarcan, 2005; Yarcan & Inelmen, 2006), or due to a greater familiarity (Baloglu, 2001).

In parallel to the negative perceptions regarding Turkey as a country, authors (Alvarez & Korzay, 2008; Öztürkmen, 2005) have remarked on the difference between the political perceptions regarding this country and its image as a holiday destination of history, sun, and beaches. Although in past years Turkey has also been affected by its outside image as a cheap mass-tourism destination (Tosun, Fletcher, & Fyall, 2006), considerable efforts are currently being made to position it as a cultural tourism destination. Specifically, the Ministry of Culture and Tourism of Turkey focuses on cultural and heritage tourism as an important center of attention in the tourism strategy of this country for the coming years. Therefore, it is crucial for Turkey to understand the factors that may help construct a more positive image of the place as a heritage tourism destination.

Cultural and historical resources at the destination have been found to influence destination choice (G. Richards, 2002; Ritchie & Crouch, 2003), and therefore it may be questioned whether the knowledge and awareness related to these resources may also be instrumental in creating a more positive image for the destination. In line with this literature, the study aims to determine whether knowledge of historical and cultural aspects of the destination is related to a more positive image for Turkey. At the same time, the study also investigates the information sources used by individuals to learn about Turkey, and determines which of these sources is most effective in order to increase the level of knowledge related to historical and cultural aspects, as well as cultural heritage at this destination.

LITERATURE REVIEW

Cultural tourism is considered to be the oldest kind of tourism. Twenty centuries ago, Roman philosopher Seneca stated "men travel widely to different places seeking different distractions because they are tired of soft living and always seek after something which eludes them" (quoted in Cabezas, 2001, p. 45). While tourism has become an international economic, social, and cultural activity, many tourist recipient communities have started to fear the negative impacts of this activity (Tosun, 2001) and its possible harm on their cultures, beliefs, social habits, and vernacular traditions. These may be avoided by developing tourism products focusing on the destination's heritage (Yunis, 2001), and creating narrating scenarios that are meaningful and pleasant to the visitors.

The terms *culture* and *heritage* are often seen together, as heritage is assigned the role of carrier of historical value of the cultural traditions of a society, from one generation to the next (Christou, 2005). As such, culture and heritage are strongly linked to tourism, as they are seen as strong attractors for tourists. This connection is manifested in the most common definitions of cultural tourism. For example, S. Richards (1997, p. 24) defines cultural tourism as "all movements of persons to specific cultural attractions, such as heritage sites, artistic and cultural manifestations, arts and drama outside their normal place of residence." In this sense, heritage tourism can be considered a subcategory of cultural tourism, and it has been defined as "tourism centred on what we have inherited, which can mean anything from historic buildings, to art works, to beautiful scenery" (Yale, 1991, p. 21). Some authors (Poria, Butler, & Airey, 2001) have stated that the motivations of the visitors and their perceptions regarding the historic and heritage characteristics of the site are paramount in classifying an activity as heritage tourism.

As tourism benefits from the existence of culture and heritage at the destination, so it may also be seen as beneficial to the protection and development of the latter (World Tourism Organization, 2001). For example, Picard (1997) commented on how culture has been instrumental in creating Bali's differentiated brand image, which has been used as an identity marker for the Balinese ethnic group within the Indonesian multiethnic nation. Tourism is also seen as an activity with economic value, beneficial for heritage preservation (Christou, 2005). Similarly, festivals and events have been determined to positively influence cohesion within a community by reinforcing social and cultural identity (Gursoy, Kim, & Uysal, 2004). In contrast, other studies have pointed to the negative impact of tourism that may cause the commodifying of culture and the simplification of historical events for the consumption of the tourists (Hughes & Allen, 2005). Culture and the performing arts may also be subject to distortion when packaged for the benefits of the tourists (Hughes & Allen, 2005). Similarly, authenticity and interpretation of historical events may also be seen as an issue in cultural and heritage tourism (Frost, 2004).

The increasing interest of destinations in promoting their heritage and historic sites to visitors has brought about important discussions related to the authenticity of the heritage and culture being promoted. The notion of "staged authenticity" is used to describe the promotion of heritage and historical sites to tourists as stages where contrived settings are presented as authentic (MacCannell, 1992). However, the tourists contrast their images of authenticity against the setting that is offered as part of the heritage experience, and these images are typically induced by mediating influences (Hughes, 1995). Other authors have contended that what is real or authentic is subject to interpretation, and that use of the past provides destination management authorities with a tool to "refashion sites and direct the tourist gaze towards a limited range of interpretations" (Waitt, 2000, p. 836).

Culture and heritage have been used to promote positive destination images (Hughes & Allen, 2005). Historical representations that convey images of the past, such as movies, have been found useful in order to create attractive destination images (Frost, 2004). The importance of imagery in destination image is stressed by MacKay and Fesenmaier (2000). These authors also contend that the image of the destination is influenced by cultural background, as aesthetic judgments and preferences are based on cultural traditions and learning processes (MacKay & Fesenmaier, 2000).

Historical knowledge is usually dependent on the interpretation of themes and sometimes unconnected accounts. This may include literary interpretation, through the description of history or stories (Goulding, 1999), or the presentation in a structured context of history and culture at museums. Tour guides have been established as important actors that may facilitate the dissemination of knowledge and the interpretation of the history and culture at the tourism sites (Reisinger & Steiner, 2006). Studies have also determined that media and technologies may be used to disseminate culture (Real, 1996). In this sense, the perceived identity of a nation and the cultural knowledge of the visitors regarding the destination are usually based on the context provided by the media and their interpretation of different elements, issues and events at the destination. Similarly, historic films have been found to generate heritage based tourism, where visitation is prompted by the heritage and historical associations of the place, rather than by its scenic value (Frost, 2004). These movies may also affect the knowledge and expectations of consumers regarding the destination (Frost, 2004).

Cultural and heritage tourists have been considered as desirable visitors, as they are typically affluent, broadly traveled and well educated (Holcomb, 1999, cited in Hughes & Allen, 2005). Various typologies (Peterson, 1994; Prentice, 1993) of cultural tourists have been used in order to identify the characteristics and motivations of these individuals. In this sense, some authors have determined that the motivations of the visitors are essential in order to classify the visit as a heritage tourism activity (Poria, Butler, & Airey, 2001). Thus heritage tourists are distinguished by their main motivation to learn and participate in a learning experience at the site (Poria, Butler, & Airey, 2006). Among the different categories of cultural and heritage tourists, classifications have identified a common group, termed as educated visitors (Prentice, 1993) and professional in their study of history (Peterson, 1994). In this regard, authors have determined that participation in cultural tourism activities requires a certain level of knowledge and familiarity (Kim, Cheng, & O'Leary, 2006; Tasci & Knutson, 2004). Furthermore, an increased demand for heritage-based activities is partly due to a growing awareness of the heritage (Waitt, 2000).

METHODOLOGY

The present research therefore examines the relationship between knowledge regarding the history and culture of a destination and the perceptions regarding the place as a heritage tourism destination, with reference to the sources of information used. The study is carried out in the context of Turkey, as perceived by Spanish individuals. The data was collected through a Web questionnaire administered to Spanish nationals in the fall of 2006. The respondents were solicited through an e-mail message sent to a list of e-mail addresses of a leisure group, and through messages posted to several Spanish Internet forums dealing with travel and leisure topics. In order to increase the participation rate, the incentive of several prizes was provided. A prescreening question was included in order to ascertain that all of the respondents were Spanish nationals. A total of 189 questionnaires were obtained, of which 157 were considered valid and usable for the research. Table 1 provides the profile of the respondents.

The questionnaire contained a scale to measure the perceptions regarding Turkey as a tourism destination, adapted from the study of Baloglu and Mangaloglu (2001). Moreover, respondents were also asked to report their knowledge of Turkish ancient, contemporary history and cultural heritage

TABLE 1 Profile of the Respondents

Profile	Frequency	Percent[a]
Gender		
Male	74	49.7
Female	75	50.3
Age		
Less than 25	9	6.0
26–35	68	45.0
36–45	54	35.8
46–55	11	7.3
56–65	7	4.6
More than 65	2	1.3
Education		
High school or less	5	3.3
University	99	65.1
Postgraduate	47	30.9
Other	1	.7
Monthly income		
Less than €600	2	1.4
€601–€1,500	14	9.7
€1,501–€3,000	57	39.6
€3,001–€5,000	43	29.9
€5,001–€7,000	15	10.4
More than €7,000	13	9.0
Visited Turkey		
Yes	75	48.1
No	81	51.9

[a]Percentages were calculated after eliminating the missing values.

and their awareness regarding ancient civilizations that have lived in the Turkish territory. This information was enriched with the use of open-ended questions to determine the respondent's recall of historical events concerning Turkey. Furthermore, the participants were also required to determine which information sources they had benefited from in order to obtain knowledge related to Turkey. The internal consistency of the scales used was high, with Cronbach's alpha figures above 80% for all of the scales included.

FINDINGS AND DISCUSSION

The perceptions of the Spanish respondents regarding Turkey as a tourism destination were relatively positive, with the most positively rated items being the perceptions regarding the historical attractions, cultural attractions and natural environment. On the other hand, the respondents showed a relatively more negative perception regarding Turkey's cleanliness and hygiene, infrastructure, and personal security. Table 2 provides a summary of these perceptions. These findings are in line with previous research regarding the perceptions of Turkey as a country with appealing attractions, but with problems of security and infrastructure (Alvarez & Korzay, 2004).

In order to determine the relationship between the respondents' knowledge regarding Turkey's history, heritage, and ancient civilizations, and their perceptions of Turkey as a tourism destination, Pearsons' correlation analysis was used. According to these tests summarized in Tables 3 and 4, there is a positive relationship regarding the knowledge of the respondents related to historical and cultural aspects of Turkey, and their perceptions of this tourism destination. These results imply that destinations that want to position

TABLE 2 Perceptions of Turkey as a Tourism Destination

Items	M^a	SD
Value for money	2.13	.812
Natural environment	1.83	.976
Climate	2.16	.789
Cultural attractions	1.78	.992
Accommodation facilities	2.60	.809
Local cuisine	2.41	1.056
Beaches and water sports	2.41	.839
Infrastructure	3.15	.864
Personal security	3.08	1.038
Historical attractions	1.69	1.066
Pollution in the environment	3.03	.845
Nightlife	2.85	.825
Cleanliness and hygiene	3.33	.881
Friendliness of the people	2.23	.919

[a]1 = most positive; 5 = least positive.

TABLE 3 Knowledge of Turkish History/Heritage and Perceptions of Turkey

Knowledge of Turkish history and heritage	M^a	SD	Relationship with perceptions of Turkey	
			Pearsons' r	p
Ancient history	2.90	1.039	0.185	0.020
Contemporary history	3.03	1.006	0.220	0.006
Cultural heritage	2.89	1.031	0.297	0.000

^{a}1 = most knowledgeable; 5 = least knowledgeable.

TABLE 4 Awareness of Ancient Civilizations and Perceptions of Turkey

Awareness of ancient civilizations	M^a	SD	Relationship with perceptions of Turkey	
			Pearsons' r	p
Hittite	3.32	1.494	0.191	0.017
Hellenistic	2.62	1.425	0.236	0.003
Seljuk	3.93	1.419	0.268	0.001
Phrygian	4.02	1.256	0.230	0.004
Urartian	4.33	1.051	0.216	0.007
Lycian	4.12	1.228	0.185	0.022
Lydian	4.06	1.288	0.226	0.005
Ionian	3.06	1.436	0.232	0.004
Persian	2.32	1.318	0.262	0.001
Roman	2.08	1.230	0.147	0.067
Byzantine	1.84	1.205	0.186	0.021
Ottoman	1.69	1.131	0.236	0.003

^{a}1 = most aware; 5 = least aware.

themselves as culture and heritage tourism destinations should pay special attention to the level of knowledge regarding the history and heritage of the place. Thus, education may be seen as an important marketing activity for the destination, as will be discussed in more detail in the next section.

At the same time, while the respondents are highly conscious regarding the connection to Turkey of the Roman, Byzantine, Ottoman, and to a certain extent Hellenistic civilizations, they have a very limited awareness of other Anatolian civilizations as related to this country (refer to Tables 3 and 4). This conclusion is also supported by the analysis of the open-ended question in the survey, for which respondents were asked to name a historical event related to Turkey. Most of the subjects answered, while some of them named more than one occurrence. The findings indicate that respondents are aware of some historical events concerning Turkey, although other less mainstream episodes were not recalled. The results and frequencies of the comments provided are summarized in Table 5. According to these answers, the highest remembered event is the fall of Constantinople and the Eastern Roman empire, while Atatürk's regime is next highest in relation

TABLE 5 Results of Open-Ended Question of Historical Event in Turkey

Comments	Frequency
Fall of Constantinople/Fall of Eastern Roman empire	39
Atatürk's regime	34
Ottoman empire	11
Eastern Roman/Byzantine empire	9
Armenian conflict/issue	8
Battle of Lepanto	7
The Trojan War	6
First World War	5
Creation of Turkish Republic	5
Fall of the Ottoman empire	5
Assault of Vienna by the Ottomans	4
Schism of Orient/Occident	4
Kurdish conflict	3
Ottoman invasions	3
Cyprus conflict	3
Turkish–Greek wars	2
Hittite empire	2
Greek history/ancient Greece	2
Battle of Gallipoli	2
Headquarters of the Pope	1
First country to give right to vote to women	1
Sultans	1
Christian tradition in Anatolia	1
Turkish war of independence	1
Birth place of important Greek philosophers	1
Battle of Malazgirt	1
Treaty of Lausanne	1
Withdrawal of Greek soldiers from Izmir	1
Christian council in Iznik	1
First Gulf War	1

to frequency. Other comments with high frequencies include mentions of the Ottoman Empire, the Armenian conflict, the battle of Lepanto, and the Trojan War.

These findings indicate that there is a limited knowledge on the ancient civilizations that lived in Anatolia. The respondents' knowledge on Turkish history seems to be limited to Constantinople and the Eastern Roman Empire, the Ottoman Empire, and Atatürk's regime. Other events that are referred to include topics mentioned in the recent press, such as the Armenian conflict, those that involved Spain or Spanish individuals, such as the battle of Lepanto, and events portrayed in recent films, such as the Trojan War and the First World War.

The study also provides insights on the sources of information mostly used by the Spanish respondents in order to learn about Turkey. The most widely used source of information is found to be word of mouth, which was used by 79% of the respondents, followed by television (51.6%) and the written press (45.2%). Books as sources of information were used by 43.3%

of the subjects, while the Internet was used by 36.3% of the respondents to learn about Turkey. Furthermore, 48.1% of the sample had visited Turkey before and was therefore able to obtain direct firsthand experience on this destination.

Moreover, the research assessed the level of effectiveness of the information sources to convey knowledge regarding the culture and heritage of Turkey and to positively affect the image of the destination. In this regard, previous experience, the Internet, and books are considered as the most effective sources for respondents to learn about the history, cultural heritage, and ancient civilizations in Turkey, as well as to create a more positive image of the destination (see Table 6). Therefore, although some of the information sources, such as word of mouth or television, were widely used to learn about the country, these sources are not found to significantly increase the level of knowledge regarding cultural or historical aspects of the country. These findings are useful in order to design an effective communication strategy for the Turkish heritage tourism product. These issues are discussed in the next section.

CONCLUSIONS

The study concluded that knowledge and awareness of individuals regarding cultural and heritage aspects of the destination are positively related to their perceptions regarding the destination. This finding provides important implications for the marketing of the heritage tourism destination. Specifically, it can be concluded that the promotion of a destination with a rich history and culture should be based not only on directly promoting the attractions and monuments, but also on increasing the knowledge regarding this historical and cultural legacy. Therefore, promotional methods that provide the possibility to convey a richer and deeper knowledge about the destination and its history may be used. Similarly, the awareness regarding cultural and historical legacy may be obtained through the participation in certain international programs, such as being on the World Heritage list, and playing an active part in the World Heritage committee. Thus, indirect promotion of the heritage tourism destination may be attained by disseminating knowledge regarding the history and culture of the destination.

Some level of awareness regarding Turkish culture and history has been achieved by international exhibitions that have been carried out in recent years with the support of the Turkish Ministry for Culture and Tourism. Cultural events in Japan during the 2003 celebrations of the Turkish year in this country, as well as the Turks' exhibition in London at the Royal Academy of Arts and at the Gulbenkian Museum in Lisbon had great interest and a positive multiplier effect on the knowledge of the visitors and their perceptions regarding Turkey as a cultural and heritage destination. Such events

TABLE 6 Users versus Nonusers of Information Sources in Relation to their Knowledge and Perceptions of Turkey

Information sources used to learn about Turkey	Knowledge of ancient history		Knowledge of contemporary history		Knowledge of cultural heritage		Awareness of ancient civilizations		Perceptions of Turkey as a tourism destination	
	t	p	t	p	t	p	t	p	t	p
Previous experience	−3.246	0.001	−3.379	0.001	−4.040	0.000	−3.686	0.000	−3.642	0.000
Word-of-mouth	0.861	0.391	−0.469	0.640	0.059	0.953	−0.578	0.564	−0.937	0.354
Web sites	−2.236	0.027	−2.891	0.004	−2.521	0.013	−3.323	0.001	−2.920	0.004
Television	−1.261	0.209	0.070	0.944	−0.720	0.473	−1.132	0.259	1.163	0.247
Written press	−0.969	0.334	−1.178	0.240	−1.058	0.292	−2.127	0.035	−1.265	0.208
Travel agent	−1.943	0.054	−0.616	0.539	−1.387	0.167	−1.694	0.092	−1.830	0.069
Books	−3.475	0.001	−4.282	0.000	−3.942	0.000	−3.978	0.000	−2.396	0.018
Tourism offices	−0.441	0.660	−1.225	0.222	−1.262	0.209	−0.987	0.325	−1.411	0.160

should be carried out in different countries in order to reach predefined target markets.

The research also determines that in relation to Turkey, there is a limited knowledge on the ancient civilizations that lived in Anatolia, while there is a higher awareness related to Byzantium, the Eastern Roman Empire, and the Ottoman Empire in relation to Turkey. This limited knowledge is also reflected on the visitation patterns of cultural tourists in the country. According to statistics related to visitation of main cultural attractions, there is a concentration of tourists in the main sites such as Topkapı, St. Sophia, and Istanbul's historical peninsula, in detriment to other cultural sites in Anatolia (Pekin, 2006). This brings congestion and carrying capacity issues, while other potentially interesting attractions are overlooked.

In order to manage heritage tourism in Turkey and to promote less visited cultural destinations, it is necessary to educate consumers, by relating these places to specific historical episodes. Thus ongoing promotional education should be carried out in the main target markets, using information sources that are able to convey extensive knowledge about the destination's historical legacy. The study provides guidance as to which information sources are most effective in order to increase the knowledge regarding the history and culture of a destination. Specifically, for Spanish people, books and Web sites are established as the most effective sources to increase historical and cultural knowledge regarding Turkey. Therefore, books on Turkey's history and Anatolian civilizations should be translated to Spanish and promoted in that country. Good quality travel books on Turkey that include in-depth information on the history of the country, including ancient history, should be marketed.

Moreover, Web sites are also found in the research as an effective information source in order to create awareness of the historical resources and to promote Turkey as a heritage tourism destination. Therefore, Turkey should not only design its official Web sites to provide rich and detailed information on the history and culture of the destination, but should also identify other Web sites that can be used in order to create awareness of Turkey's history among potential visitors. Stories about Turkey and its historical legacy can be provided through travel Web sites, such as straightuptraveler.com or lonelyplanet.com, or in electronic newsletters, such as e-Turbo News. At the same time travel blogs and communities, such as travelblog.com or igoyougo.com, can be sponsored, in order to disseminate stories that paint Turkey as a heritage tourism destination. The use of the Internet medium to provide information about Turkey's history, heritage and culture has the advantage that individuals may decide on the level of depth required.

Previous experience is also found in this research to increase the level of knowledge regarding the history and culture of the destination, while also bringing about more positive perceptions of the place. In this sense, the role of the tour guides may be essential, as they facilitate the inter-pretation of the historical sites, and provide information that increases the knowledge of the tourist. However, word-of-mouth, despite being the most widely used source of information, does not seem to be so successful. The effectiveness of word-of-mouth may be increased and encouraged through the creation of memorable experiences and their dissemination through souvenirs and memorabilia. In this sense, connections to the past may be established through the act of shopping, while the experience of the tourists may be shaped by the souvenirs offered (Gazin-Schwartz, 2004). Television is also widely used to learn about Turkey, and documentaries focusing on ancient civilizations of Anatolia may be employed in order to counteract the mostly negative influence of the press regarding Turkey (Alvarez & Korzay, 2008). Historic films may also be used in order to promote her-itage tourism in Turkey, as these may result in a greater understanding and appreciation of the past by the viewers (Rosenstone, 1995, cited in Frost, 2004).

According to Goulding (1999), the experience of the past is depen-dent on the interpretation of the history and the representation of ethnic groups. As individuals seek to understand certain historical events, specific interpretations may be induced by the media or other mediating influences (Hughes, 1995). In this sense, the promotion of the place that is performed by the destination authorities may influence the knowledge and percep-tions that foreign tourists have regarding Turkey, through the selection of specific information and historical episodes. In the case of Turkey, the pro-motional campaigns that are carried out mainly by the Ministry of Culture and Tourism focus on conveying an image of Turkey that associates it to its historical legacy. However the symbols used and the information conveyed could be expanded to include less well-known aspects of Turkey's past and its ancient civilizations.

The interpretation of Turkish history in museums and exhibitions should also be questioned as to whether a sufficient representation of ancient civ-ilizations of Anatolia is provided. While better signage and printed material at sites is necessary, a special guide training on cultural heritage sites of Turkey may need to be undertaken. Furthermore, technology and audio-visual material should be incorporated to facilitate the interpretation of the historical and cultural exhibits and to allow visitors to decide on the desired level of in-depth knowledge regarding the site.

The necessity to manage various information sources and to increase the knowledge and information regarding the history, heritage, and culture of the destination suggests the need for a collaborative approach, due to the variety of stakeholders and participating actors (Fyall, Callod, & Edwards, 2003; Fyall & Garrod, 2004; Wang & Fesenmaier, 2007). Therefore, the pro-motion and positioning of a destination such as Turkey as a heritage tourism destination should be based on a strong collaboration between national and local authorities, in conjunction with non-governmental organizations and the private sector. A promotional strategy should aim at increasing the knowledge and awareness regarding the history and culture of the destination, at different levels and through various vehicles, as explained previously. Thus, the efforts to promote the destination should be paralleled by other activities carried out through historians, writers, journalists, museum curators, film makers, et cetera.

Although there have been several studies regarding the competitiveness of Turkey as an international tourism destination (for example, Kozak, 2001, 2002), these have not specifically considered the cultural tourism product. In view of the importance of this market in Turkey's tourism strategy, future investigations should examine the competitiveness of this destination in relation to cultural and heritage tourism. The present research has focused on perceptions of the destination and the awareness of the individuals regarding the culture and history of the place. However, other indicators that may establish the competitiveness of the destination in relation to cultural and heritage tourism should be researched. These may include subjective measures, such as the uniqueness of the culture, and objectives ones, such as the age of the culture, the investment in cultural facilities, or the extent of historical documentation. Furthermore, future investigations may also consider the impact of cultural tourism in Turkey on the profitability and sustainability of the destination, as well as the wellbeing of the residents.

Other than the consumption of the past through historic sites and attractions, cultural tourism also focuses on experiencing forms of art and indigenous cultures. The present research focuses on the role of historical knowledge and awareness of ancient civilizations, and therefore the focal point of the study is on heritage tourism. However, further research should investigate cultural tourism in Turkey from the perspective of the arts, especially as Istanbul has been selected as the European Capital of Culture in 2010. The creative and performing arts may also serve as attractors of the destination (European Travel Commission, 2005), especially in combination with business and conventions tourism.

REFERENCES

Alvarez, M. D., & Korzay, M. (2004). The image of the host community and its impact on satisfaction and post-purchase behavior. In *The role of education in quality destination management: Proceedings of the WTO Education Council Conference in Beijing, China, October 23, 2003* (pp. 98–119). Madrid, Spain: World Tourism Organization.

Alvarez, M. D., & Korzay, M. (2008). Influence of politics and media in the perceptions of Turkey as a tourism destination. *Tourism Review, 63*(2), 38–46.

Baloglu, S. (2001). Image variations of Turkey by familiarity index: Informational and experiential dimensions. *Tourism Management*, *22*(2), 127–133.

Baloglu, S., & Mangaloglu, M. (2001). Tourism destination images of Turkey, Egypt, Greece, and Italy as perceived by U.S.-based tour operators and travel agents. *Tourism Management*, *22*, 1–9.

Bigné, J. E., Sánchez, M. I., & Sánchez, J. (2001). Tourism image, evaluation variables and after purchase behaviour: Inter-relationship. *Tourism Management*, *22*, 607–617.

Boria, E. (2006). One stereotype, many representations: Turkey in Italian politics. *Geopolitics*, *11*, 484–506.

Cabezas, V. G. (2001). Trends and profiles of cultural tourism in the global tourism scenario. In *Cultural heritage and tourism development: A report on the International Conference on Cultural Tourism* (pp. 45–48), Madrid, Spain: World Tourism Organization.

Christou, E. (2005). Heritage and cultural tourism: A marketing-focused approach. In M. Sigala & D. Leslie, *International cultural tourism: Management, implications and cases* (pp. 3–15). Oxford, England: Butterworth-Heinemann.

Chon, K. S. (1990). The role of destination image in tourism: A review and discussion. *Tourist Review*, *45*, 2–9.

Dülger, S., Girişken, G., Yıldız, E., & Yarcan, Ş. (2005). Pre- and post-visit images of Turkey: A descriptive study of U.S. travelers. *D.A.Ü. Tourism Araştırmalar Dergisi*, *6*(1/2), 35–57.

European Travel Commission. (2005). *City tourism and culture: The European experience*. Madrid, Spain: World Tourism Organization and European Travel Commission.

Frost, W. (2004). Braveheart-ed Ned Kelly: Historic films, heritage tourism and destination image. *Tourism Management*, *27*, 247–254.

Fyall, A., Callod, C., & Edwards, B. (2003). Relationship marketing: The challenge for destinations. *Annals of Tourism Research*, *30*, 644–659.

Fyall, A., & Garrod, B. (2004). *Tourism marketing: A collaborative approach*. Cleveland, OH: Channel View Publications

Gazin-Schwartz, A. (2004). Mementos from the past: Material culture of tourism at Stonehenge and Avebury. In Y. Rowan & U. Baram (Eds.), *Marketing heritage: Archeology and the consumption of the past*. Oxford, England: Altamira Press.

Goulding, C. (1999). Interpretation and presentation. In A. Leask & I. Yeoman (Eds.), *Heritage visitor attractions: An operations management perspective* (pp. 54–68). London, England: Cassell.

Gursoy, D., Kim, K., & Uysal, M. (2004). Perceived impacts of festivals and special events by organizers: An extension and validation. *Tourism Management*, *25*, 171–181.

Holcomb, B. (1999). Marketing cities for tourism. In D. Judd & S. Fainstain (Eds.), *The tourist city* (pp. 54–70). New Haven, CT: Yale University Press.

Hughes, G. (1995). Authenticity in tourism. *Annals of Tourism Research*, *22*, 781–803.

Hughes, H., & Allen, D. (2005). Cultural tourism in Central and Eastern Europe: The views of "induced image formation agents." *Tourism Management*, *26*, 173–183.

Kim, H., Cheng, C., & O'Leary, J. (2006). Understanding participation patterns and trends in tourism cultural attractions. *Tourism Management*, *28*, 1366–1371.

Kozak, M. (2001). Comparative assessment of tourist satisfaction with destinations across two nationalities. *Tourism Management*, *22*, 391–401.

Kozak, M. (2002). Destination benchmarking. *Annals of Tourism Research*, *29*, 497–519.

MacCannell, D. (1992). *Empty meeting grounds*. London, England: Routledge.

MacKay, K. J., & Fesenmaier, D. R. (2000). An exploration of cross-cultural destination image assessment. *Journal of Travel Research*, *38*, 417–423.

Öztürkmen, A. (2005). Turkish tourism at the door of Europe: Perceptions of image in historical and contemporary perspectives. *Middle Eastern Studies*, *41*, 605–621.

Pekin, F. (2006). Kültür Turizmi ve İstanbul. In A. E. Bilgili (Ed.), *Istanbul Kültür Turizm*. Istanbul, Turkey: Istanbul Directorate for Culture and Tourism.

Peterson, K. (1994). The heritage resource as seen by the tourist: The heritage connection. In J. Van Harssel (Ed.), *Tourism: An exploration* (3rd ed., (pp. 242–249). Englewood Cliffs, NJ: Prentice Hall.

Picard, M. (1997). Cultural tourism, nation building and regional culture: The making of a Balinese identity. In M. Picard & R. E. Wood, *Tourism, ethnicity and the state in Asian and Pacific societies* (pp. 181–214). Honolulu, HI: University of Hawaii Press.

Poria, Y., Butler, R., & Airey, D. (2001). Clarifying heritage tourism. *Annals of Tourism Research*, *28*, 1047–1049.

Poria, Y., Butler, R., & Airey, D. (2006). Tourists perceptions of heritage exhibits: A comparative study from Israel. *Journal of Heritage Tourism*, *1*(1), 51–72.

Prentice, R. C. (1993). *Tourism and heritage attractions*. London, England: Routledge.

Real, M. R. (1996). *Exploring media culture*. Thousand Oaks, CA: Sage.

Reisinger, Y., & Steiner, C. (2006). Reconceptualising interpretation: The role of tour guides in authentic tourism. *Current Issues in Tourism*, *9*, 481–498.

Richards, S. (1997). *National heritage tourism forum, review and summary*. Cleveland, OH: Ohio Division of Travel and Tourism.

Richards, G. (2002). Tourism attraction systems: Exploring cultural behavior. *Annals of Tourism Research*, *29*, 1048–1064.

Ritchie, B. J. R., & Crouch, G. L. (2003). *The competitive destination*. Cambridge, MA: CABI.

Rosenstone, R. A. (1995). *Visions of the past: The challenge of film to the idea of history*. Cambridge, MA: Harvard University Press.

Sirakaya, E., Uysal, M., & Yoshioka, C. F. (2003). Segmenting the Japanese tour market to Turkey. *Journal of Travel Research*, *41*, 293–304.

Sönmez, S., & Sirakaya, E. (2002). A distorted destination image? The case of Turkey. *Journal of Travel Research*, *41*, 185–196.

Tasci, A. D. A., Gartner, W. C., & Cavusgil, S. T. (2007). Measurement of destination brand bias using a quasi-experimental design. *Tourism Management*, *28*, 1529–1540.

Tasci, A. D. A., & Knutson, B. J. (2004). An argument for providing authenticity and familiarity in tourism destinations. *Journal of Hospitality and Leisure Marketing*, *11*(1), 85–109.

Tosun, C. (2001). Challenges of sustainable tourism development in the developing world: The case of Turkey. *Tourism Management*, *22*, 289–303.

Tosun, C., Fletcher, J., & Fyall, A. (2006). Turkey: EU membership implications for tourism development. In D. Hall, D. Smith, & B. Marciszewska (Eds.), *Tourism in the new Europe: The challenges and opportunities of EU enlargement* (pp. 270–287), Cambridge, MA: CABI.

Um, S., & Crompton, J. L. (1990). Attitude determinants in tourism destination choice. *Annals of Tourism Research*, *17*, 432–448.

Waitt, G. (2000). Consuming heritage: Perceived historical authenticity. *Annals of Tourism Research*, *27*, 835–862.

Wang, Y., & Fesenmaier, D. R. (2007). Collaborative destination marketing: A case study of Elkhart county, Indiana. *Tourism Management*, *28*, 863–875.

Woodside, A. G., & Lysonski, S. (1989). A general model of traveler destination choice. *Journal of Travel Research*, *28*(4), 8–14.

World Tourism Organization. (2001). *Cultural heritage and tourism development: A report on the International Conference on Cultural Tourism*. Madrid, Spain: Author.

Yale, P. (2001). *From tourist attractions to heritage tourism*. Huntingdon, England: ELM.

Yarcan, S., & Inelmen, K. (2006). Perceived image of Turkey by U.S.-citizen cultural tourists. *Anatolia: An International Journal of Tourism and Hospitality Research*, *17*, 305–312.

Yunis, E. (2001). Cultural heritage tourism and sustainable development. In *Cultural Heritage and Tourism Development: A Report on the International Conference on Cultural Tourism* (pp. 85–88). Madrid, Spain: World Tourism Organization.

Balancing Tourism and Religious Experience: Understanding Devotees' Perspectives on Thaipusam in Batu Caves, Selangor, Malaysia

AZILAH KASIM

Department of Tourism and Hospitality, Social Sciences Division, College of Arts and Sciences, Universiti Utara Malaysia, Sintok, Kedah, Malaysia

Among the many personas of cultural heritage offered to global tourism, religious or faith-based tourism is perhaps the least prominent. However, this often-ignored component of tourism resources is turning into a booming business, as can be seen in the case of Mecca and Jerusalem. In essence, religious tourism is a good example of pro-poor tourism because it can generate good tourism income, develop the local economy, and bring about other possible benefits such as employment and local access to outside goods and services. However, the excitement of making profit from religious tourism should not be allowed to overshadow its traditional role of promoting spiritual healing and piety. This article argues that understanding the significance of a religious event amongst its followers will preserve the real purpose of religious travel and tourism and provide insights of a balanced management approach of a religious tourism destination. Using Malaysia as a study context, the article highlights qualitative findings from an open-ended questions survey on Hindu parents of University Utara Malaysia students. The findings highlight the meaning and importance of Thaipusam amongst the devotees, the balance of tourism and religious activities while at the sacred site as well as issues, concerns and improvements required to increase their quality of experience in Batu Caves. The article ends with a discussion on the implications of the findings on the management of a religious tourism destination.

INTRODUCTION

Malaysia has long regarded tourism as its second biggest source of foreign exchange earner. Driven by government policy towards accelerating the domestic private sector and stimulating the services to lead economic growth, many cultural, natural and man made resources have been developed or managed partly or solely for tourism. After the economic downturn in 1999 up until 2001, which affected tourism tremendously, the Malaysian economy has since turned around to provide positive consistent growth in gross domestic product from 2002 onwards. There was a healthy growth of disposable income, thereby stimulating domestic travel. The strong Asia Pacific economic recovery of neighboring countries also helped contribute to the Malaysian tourism growth, with the increase of regional travel from selected countries within the South East Asian Region. With the country's vast array of tourism options, coupled by positive government encouragement, Malaysia has managed to position itself as a destination that "has it all" through the Malaysia Truly Asia campaign. This is set to continue against the backdrop of a booming Asia Pacific tourist industry.

Religious Tourism

Mankind has an innate desire to observe and seek understanding of the different cultures that exist in the world. These desires to observe and understand different ways of life, traditions, values, and belief systems constitute the very platform of tourism. For domestic tourists, cultural heritage can stimulate a greater understanding in the local history, which may transcend into the feeling of pride and patriotism. For international tourists, this tourism resource can nurture a sense of respect and understanding of other cultures. However, presenting culture as a tourism asset may, in due time, lead to commodification of culture which, as theorized by George (2004), may impede a community's effort to achieve sustainability by unbalancing other critical community capital assets. In fact, he contends that tourism development runs the risk of invoking a metamorphosis of community, whereas the "old" traditional community culture eventually dies and is replaced with the birth of a "new" culture. It is argued here that such transformation should be mitigated if not prevented, especially when dealing with religious tourism. Understanding and addressing devotees interests and concerns can help bring a balanced approach to management, which in essence will delay such transformation.

Amongst the many personas of cultural heritage offered to the global market, religious or faith-based tourism is perhaps the least prominent. Religious or faith-based tourism refers to travel to a specific location or destination, during a specified time of the year, to either observe or participate in some religious rituals according to ones belief. To the mass tourists, religious based tourism resources are often included as add-ons or side trips. For example, a tourist in Istanbul may visit the Blue Mosque and observe the praying of Moslems, as part of their overall visit to other attractions such as the Hiya Sofea, the Spice Market, the Grand Bazaar, and the Hammam.

In the literature, various perspectives have been applied to the study of religious tourism. Turner (1973) for example, was the first researcher to use sociological–anthropological approach in studying the balance between tourism and pilgrimage. Nolan and Nolan (1992) were the first to use the geographical approach. Smith, (1992) used the socioeconomic perspective to examine impacts of religious tourism while Uriely et al. (2003) were among the earliest researchers studying local residents perception on religious tourism. This study is different because it looks at devotees' perception on religious tourism in order to improve the management of a religious tourism destination.

In the traditional sense of the word, religious ceremony symbolizes the relationship between nature, god, and the society. But increasingly, religious ceremony has become an attraction that spurs faith-based travel. Increasingly, faith-based travel is turning into a booming business. In Mecca, for example, travel and tourism agents have long profited from assisting and managing the hundreds of thousands of pilgrims who visit the holy land on an annual basis. It is projected that there will be approximately 10 million international tourist arrivals to Mecca in 2011, spending about 7.8 billion dollars on hotels and restaurants alone (Economist Intelligence Unit in Zawya, n.d.).

Religious tourism has expanded into an integral part of regular tourism as people seek to enjoy their travel even though their main travel intention is spirituality. As noted by Kevin Wright, religious tour director of Globus Tours (in Cogswell, 2006), what most people are experiencing and wanting now is a balance between traditional sightseeing and faith-based travel. They want to experience some nice Italian meals while visiting the Vatican in Italy; they may choose to raft on the Colorado River, not only to describe nature from a creationist perspective, but also to enjoy the experience; do a grand tour of Central America in the name of volunteer mission; or engage in shopping after performing the Hajj.

In fact, according to a Mintel report in 2005, drive from consumers for more authentic experience, such as immersing themselves in the spiritual and cultural traditions associated with specific religions and pilgrimage sites, is one of the key forces beside faith that drive the growth of religion and pilgrimage. Indeed, giving tourists the opportunity to experience local public culture *in situ* has been proposed by Englehardt (2007) as one of the key ways to provide authentic rather than "staged" or "reconstructed" experience. This can be done in several ways; through direct participation of visitors in public events and festivals; through establishing restaurants serving ethnic delicacies; through virtual reconstructions such as museums and interpretive centers; as well as through staged performances specifically designed to be staged for a discerning audience (Englehardt, 2007).

Kamil (2000) argues that the people who make their way to a religious tourism destination want to share a religious experience. The point of their visit is not to view, but to participate; to live the past in the present and not be limited to just sightseeing and picture-taking. As Kamil stresses (p. 4):

> What makes it come alive is participation; to mingle amidst those engaged in worship: the act of bowing, crossing oneself, touching an icon, or as on the occasion when I chanced to be at the church during a mass baptism, see white-clad babies with golden crowns blessed by the bishop in full ecclesiastical regalia. To be a witness to the faith, simplicity and unity of religion; this is what religious tourism should be about.

Indeed, faith-based travel is fast becoming a money-spinner for many tour and travel operators. While there is nothing wrong with making money out of religious tourism, it is argued here that the excitement of making profit should not be allowed to overshadow the traditional role of religious ceremony to promote spiritual healing and piety. George's (2004) theory on the effect of commodification, and Englehardt's emphasis on the value of authenticity in cultural tourism, should be used as a guide in offering religious events and ceremonies as tourism products. There is a need to understand the significance of a religious event in its followers in order to maintain the real purpose of religious travel and tourism. It will help tourism planners and decision makers to "keep it real" and not be tempted to over-commercialize the products and services associated with religious tourism.

This article uses qualitative data, personal observation, and secondary data, to study the significance of Thaipusam in influencing Hindu people's journeying. Specifically, it looks at the meaning of Thaipusam to its devo-tees, intrinsic and extrinsic motivations for choosing Batu Caves for fulfilling their vows (which essentially boost domestic travel as they would congregate from all over Malaysia just to celebrate the 7 days celebration), the problem that exists, and how these problems may be mitigated to ensure a better reli-gious tourism for them. In doing so, it explores the Thaipusam phenomenon in details, explaining the existing situation of religious tourism in Batu Caves and what should be done to ensure a sustained religious tourism.

Religious Tourism in Malaysia

One of the most diverse cultural resources can be found in the Asia Pacific. The crossings of cultures over thousands of years are manifested in the form of historical monuments such as Ankor Wat, Borobudur, and the lesser known Lembah Bujang as well as a plethora of religious and cultural mix. This is also where major religions—Buddhism, Hinduism, and many minor ones, were born (World Heritage Report, 2004). Asia Pacific undoubtedly forms an extremely attractive and diversified tourism product, which has something to offer to tourists from all walks of life.

Like the rest of Asia Pacific, Malaysia is also rich in unique and exotic cultural resources and celebrations. Its people enjoy numerous cultural and religious celebrations. Lifestyles are conveyed through religions, festivals, costumes, cuisines, arts and crafts, architecture, music, and dance. This gives the country the edge in relation to offering cultural and religious celebrations as tourism products.

One of the most famous resources is Batu Caves, glorified as a result of a unique religious celebration called Thaipusam. Thaipusam was first celebrated in 1888 after the temple founder, Mr. Kayaroganam Pillai, dreamed of being requested by God Sakti to build a shrine for her son Murukan on top of the Bukit Batu. This led to the building of wooden staircases to the temple, which were replaced with concrete in 1939 to accommodate increasing number of visitors. The hill was gazetted by the British for public recreation in 1930.

Thaipusam, a day of penance and thanksgiving for Hindu devotees, is held in honour of Lord Muruga or Lord Subramaniam (Belle, 2005). Although Thaipusam is also observed in many other centres including Penang, Ipoh, Johor Bharu, Sungai Petani, Muar, Maran, and increasingly among the small Indian communities stationed in the major East Malaysian cities, the festival is best experienced in Kuala Lumpur where the deity's jeweled chariot is led in a mass procession through the streets of the city, culminating at the Batu Caves in Selangor. Consequently, Batu Caves, located in Gombak district and only 15 km north of Kuala Lumpur, is said to be the most popular tourist destination in Selangor. It has never ceased to attract both local and foreign visitors as a constant stream of tourist buses arrives daily, either to witness the procession of Thaipusam or to marvel at the uniqueness of the temple inside the cave. International visitors come from the United Kingdom, United States, Australia, and other European countries.

Thaipusam

The intensity of the Thaipusam celebration is well known in the Malaysian tourism industry. During the Thaipusam festival, a large number of Hindu devotees (1 million in 2009 according to www.whatsonwhen.com) from all over Malaysia would choose to gather at Batu Caves to climb up its 272 steps and pray at it majestic temple. Thaipusam is a religious festival that occurs in the Hindu month of Thai, usually around the last week of January or the first week of February (Belle, 2005). Although Thaipusam is essentially a Tamil festival, it now draws not only Hindus from every regional Indian background, but also Sikhs, members of Malaysia's miniscule Sinhalese community, and Chinese devotees (Ramachandran, 1994). During this time Hindus pay annual homage to Lord Muruga, making offerings and asking for the Lord's forgiveness and blessings. The highlight of this celebration is the kavadi procession up the 272 steps up jagged face of a limestone crop to the three main caves. The activity demonstrates what Luchman and Nakagoshi (2006) refer to as the long developed interrelationship between human and nature that explains the use of nature (in this case a cave within a limestone hill) as a site of religious–traditional value.

The Significance of Thaipusam in Motivating Domestic Travel Among the Malaysian Indian Community

Kamil's (2000) analysis that religious tourism should be about sharing a religious experience is a correct and important one. Religious tourism should be about participating, mingling, and to become a witness to the faith in a simple but united way. However, a religious tourism that has become too big and too exposed to the outside world may run the risk of commodification, and could lose its authenticity and uniqueness. As George (2004) found empirically, commodification of culture may eventually transform a community. Traditional community may become weaker and finally disappears, replaced by the emergence of a new culture. When this takes place, a community's effort towards preserving the authenticity of a cultural experience may be impeded. Thaipusam in Batu Caves, being the largest religious gathering in Malaysia, may be exposed to such risk, unless a conscious effort is made to understand the event from the perspective of the local devotees, and what they think of what should be. This article highlights an attempt at this. Specifically it looks at the role of Thaipusam in motivating domestic travel among the Indian community. It is argued that understanding devotees' perspectives in religious tourism can help keep destination manager and/or marketer become more "grounded" and balanced in their management approach. As Weidenfeld et al. (2008) accurately pointed out, tourism and religion should have a cohabitual or even complementary relationship to enhance the tourist experience.

The method for collecting data on the perspective of local devotees was through an open-ended-questions survey mailed to 250 randomly selected addresses of parents of Indian students in University Utara Malaysia. The survey questions were designed to seek information on the significance, issues, or concerns as well as perspectives on how to improve their religious (Thaipusam) experience in Batu Caves. The word *significance* in this study is defined as the importance, the preference and the desire for improvement of Thaipusam. As it is beyond the scope of this article to academically dwell on the link of the aforementioned constructs, a simple but logical explanation of the chosen operational definition is offered: In dictionaries, a synonym of the word *significance* is *importance*. When something is important, it has a "superior worth" (Importance, n.d.), which merits priority. In other words, we "prefer" it to take place under certain conditions that we believe to be increasing the probability—or improving—a more successful occurrence of it.

At the time of the open-ended questions survey, the population of Indian students who are Hindus in University Utara Malaysia was approximately 2,500. Hence, the study uses the mailing list of these students to reach the students parents who are Hindu devotees and may be inclined to travel to Batu Caves for Thaipusam. Following the "rule of thumb" of 10% of the sample population, 250 was considered an adequate sample size. Of the targeted sample, 190 completed survey answers were received back from those who has fulfilled their vows at least once in Batu Caves in the last 3 years, and were used for this article.

The study adopts qualitative approach because according to Strauss and Corbin (1990), a qualitative approach helps to discover the uniqueness of each particular situation by explaining and understanding the context-specific phenomenon through naturalistic, qualitative inquiry. Open-ended questions were asked to solicit information such as (a) the real meaning and importance of Thaipusam; (b) reasons for choosing Batu Caves as opposed to other sacred sites for fulfilling their vows; (c) tourism related experiences at the sacred site; (d) problems or disruptions to their religious experiences and (e) suggestions for minimizing those problems and disruptions. The themes that emerged are as follows, exemplified with direct quotations from some of the respondents.

To understand the significance of Thaipusam, local devotees are asked what Thaipusam really means to them. Respondents as a whole relate Thaipusam to a day of joy, as it is a day Lord Muruga, a very important deity in Hinduism, was born. The day gives an opportunity for "rebirth" of oneself or "renewal" from past sins and misdemeanors because those who seek forgiveness will be forgiven, subject to the level of "purification."

> Praying [during Thaipusam] can help make your wishes come true. I will pray [during Thaipusam] for my children. I want them to be successful in their exams.

The purification they went through involves a month-long ritual "cleansing" process to prepare themselves in terms of endurance, during which they deny themselves alcohol, tobacco, and sex and to do regular meditation. They describe the 3-day procession, which begins by escorting a statue of Lord Maruga from the Sri Maha Mariamman temple to the Caves, as an "honor" to them, a chance to be closer to deity. The state of being in a trance, and indulging in masochistic acts of self-mutilation, body piercing, and heavy kavadi dragging is seen as very cleansing to their soul.

It [the cleansing ritual] is an experience I would repeat again and again to show God my love. When I am carrying kavadi I don't feel any pain. No word can describe how I feel.

To three quarters of the respondents, Thaipusam is a more important celebration than Deepavali. This is in contrast to popular belief that Deepavali is the main celebration for the Indian community in Malaysia. However, there are those who believe that both festivals are of equal importance, and not comparable as they are for different functions:

Thaipusam is more to God but we celebrate Deepavali for a hope for good things and throw away the bad things. Thaipusam is more to religion. We cannot say which is important. Both have their own importance.

No. Because both of the festivals are different: Where Deepavali means "festivals of lights" signifies the triumph of good over evil. We also take oil bath, doing a lot of sweets, put oil lamps and also visit temples. This festival signifies the victory of Lord Krishna over the demon, Ravana.

As a religious tourism destination, Batu Caves is not exempted from competition because Thaipusam can be celebrated at temples located in several states in Malaysia including Penang, Perak, and Melaka. In other words, devotees have a choice of doing their rituals in any of the states. In the presence of competition, a tourism destination must posess unique attributes that can draw tourists. Thus, the study sought understanding on why Batu Caves is a preferred celebration destination for Thaipusam and why an overwhelming (and steadily growing) number of devotees flock to the site annually. Among the themes that can be picked from the majority of respondents include "cave uniqueness" and "temple magnificence," which can be interpreted as their awe of the surroundings that possibly bring a greater feeling of being close to their god. Other themes include "crowd" and "feeling merry," which can be interpreted as the feeling of merriment brought about by the social surrounding and being part of a big gathering of devotees which makes celebration in Batu Caves more exciting than in other sites. A few excerpts indicating the aforementioned findings are the following:

There's always a strange feeling of calm in me whenever I accompany my [kavadi/ornate/milk jugs carrying] family members into the [huge opening] of the cave.

The higher I climb the steps (up to the cave mouth) the closer I feel to God . . . It's tiring yes, but its all (rewarding) in the end.

My friends and families are all over Malaysia. Batu Caves is like a meeting point for us. It's exciting to travel because you know you will see familiar faces. I feel good (when doing) the ritual with people I know.

To tourists or devotees who are just accompanying their family members make sacrifice to Lord Muruga, Thaipusam offers a remarkable sight of thousands of followers in a trance-like state, carrying milk jugs, body-piercing kavadis, or ornate frames (Belle, 2005). This phenomenon makes Thaipusam in Batu Caves the biggest and most intense religious celebration in Malaysia. In some cases the effect of the ongoing religious procession were so powerful that some onlookers also experience spontaneous trance states, manifested by screams, shouts, or wild dancing. Nonetheless, according to Collins (1997) local devotees regard the trance state of onlookers as superficial because they believe that only *arul,*(the trance-like state of the followers carrying kavadis, ornate frames, and milk jugs in the procession) is recognized as symbolic of the grace of the deity and is therefore sought and desired throughout Thaipusam. Those spontaneous trance states is thought of as representing the unwanted intrusion of disruptive lower deities, or even malign spirits as those individuals have neither fasted nor purified themselves, accordingly (Collins, 1997). From tourism perspectives however, such condition is argued to be heightening the peculiarity of the whole event. Indirectly, this can add to tourists' excitement as they marvel at the unique-ness of the ceremony, the culture associated with it, and the natural land-scape of Batu Caves. As Wendenfelt et al. (2008) put it, tourism and religious experience should exist in complimentary and not competitive environment.

Wendenfelt et al. (2008) also emphasized that if religious tourism is to have any spiritual meaning to tourists, it should combine a reverence for the past with participation in the present. In other words, tourists experiencing religious tourism should not have to have a less touristic experience simply because they are fulfilling their sipiritual beliefs. For this reason, the study seeks to understand if Thaipusam do allow the coexistence of both elements by asking the respondents to elaborate if they can have 'fun' during their visit to Batu Caves. Three quarter of the respondents agree, but define fun as the happy feeling of "being with" family and fellow devotees. They also attribute fun to the general feeling of "being able to seek purification" of the soul, to not doing it alone, but with a "mass of other people" with the same goal, and to the joy of buying ritual related products such as flowers, et cetera. Here the seeking of happiness and joy, the uplifting of spirit for being somewhere far from home, and the tendency to spend while being away from home among the devotees and the onlookers of Thaipusam celebration are actually similar to attributes of tourism in general. Examples of quotes are as the following:

> I do enjoy myself . . . being [in Batu Caves] with people I know . . . I [carry] kavadi sometimes and there are always many people who will help me [fix up the kavadi] and support me.

> There are so many vendors [at Batu Caves] selling beautiful things. I enjoy going around looking at the nice things they have.

Belle's observation in 2005 on tourist behavior and tourist presence was reinvestigated in this study. The majority of respondents regard tourist behavior during Thaipusam as appropriate, which is similar to what Belle (2005) concluded on tourist behavior:

> I don't mind [the tourists] looking at me. They are just looking. It's ok. Their faces are funny though—they look really scared!!

> So far I have no problems with [onlookers]. When I am in the moment all I think about is God and that He accepts [my sacrifice].

On the other hand, in terms of tourist presence what emerged was a general discontent on overcrowding. They blamed tour operators for being inconsiderate about the holiness of the event when deciding to bring tourists to Batu Caves.

> Every year more [tourists] come. They come, take pictures, that's it.

> I'd like them to show more respect . . . I mean show that they care . . . and not wear and behave like they are in a pub or something . . . smoking, shouting.

> [Batu Caves] has been so crowded lately . . . [tourist] buses, cars . . . we have parking problem. They should put more parking [spaces] if they want to allow more people!

> [Tour operators] just want to make money . . . I don't think they really care [about Thaipusam] . . . that's not what they want to do.

The aforementioned observation of tour operators approach in Batu Caves can be interpreted as "business as usual" with scant regard for cultural or spiritual value of religious tourism. Tourists' negative behaviors such as improper dressing, smoking, drinking alcohol, and making loud interruptive noises within the shrines' vicinity (as indicated by some respondents) are indicative of a lack of tendency by some tour operators to nurture a more caring and respectful tourist behavior. The intrusions of mass tourism have long been a matter of deep concern to many Hindus because they regard Batu Caves as a sacred site, which must be protected in terms of ritual purity and from pollution (Wan Hashim, 1983).

These negative aspects only illustrate further what many authors such as Erb (2000) and Walker et al. (2000) have known all along; that while tourism growth lead to economic benefits, it also brings social and ecological impacts. Clearly, the intrusion of mass tourism must be properly mitigated. Tourism has been known to consume both natural and human-made resources of the host nation, and is certainly prone to affect cultural ones, too. Such is the case with Egypt (see Weeks et al., 2006) which has sent the Egyptian authorities scrambling for solutions to deal with the problem.

Fortunately, Malaysian authorities strongly oppose the "human zoo" approach to tourism, and have taken steps to ensure that the cultural integrity of religions and belief systems are respected. Attempts by tourism companies to promote Thaipusam as a "gape and wonder" spectacle have been discouraged by the Malaysian authorities (Said, in Khan et. al, 1992). This is in contrast to Singapore where a series of advertisements released by the Singapore Tourist authorities in 1984/85 promoted Thaipusam as an "extraordinary spectacle" (Saturday Travel Section in Belle, 2005).

In other words, Batu Caves and the Thaipusam celebrations have been saved from enduring typical problems of heritage tourism such as what Englehardt (2007) refered to as the commercialization of the host culture that transforms the "product" into an easily comprehended commodity for the quick consumption of a large number of tourists. In contrast to places like Toraja, Indonesia, for example, where sacred funeral services were being adapted to meet tourists' needs; religious rituals and ethnic rites in Batu Caves have not been reduced and sanitized to conform to tourist expectations and schedules. This demonstrates the typical problem of contemporary culture tourism. On one hand, tourists increasingly seek exotic and unique cultural spectacles and experiences at any cost. On the other hand, tourism can degrade local culture and even reinvent it to fit the needs of the industry. As a result, host communities find culture and tradition under threat from the purchasing power of the tourism industry. Instead of getting rich and authentic cultural experiences, tourists get staged authenticity (Englehardt, 2007; Sofield, 2000).

Regarding how to improve the negative aspects of Thaipusam, most suggestions address the issue of crowding. These suggestions can be themed as regulate, more parking spaces, and divert tourists to other Thaipusam religious site:

> [Relevant authorities] must regulate . . . otherwise they park randomly alongside the road . . . it's such a hassle for [devotees] because we have to walk a long way to the site.

> I think the government really try [*sic*] but I don't know why the numbers keep increasing.

> May be they [tour operators] should not concentrate on Batu Caves only. We have Thaipusam at other sites, also.

In any case, Thaipusam cannot be closed to tourism because travel for purposes of religion, health, education, and cultural or linguistic exchange are particularly beneficial forms of tourism, which deserve encouragement.

From the economic point of view, the Indian community is generally still far behind compared to other ethnic communities in the country. Therefore, tourism during Thaipusam (albeit in a more controlled and properly managed form) presents viable opportunities for local economic development. As has been found elsewhere (see Deloitte & Touche, 1999; Ashley, Roe, & Goodwin 2001), tourism does have some advantages over other sectors for delivering pro-poor growth such as opportunity for local access to markets for other goods and services as well as potential for linkage between tourism with other economic sectors such as agriculture and fisheries to create initial demand for a good or service that can then itself become a growth sector. Another advantage is that tourism provides relatively labor-intensive opportunities more so than manufacturing and nonagricultural production and can be built on natural resources and culture, which are assets that some of the poor have.

At the same time, too much reliance on international tourism is not the answer. International tourism operates in a market economy and it is very much influenced by international market forces. Whenever new destinations emerge with cheaper and more attractive offerings, others will struggle to remain competitive and some will decline. Tour operators will respond to these new opportunities and will switch operations to the more competitively priced destination. Thus, product that is not unique or fail to retain its attractiveness will loose out. Such may not be the case for Thaipusam in Batu Caves now, but its status as a tourism product offered to international tourists still exposes it to such risk.

For the aforementioned reasons, it is important to rely also on domestic tourism—in this case tourism related activities of devotees—to develop pro-poor growth. Domestic tourism is more dependable because countries with significant domestic and regional tourism industries tend to suffer less from problems such as political instability and security concerns (as they have more knowledge on what really goes on in the country, and therefore are less prone to baseless news that could trigger fear for travel). Domestic tourism can also cushion the impact of low arrival of international tourists during low season. This has been proven in the case of Batu Caves, when the Thaipusam ceremony was celebrated as normal in 1998 even as the country experienced the worse economic and tourism downturn in its history (Zuko, n.d.). Granted, domestic tourism by itself does not increase the gross domestic production or employment. But in the case of Thaipusam in Batu Caves, the excitement and joy that come from this unique cultural phenomenon has indirectly drawn international tourists to come and witness it. The point here is that, if a cultural heritage is successful in drawing domestic tourists, it will also be able to draw international tourists and spin the economy. However, care is needed to ensure that rituals are kept authentic and followers can fulfill their religious faith properly.

CONCLUSION

Guided by George's (2004) theory on the effect of commodification, as well as Englehardt's (2007) and Kamil's (2000) emphasis on the value of authenticity in cultural tourism, this article have looked at the issue of commodification of culture within the specific context of Thaipusam celebration in Batu Caves, Selangor, Malaysia. To illustrate its main premise that the excitement of making tourism profit should not be allowed to overshadow the traditional role of religious ceremony, the article presented local devotees' perspectives on the significance of the Thaipusam, problems that may exists and ways to reduce the problems. The findings indicate that to local devotees, Thaipusam is an important event that brings them together as a community and brings them closer to God. They find fulfilling their religious call in Batu Caves to be more special, due to the temple's size and uniqueness, as well as the bigger number of devotees there. Devotees do enjoy their experience which indicates that in Batu Caves, tourism and religious experience do exist in complimentary and competitive environment (see Wendenfelt et al., 2008). However, the same balance is not achieved when it relates to the mass tourists as they bring about the problem of overcrowding.

The implication of the aforementioned findings is that offering religious events and ceremonies as tourism products must be guided by a sense of understanding about the real purpose of the event. Understanding a religious event from the perspective of devotees can help tourism planners and decision makers to keep it real, to nurture what is important (in this case the togetherness of a community and their closeness to god) and not be tempted to overcommercialize the products and services associated with religious tourism.

Granted, these findings may be subjected to bias in sampling because the data involve only those in the list of parents of UUM students who are Hindus. Thus, future research on the topic would benefit from a bigger sample and better sampling frame such as the total population of Hindu devotees in Malaysia.

Nonetheless, it is to have a sustained cultural tourism product, commodification of the resource must be avoided so as to preserve its authenticity (George, 2004; Englehardt, 2007). Cultural heritage sites may be exotic and seductive attractions to tourists. But to a local or a believer, those sites are more than just an attraction. They are places of worship, to be near God, to show spiritual appreciation and to seek forgiveness. These attributes require tourism to be limited, conducted respectfully and be managed carefully.

To reduce overcrowding of a religious site, as have been evident in the case of Batu Caves, developing a niche market for religious tourism may be a way to mitigate potential negative impacts of religious tourism. As has been discussed, mass tourism will expose sacred and important destinations such as Batu Caves to disrespectful tourists who may not even be interested in religious tourism in the first place.

The sanctity of a religious tourism product to its devotees warrants a more sensitive approach from destination marketing organization. Among required policy would be enhancing tour operators' sensitivity and respect for such product in terms of culture, as well as ecology. This is to reduce problems such as overcrowding and disruptive behaviors of tourists as found in this study.

In addition, since tourism thrives on novelty and uniqueness, a religious tourism destination must maintain its uniqueness. Kamil (2000) points out that seldom-exposed authentic activities are an interest of tourists to enjoy and experience. Luchman and Nakagoshi (2006) add to this the importance of promoting experience that is based on religious spirits interest if we were to balance nature conservation and tourism development.

Therefore the key is not to shut local rituals from tourism, but to ensure its sustainability through proper care. Ensuring sustainability in this context can be accomplished by:

1. Managing against overcommercialization of a religious tourism resource;
2. Keeping rituals authentic;
3. Educating onlookers on the "do's" and "don'ts" of a particular religious ceremony and encouraging a sense of respect; and
4. Encouraging donations or pledges to generate money to help support the continuity of the rituals.

In sum, a religious tourism product such as Thaipusam in Batu Caves must be preserved as both a sacred activity and as an attractive tourism activity. It should not be allowed to lose its authentic appeal through commodification process that comes naturally with too much tourism. It must be preserved first and foremost for the devotees, by understanding

TABLE 1 Tourist Arrivals and Receipts to Malaysia

Year	Arrivals (million)	Receipts (RM millions)
1995	7.46	9,174.9
1996	7.14	10,354.1
1997	6.21	9,699.6
1998	5.55	8,580.4
1999	7.93	12,321.3
2000	10.22	17,335.4
2001	12.78	24,221.5
2002	13.29	25,781.1
2003	10.58	21,291.1
2004	15.70	29,651.4

Source: Tourism Malaysia, 2005.

and respecting the significance of the site to them. Their religious experience should be enhanced by minimimizing problems and ensuring balance between their experience, and tourism activities that takes place in and around the site. A more grounded and balanced management approach will not only help ensure natural and cultural sustainability of a religious site and but also maintain tourism activity at a healthy level. In such a way, we could, in the end, have a win-win situation.

REFERENCES

Ashley, C., Roe, D., & Goodwin, D. (2004). Pro-poor tourism info sheets. Pro-poor tourism partnership. Retrieved from http://www.propoortourism.org.uk/info_sheets/3%20info%20sheet.pdf

Belle, C. V. (2005). Thaipusam in Malaysia: A Hindu festival misunderstood? Retrieved from http://tux.lib.deakin.edu.au/adt-VDU/uploads/approved/adt-VDU20050705.110706/public/01front.pdf

Cogswell, D. (2006, March 13), Faith tourism surges. *Travel Weekly*. Retrieved on October 13, 2007 from www.travelweekly.com

Collins, E. F. (1997). *Pierced by Murugan's lance: Ritual, power and moral redemption among Malaysian Hindus*. Dekalb, IL: Northern Illinois University Press.

Deloitte and Touche International Institute for Economic Development and Overseas Development Institute. (1999). *Sustainable tourism and poverty elimination study. A report to the Department for International Development*. Retrieved from http://www.propoortourism.org.uk/dfid_report.pdf

Englehardt, R. (2007, February 27). *Protecting indigenous cultures within tourism environment: A rights-based approach empowering local stakeholders*. Ambassador Bill Lane Jr. Lecture on Sustainable Tourism, University of Hawai'i at Manoa School of Travel Industry Management, Manoa, Hawaii.

Erb, M. (2000). Understanding tourists: Interpretation from Indonesia. *Annals of Tourism Assessment Review, 20*, 513–535.

George, E. W. (2004). Commodifying local culture for tourism development: The case of one rural community in Atlantic Canada, Ph.D. Thesis, University of Guelph, (HN103.5 .G56 2004)

Importance. (n.d.). In *Merriam-Webster's online dictionary* (11th ed.). Retrieved from http://www.merriam-webster.com/dictionary/importance

Kamil, J. (2000, January). Religious tourism as big business. *Al Ahram Weekly, 469*.

Luchman, H., & Nakagoshi, N. (2006, June). *Kasodo, tourism, and local people perspectives for Tengger Highland Conservation*. Presented at Survival of the Commons: Mounting Challenges and New Realities, the Eleventh Conference of the International Association for the Study of Common Property, Bali, Indonesia. Retrieved from dlc.dlib.indiana.edu/archive/00001914/00/Hakim_Luchman.pdf

Mintel. (2005). Travel and tourism analyst. *Religious Tourism—International Research, 27*, 709–736.

Muhammad, I. S. (1992). Ethnic perspectives of the left in Malaysia. In J. S. Khan & L. K. Wah (Eds.), *Fragmented vision: Culture and politics in contemporary Malaysia* (pp. 254–281). Sydney, Australia: Asian Studies Association of Australia; Allen and Unwin.

Nolan, M., & Nolan, S. (1992). Religious sites as tourism attractions in Europe. *Annals of Tourism Research*, *19*, 68–78.

Ramachandran, S. (1994). *Indian plantation labour in Malaysia*. Kuala Lumpur, Malaysia: S. Abdul Majeed.

Smith, V. (1992). Introduction: The quest in guest. *Annals of Tourism Research*, *19*, 1–17.

Sofield, T. H. B. (2000). *Re-thinking and re-conceptualising social and cultural issues of tourism development in South and Southeast Asia*. Murdoch, Australia: Murdoch University Press.

Tourism Malaysia. (2005). Tourist arrivals and receipts to Malaysia. Retrieved February 15, 2009, from http://www.scribd.com/doc/20353435/Malaysia-International-Tourist-Arrivals-and-Receipts

Turner, V. (1973). The centre out there: Pilgrim's goals. *History of Religion*, *12*, 191–230.

Uriely, N., Israeli, A., & Reichel, A. (2003). Religious identity and residents' attitudes toward heritage tourism development: The case of Nazareth. *Journal of Hospitality and Tourism Research*, *27*(1), 69–84.

Walker, J. L., Mitchel, B., & Wismer, S. (2000). Impact during project anticipation in Molas, Indonesia: Implication for social impact assessment. *Environmental Impact Assessment Review*, *20*, 513–555.

Wan, H. (1983). *Race relations in Malaysia*. Kuala Lumpur, Malaysia: Heinemann Educational Books (Asia).

Weeks, K. R., Hetherington, N. J., & Jones, L. T. (2006). The Valley of the Kings, Luxor, Egypt site management master plan. *The Theban Mapping Project, Cairo*. Retrieved from http://www.thebanmappingproject.com/about/KVMasterplan/KVM_CH3.pdf

Weidenfeld, A., & Ron, A. S. (2008). Religious needs in the tourism industry. *Anatolia: An International Journal of Tourism and Hospitality Research*, *19*, 357–361.

Whatsonwhen. (n.d.). Retrieved from http://www.whatsonwhen.com

World Heritage Report. (2004). *The state of world heritage in the Asia-Pacific region 2003*. Paris, France: UNESCO World Heritage Centre. Retrieved from whc.unesco.org/documents/publi_wh_papers_12_en.pdf

Zawya. (n.d.). *Saudi Arabia: Travel and tourism forecast*. Retrieved from http://www.zawya.com/printstory.cfm?storyid=EIU20081101211523375&l=000000080828

Zuko.com. (n.d.). *Exotic and mysterious places*. Retrieved from http://www.zuko.com/travelogues/Travel_Exotic_Mysterious_Batu_Caves.asp

The Potential for Northern Ireland to Promote Politico-Religious Tourism: An Industry Perspective

MARIA TERESA SIMONE-CHARTERIS and STEPHEN W. BOYD

Department of Hospitality and Tourism Management, University of Ulster, Coleraine Campus, Coleraine, Northern Ireland

Recent years have seen cultural heritage tourism mature as a distinct body of academic inquiry. Culture, however, is a broad concept. As a consequence, cultural heritage tourism can be segmented into more specific subcategories. Among these are religious and political tourism. A review of the literature on political tourism and religious tourism reveals that tourists who have interest in things political and religious share similar motivations and often make use of similar attractions. However, the interrelation between religious and political tourism is an issue that has barely been addressed within academia. Possible connection here, it is argued by the authors, to be particularly evident in Northern Ireland. This study presents the views of public and private tourism sector organizations across Northern Ireland on the potential to link political and religious tourism as a definable niche product, what the authors have labeled as politico-religious tourism and investigates their willingness to collaborate to develop this new niche product.

INTRODUCTION

The growing sophistication of travelers resulting, to some extent, from demographic, economic, and technological changes in society, has contributed to a shift from traditional forms of tourism characterized by inclusive tours focused on undifferentiated sun and sea locations towards more engaging and "meaningful" holidays (Weiler & Hall, 1992). Today's visitors no longer want to spend their time sun-baking by the side of five-star hotel pools, or whittling away their wealth in glitzy shopping malls (Frew, 1989 as cited in Hall & Weiler, 1992). They are more interested in discovering, experiencing, participating in, learning about, and being included in the everyday life of the destinations (Robinson & Novelli, 2005). Increasingly, according to Kneafsey (1994, p. 105) "Culture is being seen as a resource and history has become a saleable commodity," hence the maturing of cultural and heritage tourism.

Culture, however, is a broad concept encompassing everything that defines a community from its way of life to tangible and intangible elements (beliefs, values, social practices, rituals and traditions, buildings, monuments, objects, sites, language, performances and festivals, and craftsmanship). As a consequence, cultural heritage tourism can be further segmented into smaller, more specific subcategories defined by specific types of attractions and events (Robinson & Novelli, 2005; M. K. Smith, 2003). These subcategories have been identified as: arts tourism (involving visits to e.g., theatre, concerts, literary sites); creative tourism (involving participation in e.g., painting, pottery, cookery); urban tourism (involving shopping, nightlife and visits to historic sites); rural tourism (e.g., visits to villages, farm-stays, National Parks); indigenous tourism (involving participation in or visits to cultural centers, performances, festivals); industrial heritage tourism (e.g., visits to regenerated waterfront developments); sport tourism (attendance of and/or participation in sport events and manifestations); gastronomy tourism (involving e.g., food festivals and wine trails); political tourism (visits to e.g., national monuments, war memorials, and cemeteries) and pilgrimage/religious tourism (involving trips to churches, temples, religious festivals and ceremonies; NITB, 2006a; Timothy & Boyd, 2003).

Religiously motivated travel is perhaps the oldest and most prevalent type of travel in human history (Kaelber, 2006; Rinschede, 1992; Sharpley & Sundaram, 2005; Sigaux, 1996; Timothy & Olsen, 2006; Vukonić, 1996) and may go back to the beginnings of many of the world's religions (Casson, 1974; Tomasi, 2002; Westwood, 1997). However, despite the pervasiveness and volume of religious tourism throughout the world, relatively little has been said about it by scholars of religion and tourism. Only recently have academics, governments and tourism agencies taken notice of the increasing numbers of religiously motivated travelers, or at least the increase in visitation to sacred sites in conjunction with the general growth of cultural and heritage tourism. As a consequence, a nascent collection of journal articles has appeared during the past 15 years and a few books have been published since 2000 that outline the history of pilgrimage and the transformation of pious journeys into modern-day tourism (Timothy & Olsen, 2006).

Political tourism has been neglected even more despite the growing numbers of "curiosity" visitors, who are interested in learning about current or recent conflicts (Causevic & Lynch, 2007), and its relation and similitude with *thanatourism* or dark tourism. Nonetheless, in the academic environments, politics has been associated with tourism mainly in relation to heritage (since history is usually told from the perspective of people in positions of power; Nic Craith, 2003; Timothy & Boyd, 2003, 2006) and tourism policy (Altinay & Bowen, 2006; Hall, 1994).

That religion and politics are connected cannot be denied: the current situation in the Middle East, the Twin Towers disaster of 2001 in New York, and the ongoing or recent conflicts in numerous destinations (e.g., Cyprus and former Yugoslavia) all highlight this link (Green, 2003). Moreover, a thorough review of the literature on religious and political tourism reveals that political and religious tourists share similar motivations and often make use of similar attractions. Nonetheless, surprisingly the opportunities and benefits that can derive from exploring the interrelation between religious and political tourism have not been examined yet. This connection is particularly evident in Northern Ireland where political attractions and sites tend to reflect a religious perspective and religious attractions and sites tend to echo a political view. However, it appears that the Northern Ireland Tourist Board (NITB) is reluctant to officially promote political tourism as a distinct niche tourism product. In fact, while it is focusing on the marketing of Northern Ireland's religious heritage through the Christian Heritage/St. Patrick Signature Project, at the same time it looks like it is shying away from the Province's political heritage potential despite the increasing popularity of the murals in Belfast and Londonderry/Derry and other attractions linked to the Province's troubled past. In contrast, private tourism organizations such as Coiste na n-Iarchimí, Belfast City Sightseeing, Shankill Tourism, Free Derry Tours, and Derry Taxi Tours have recognized the potential for political tourism and are trying to further develop it in order to satisfy a growing demand.

In order to start a serious academic debate in the literature regarding religious and political tourism, this study investigates the views of public and private tourist sector organizations within Northern Ireland on the development and promotion of politico-religious tourism in the Province, and if willingness exists, among the different players, to collaborate in order to assist opportunities associated with political and religious sites and attractions. The aim of the authors was also to open up debate in what connections may exist in visitor motivations between religious and political tourism. While this research is at the stage of a single case study, the argument that is made by the authors is that connections may be recognized through the shared motivations of visitors who have the propensity to visit places of religious and political association, and where the two exist together. Therefore, they call for comprehensive research that goes beyond individual case studies, but that embraces comparative investigations to uncover similarities and differences.

Similarities between the motivations of religious and political tourists however, are not investigated in this article through the perspective of visitors, but rather through those industry sectors that are responsible for delivering products to this niche market as they are believed to be useful for market segmentation and product positioning purposes.

This article comprises of six sections. The first section reviews the relevant literature regarding pilgrimage and religious travel and political tourism, at the end of which the authors argue that political and religious tourists share similar motivations and that connections between religious and political tourism exist. The second section focuses on tourism in Northern Ireland and highlights the increase in popularity of attractions associated with religion and politics. The third section explains the methodology employed to conduct the study and the rationale for adopting it. Linked to this is the presentation of the main findings, which reveals the current situation in Northern Ireland with regard to the development and promotion of religious and political tourism. In the fifth section the results are discussed and commentary is offered on how they relate to existing research in the areas of religious and political tourism. The last section summarizes the findings of the study, highlights its limitations, and provides suggestions for future research.

LITERATURE REVIEW

Religious Travel

Traditionally, religiously motivated travel has coincided with pilgrimages usually undertaken for motives such as visiting a site where a miracle took place or where one is expected to occur in the future, fulfilling a commandment or religious requirement, obtaining forgiveness for sins, praying and seeking a cure for illness (Timothy & Boyd, 2003).

According to Vukonić (2002) though, travel with the primary goal of visiting sacred sites often includes visits to neighboring tourist sites and vice versa. For example, pilgrims at Lourdes (France) commonly include visits to Andorra to the East, Biarritz to the West, and the Spanish Pyrenees to the South in their travels. Similarly, pilgrims to Fatima (Portugal) along the way visit the Atlantic Coast and historical cities in the hinterland. Travels to Medjugorje (Bosnia-Herzegovina) include visits to numerous Adriatic tourist sites. Likewise, Santiago de Compostela is usually one stop of a multifaceted vacation including the Spanish seaside, culture, and gastronomy (Santos, 2002).

In addition, as a result of marketing and a growing general interest in cultural tourism (Robinson & Novelli, 2005; Timothy & Boyd, 2003), religious sites are being commodified and packaged for a tourism audience (Olsen, 2006). As a consequence, pilgrimages and other religious journeys are becoming tied to other types of tourism, and religious places are being visited for a variety of reasons such as their architecture and historical importance, some of which have nothing to do with religion directly (Digance, 2003; Poria, Butler, & Airey, 2003; Vukonić, 2002). This view is in line with Rinschede's (1992, p. 52) definition of religious tourism as "That type of tourism whose participants are motivated either exclusively or in part for religious reasons."

Thus, religious sites are simultaneously sacred and secular as they are visited by both pilgrims and religious travelers and tourists (Collins-Kreiner & Gatrell, 2006). V. L. Smith (1992), in order to conceptualize the varying relationship between pilgrims and tourists, placed them on a continuum (see Figure 1). At one end of the spectrum lies sacred pilgrimage (a journey driven by faith, religion, and spiritual fulfillment) while at the opposite end lies the secular tourist (driven by more materialistic motivations). Situated between the two are infinite possibilities of sacred-secular combinations of religious tourists who are "more pilgrims than tourists" or "more tourists than pilgrims."

This scenario is further complicated by the combination of pilgrimage travel with New Age Spirituality (Rountree, 2002). According to Baum (2000), the concept of religion has shifted with the advent of modern secularizing trends such as postindustrialism, cultural pluralism, and scientific rationality.

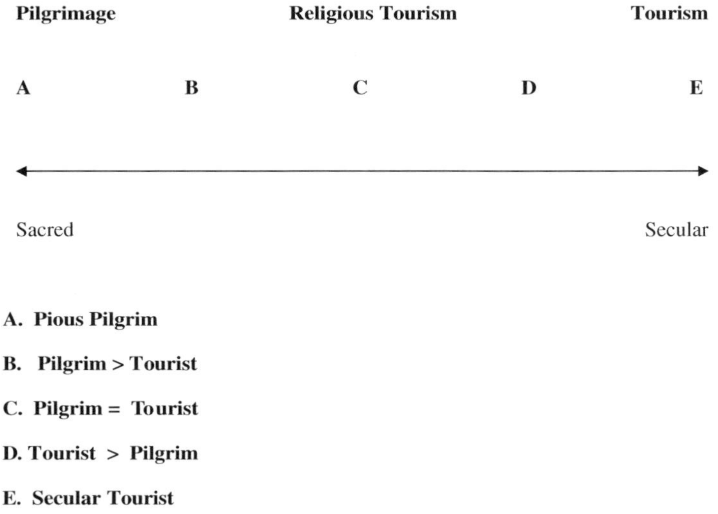

Pilgrimage		Religious Tourism		Tourism
A	B	C	D	E

Sacred   Secular

A. Pious Pilgrim

B. Pilgrim > Tourist

C. Pilgrim = Tourist

D. Tourist > Pilgrim

E. Secular Tourist

FIGURE 1 Pilgrim-tourist continuum.
Source: V.L. Smith (1992).

As such, the term *religion* is used in everyday public discourse to refer to things outside the realm of traditional religious institutions. As a result of both secularizing trends and the changing use of the word, religion is being increasingly seen as a privatized and pluralized experience where the spiritual and the religious are separate (Olsen & Timothy, 2006). As Heelas (1998, p. 5) notes: "people have what they take to be 'spiritual' experiences without having to hold religious 'beliefs'." Thus, many people who consider themselves spiritual would not see themselves as religious and vice versa. Because of this, modern society has expanded what it defines as sacred, bringing about the creation of new sites of sacrality, with travel to these sites being termed pilgrimage in its own right because rather than pilgrimage being travel to sites where heaven and earth converge, it is considered to be journeys "undertaken by a person in quest of a place or a state that he or she believes to embody a *valued ideal*" (Morinis, 1992, p. 4).

In this light then, the concept of pilgrimage has been extended to include travel to places symbolizing nationalistic values and ideals such as the Wailing Wall in Jerusalem in representation of all of Judaism (Guth, 1995; Rinschede, 1992; Zelinsky, 1990); disaster sites such as Ground Zero in New York and the Paris underpass where Princess Diana was killed (Blasi, 2002; Conran, 2002; Kaelber, 2006; Lennon & Foley, 2000); war memorials and cemeteries designed to commemorate famous war heroes, political figures, and military chiefs such as Alexander the Great and Napoleon (Johnstone, 1994; Lloyd, 1998; Seaton, 2002; V. L. Smith, 1996); historical sites that contribute to national and cultural identity such as the Turkish Gallipoli Peninsula for Australians and New Zealanders (Hall, 2002, 2006); and places related to the lives of literary writers and the settings of their novels (Herbert, 2001). Even places traditionally associated with secular tourism are now regarded as pilgrimage sites such as those associated with music stars like Elvis Presley's mansion (Graceland) in Memphis, Tennessee (Alderman, 2002); nostalgic tourist attractions such as Walt Disney World (Knight, 1999); sporting events (Gammon, 2004) and even shopping malls (Pahl, 2003).

It follows that many people travel to a widening variety of sacred sites not only for religious or spiritual purposes, but also because they are marked and marketed as heritage or cultural attractions (Timothy & Boyd, 2003). They may visit because they have an educational interest in learning more about the history of a site or understanding a particular religious faith and its culture and beliefs; for nostalgic reasons or patriotic stirrings; for a chance to admire architectural or natural wonders; in search of authentic experiences; or simply out of curiosity (Olsen & Timothy, 2006; Shackley, 2001a, 2002).

Political Tourism

As noted previously, little research has been carried out on political tourism, which is also referred to as "politically oriented tourism" (Brin, 2006), "terror tourism" (Northern Ireland Assembly Official Report, 2008), "troubles tourism" (Belfast City Council, 2006; McDowell, 2008), and "phoenix tourism" (Causevic & Lynch, 2007). As a consequence, a clear definition for a political tourist and an agreed upon typology of such tourists are virtually absent from tourism discourse. In a recent publication, Henderson (2007, p. 244) while discussing the relationship between communism, heritage, and tourism in East Asia referred to "political heritage" as to that type of heritage, which "includes features based on war, colonialism and the physical and less palpable legacies of different regimes." In 1992, Rinschede defined political tourism as "diplomatic tourism, tourism at political events, and tourism at national monuments" (Rinschede, 1992, p. 52). This definition, however, is over one and a half decades old and does not take into consideration the growing numbers of political tourists and activists who arrive in areas affected by political unrest on fact-finding missions to learn first-hand about events they see so often on their television screens (Solidarity Boosts P.A. Tourism, 2006; Burnhill, 2007).

These more adventurous or ideologically driven visitors are not afraid of political strife or violent episodes. Quite the contrary, they come because of them (Burnhill, 2007). It follows then that political instability can be an impetus rather than an impediment to visit a given destination either when political instability is a thing of the past, or when conflicts are current and ongoing (Brin, 2006). For example, in Berlin in Germany tourists are allured by remaining segments of the now gone Berlin Wall, which divided the city during the Cold War (Timothy, 2001). In China, visitors are attracted to Beijing's Tiananmen Square, which was the theater of the student protests of 1989 culminating in the Tiananmen Square Massacre (Hall & O'Sullivan, 1996). In South Africa, around 2,000 tourists per day visit Robben Island Museum to learn about apartheid (Shackley, 2001b). In Jerusalem, Israel, visitors take private or organized excursions to sites related to the Israeli-Palestinian Conflict (Brin, 2006; Clarke, 2000). Similarly, in Northern Ireland, political tourists are interested in learning about the recent 'Troubles' through living history tours, which show the conflict from the perspective of one of the sides involved depending on the tour taken.

Moreover, according to Brin (2006), Crooke (2005) and McDowell (2008), a political process takes place when tourists visit destinations, which were once affected by conflict in the past or where conflict is still ongoing. Tourists are willing to pay in order to be taken to unstable and possibly dangerous places and be shown things to satisfy their curiosity and provide them with a unique experience. On the other hand, when they go on a tour organized by official or unofficial representatives of one of the belligerent sides to a conflict, tourists are, in effect, a "captive audience." They are told and shown things carefully selected by their hosts to further their political claims. Once they go home, the tourists are ready and willing to propagate a certain political agenda to their friends and relatives. Hence, tourists become political allies (Brin, 2006; Crooke, 2005; Henderson, 2007; McDowell, 2008). Earlier, Richter (1983) suggested that specific itineraries might be viewed as representing ideological values of the tourists and their political beliefs and convictions. According to her, tourists going away on vacation to a country experiencing political instability are themselves "politically natured." They might not side with any one side of the conflict in the destination, but are intrigued by the very conflict: its causes and background, its current implications on the hosts and its presence in everyday life.

It follows that most hosts hope to promote a political agenda and that some visitors are more inclined than others to become potential agents, won-over carriers who can propagate desired political messages upon returning to their countries and communities. But what about the more politically neutral tourists, who accidentally visit political attractions, or who visit political attractions and other types of attractions during their visit to a destination? What are the motivations that drive them? The motivations of political tourists are difficult to categorize due to lack of research on political tourism. The extant literature indicates that people are inspired to visit political attractions because they want to learn first-hand about past or current events they see or have seen on their television screens; to show support or solidarity (e.g., visits to Cuba to protest against the U.S. ban on travel to the destination); in search of authenticity (e.g., visits to Jerusalem, Israel); for nostalgic, commemorative, or nationalistic reasons; because they empathize with the victims (e.g., visits of Irish people to Robben Island Museum), for educational purposes (e.g., visits to the Museum of Free Derry in Londonderry/Derry, Northern Ireland); out of curiosity (e.g., visits to murals in Belfast and Londonderry/Derry in Northern Ireland); or to enjoy the "thrill" of political violence (Brin, 2006; Causevic & Lynch, 2007; Clarke, 2000; Shackley, 2001b; Solidarity Boosts P.A. Tourism, 2005; Burnhill, 2007).

Hence, political tourism can be defined as travel to sites, attractions, and events associated with war, conflict, and political unrest for educational, commemorative, or diplomatic reasons; to show solidarity or empathy; out of curiosity; in search of authenticity; to enjoy the thrill of political violence; or for a combination of these.

POLITICAL AND RELIGIOUS TOURISM INTERFACE

The review of the literature on religious and political tourism indicates that political and religious tourists are inspired to visit cultural heritage attractions by similar motivations. Figure 2 illustrates that while motivations are different for religious and political tourists, there are a range of shared motivations including: educational interest in the history of a site or event, nostalgic, patriotic, or commemorative reasons, the desire for authentic experiences, and curiosity. The concept of motivation has been considered useful for

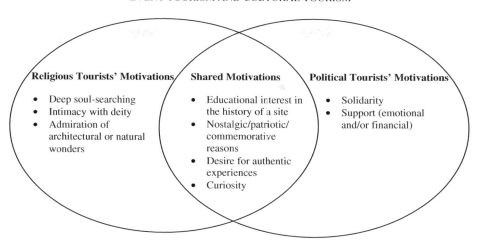

FIGURE 2 Motivations of religious and political tourists.
Source: Simone-Charteris and Boyd (2008).

developing marketing strategies, appropriate advertising appeals, and as the basis for market segmentation and product positioning in tourism in many empirical investigations (Crompton, 1979; Card & Kestel, 1988; Ryan & Glendon, 1998; Yavuz, Baloglu, & Uysal, 1998). According to Kozak (2002, p. 222), "dipending upon the empirical findings, destination management would either promote attributes that best match tourists motivations or concentrate on a different market where tourist motivations and destination resources match each other." The argument the authors are putting forth in this article is that because religious and political tourists share similar motivations and because in Northern Ireland numerous attractions related to the history of the troubles have both religious and political connotations, it would make sense to promote political and religious tourism not as two separate identities, but together as politico-religious tourism.

The following section focuses on tourism in Northern Ireland. It explains how the industry has been affected first by the troubles and then by the peace process and highlights the increase in popularity of attractions associated with religion and politics.

THE CONTEXT: TOURISM IN NORTHERN IRELAND

Northern Ireland has a long history (circa 30 years) of terrorism, which has been beamed by the media across the English-speaking world and even worldwide (Boyd, 2000; Wall, 1996). Not surprisingly, the region's tourism industry has been affected in terms of receipts and visitors, unsuitable tourism developments because of a poor economic and social image, and a lack of suitable infrastructure (Boyd, 2000; Wall, 1996; Wilson, 1993).

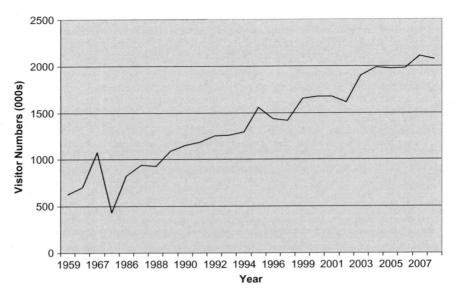

FIGURE 3 Visitors numbers to Northern Ireland over time (1959–2008). (Color figure available online).

Figure 3, however, reveals that prior to the civil unrest at the end of the 1960s, Northern Ireland enjoyed visitor numbers that approached one million visitors in 1967; a fact often forgotten about when discussions take place about tourism and Northern Ireland. But decline was rapid once civil unrest broke out in 1969; the year 1972 saw visitor numbers shrink by over 50% in a period of only 5 years to 435,000. This is not surprising as the early 1970s witnessed some of the worst violence the Province (Northern Ireland) had to endure during the troubles. However, the peace process and the Good Friday Agreement of 1998 have generated significant improvements for the tourism industry. In fact, since the signing of the Agreement between Westminster, Dublin and the majority of the political parties within the region, Northern Ireland has experienced a steady growth in international visitor flows (NITB, 2003, 2005, 2006b, 2007, 2008b) and by 2007, the Province recorded for its first time over two million visitors (see Figure 3), where the sector contributed £535m to the local economy (NITB, 2008b).

Nonetheless, Northern Ireland temperate climate and location on the periphery of Western Europe do not make it an obvious holiday destination. As a consequence, diversification of the tourism product and the development of niche markets are essential to enable Northern Ireland to compete in the international market and attract the overseas holidaymaker (Devine & Connor, 2005).

Northern Ireland is primarily regarded as a bicultural society, as a region that is largely divided between two ethnic identities: British and Irish, Unionists and Nationalists, Protestants and Catholics, Orange and Green (Nic

Craith, 2003). Religion and politics are inextricably linked in Northern Ireland and the political structure has a tendency to reflect the religious orientation of the two main communities forming the Northern Ireland society. The Northern Ireland Assembly, in fact, which has full authority to make laws and take decisions on the functions of the Northern Ireland Government Departments comprises of five main parties: the Democratic Unionist Party (DUP), Sinn Féin (SF), the Ulster Unionist Party (UUP), the Social Democratic and Labor Party (SDLP), and the Alliance Party of Northern Ireland (APNI; Northern Ireland Assembly, 2009). Of these the DUP has links to Protestant churches, Sinn Féin to the Roman Catholic Church, the UUP is linked to Protestant churches but is more moderate than the DUP, the SDLP is a nationalist party but is more moderate than Sinn Féin, and the APNI is a cross-community anti-sectarian party. The Province has a long-established heritage steeped in the different histories of the two main communities forming the Northern Ireland society (Graham, 1994). According to Devine and Connor (2005, p. 10) "to discover the real Northern Ireland the 'Troubles' should not be hidden but explored. The different cultures of both the Catholic and Protestant communities should not be concealed but celebrated and promoted to the tourist." This view is supported by Boyd (2000), who maintains that there will always be an element of visitors to Northern Ireland who want to see landmarks that reflect a turbulent past:

> Many visitors since the early 1980s when visiting Belfast insisted in seeing sections of the wall that separated the two communities, and had to walk up sections of both the Shankill Road (Protestant) and Falls Road (Catholic) in west Belfast. As many countries, particularly those changing from a system of communist-state control to more of a democracy, are rushing to remove symbols and tangible elements of their dark past, Northern Ireland would do well to consider the importance of maintaining certain symbols, icons, buildings, and places to reflect and commemorate the past. (Boyd, 2000, p. 167)

Murals, for example, are part of the wider culture of both communities in Prostestant and Catholic Northern Ireland. While some people celebrate the paintings and consider them an expression of popular culture, political resistance, or working-class defiance, others consider them as expressions of power or even as acts of intimidation. Thus, murals provoke opposition as much as they generate support (McCormick & Jarman, 2005). Despite the controversy they generate, murals have become popular with the media, which use them to convey a sense of distinctiveness, place and authenticity. However, they have become even more popular with tourists, who see them as a *matériel* remnant of the conflict, a legacy of the last 30 years, a remainder of a past that should not be forgotten or concealed (McCormick & Jarman, 2005; Peace Line Tours, 2006). Murals are generally considered as political tourist attractions. However, they also express a religious perspective.

Currently, religious tourism and political tourism occupy very different places on the agendas of public and political bodies. In fact, considerable emphasis is placed on the development of a Christian heritage/St. Patrick Signature Project with the outcome of a Christian heritage trail being developed across the Province. Conversely, political tourism is still being debated in the Northern Ireland Assembly, does not appear in any of the tourist material produced by the Northern Ireland Tourist Board, rather is addressed through a select few private sector tourist companies and organizations.

The article now shifts to presenting the methodology that was employed to carry out the study followed by the results and wider discussion and implications.

STUDY METHODS

A qualitative research strategy was adopted as the most suitable approach for an exploratory study of this kind. It is argued that semistructured and in-depth interviews provide the researcher with the opportunity to "probe" answers to encourage interviewees to explain or build on their responses. It is also believed that probing may lead the discussion into areas that had not been previously considered, but which are significant and favors the collection of rich and detailed data (Saunders, Lewis, & Thornhill, 2007). Given the complexity of the questions selected for the interviews and the uncertainty about respondents' reactions to questions regarding political and religious aspects of the tourist experience in particular, semistructured interviews were chosen by the authors to obtain data. The interviews were conducted with experts, managers, and senior officers of private and public institutions within the tourism industry over a two month period in the spring of 2008. As respondents were sometimes located in different counties from that of the interviewer, a combination of face-to-face and telephone interviews was employed. Since the research aims to investigate an issue in-depth from a qualitative perspective, a purposeful sampling method was employed to choose the appropriate experts to interview. This allowed the researchers to select cases (interviewees) that would best answer the study aims (Hemmington, 1999; Patton, 2002).

Based on their experience, role, and influence in policymaking in tourism, 23 key experts were chosen among visitor and convention bureaus, city councils, the Northern Ireland Tourist Board, the Orange Order, organizations involved with walking, bus and taxi tours, community organizations, and two museums (see Table 1). Representatives were included with very different viewpoints in order to ensure that as complete a spectrum of opinion as possible was gained. Such a diverse range of experts also added

TABLE 1 Interviewees and Their Job Titles

Sector	Name of the institutions	Job titles
Public	Northern Ireland Tourist Board	Product Marketing Manager—Culture and Heritage
	Northern Ireland Tourist Board	The St. Patrick & Christian Heritage Signature Project Manager
	Northern Ireland Tourist Board	The Walled City of Derry Signature Project Manager
	Belfast City Council	Cultural Tourism Officer
	Derry City Council	Assistant Economic Development Officer
	Armagh City & District Council	Tourism Development Officer
	Down District Council	Tourism Development Manager
Public/Private	Belfast Visitor & Convention Bureau	Leisure Tourism Manager
	Belfast Visitor & Convention Bureau	Renewing Communities Visitor Servicing Project Officer
	Derry Visitor & Convention Bureau	Sales & Marketing Manager
	Armagh Down Tourism Partnership	Chief Executive
Private	Belfast City Sightseeing	Business Development Manager
	Coiste na n-Iarchimí	Coordinator for Coiste na n-Iarchimí Irish Political Tours
	Shankill Tourism	Tourism, Culture, and Art Development Officer
	TaxiTrax	Chairman
	Derry Taxi Tours	Chairman
	Free Derry Tours	Coordinator Manager
	The Apprentice Boys of Derry Memorial Hall	General Secretary
	Top Tours Ireland	Proprietor
	Armagh Guided Tours	Founder
	Legendary Days Out	Co-founder
	St Patrick's Centre	Director
	Orange Order	Belfast Orangefest Development Officer

Source: Simone-Charteris and Boyd (2008).

richness to the research. Each participant was further probed when necessary for any additional information (Saunders et al., 2007). All conversations were recorded: face-to-face interviews were recorded on a Dictaphone and telephone interviews via a telephone conversation recorder. This not only allowed to control bias and to produce reliable data for analysis, but also enabled the authors to concentrate more fully and listen attentively to the interviewees' responses (Saunders et al., 2007). All recordings were transcribed in verbatim format soon after completion, while still fresh in the researchers' minds, and notes were produced during the transcription process. This was important in terms of capturing and reflecting all verbal and nonverbal aspects of the interviews and observations.

The transcripts and notes were analyzed according to key themes (content analysis) which are used to present the findings of the research. By looking for key terms and phrases, lengthy transcripts of key-informant interviews, were reduced to manageable blocks of text (Stemler, 2001), from which relevant quotes have been selected. Since some respondents expressed the wish not to be identified, on occasions, the authors were unable to state the respondents' names. When this was the case, the organizations the respondents represented were stated instead.

There emerged a number of limitations to the research approach adopted. It is accepted that the findings are based on the authors' interpretations of the statements interviewees made on various topics. However, this is defended on the basis that the method allowed for an exact copy of the interview to be written down. Second, it is recognized that in the case of some interviewees their responses are very biased because of poor lines of communication between leading public sector bodies and private sector operators. The authors have experience in conducting deep interviews from a semistructured interview schedule, and are cognizant of the importance of ensuring that objectivity (minimizing bias) is maintained in the interpretation of both direct quotes and large sections of conversations and recognizing where lack of factual basis shapes opinions.

FINDINGS

The presentation of the key findings is structured around six main areas: the importance of religious tourism in terms of attracting visitors to Northern Ireland, the attractiveness of political tourism to out-of-state visitors, the potential for religious and political tourism to be promoted as politico-religious tourism, the willingness on behalf of tourist organizations to collaborate with the public and private sectors in order to assist opportunities associated with political and religious tourism, the willingness among the different tourist bodies to collaborate with political and religious institutions, and the role played by public and private tourist organizations in the development and promotion of religious and/or political tourism.

The Attractiveness of Religious Tourism to Out-of-State Visitors

All participants agreed that religious tourism or Christian heritage tourism as some preferred to refer to it, plays an important role in attracting visitors to Northern Ireland. The majority of interviewees described the link with St. Patrick and the numerous Christian sites associated with it, as something unique to the Province. Interviewees also unanimously believed that the Northern Ireland Tourist Board's St. Patrick & Christian Heritage Signature Project has potential to further improve the existing Christian heritage product and attract out-of-state visitors. Most interviewees, however, were dubious that the visitors' reasons are purely of a religious nature and believed that the market interested in visiting Christian heritage sites is represented by "culturalists and sightseers." One informant stated: "[Visitors] are not specifically looking for a religious experience; however they are interested in cultural experiences, architecture, authentic/unique experiences, heritage sites, etc." (Northern Ireland Tourist Board, personal communication, June 29, 2008). Moreover, some participants attributed the visitors' interest in the religious history of Northern Ireland to the interconnection of religion with politics, history, and culture in the Province. As one informant noted:

> In many ways you have got a political interest in the religious institutions in terms of something like St. Columb's Cathedral [in Londonderry/Derry] because it has Siege artifacts, which connects it to the political history . . . There is definitely an interest [in religious tourism]: whether it's because of religious, historical, or political reasons it's difficult to say. (M. Cooper, personal communication, June 25, 2008)

The Attractiveness of Political Tourism to Out-of-State Visitors

All interviewees also agreed that political tourism contributes to attracting visitors to Northern Ireland. Although some informants were uncertain whether political tourism is the main reason for visiting, they all agreed that when people are in the Province they want to find out more about the political history as well as engage in other more traditional activities. On the other hand, all participants stressed the importance of handling political tourism sensitively and in a balanced way because of its controversial nature. One informant commented that:

> We did research on this last year and the research told us that over 55% [of visitors] were on the tour purely because of politics; on the top of that 75% of people took the tour because it included some political aspect; there was only a very small amount, less than 5% that had no interest in politics at all . . . What the customers are telling us is that what is unique about Belfast is our political heritage, that political difference, they don't see it in any other city . . . People never had the chance to come here before, they are curious, so as long as things are done sensitively and in a balanced way, there is no reason why politics can't be at the heart of the tourism product . . . The unique selling point is our political divide and especially the evolution of that into peace. I would say that Northern Ireland now is regarded as one of the prime changed societies in the world for the likes of peace and conflict resolution. That is why [visitors] are here. (A. McCormack, personal communication, May 12, 2008)

The controversial nature of political tourism was also reflected by the resistance of some interviewees (both from the public and private sectors) to use the term political tourism. This was stated by one of the informants: "I wouldn't say political tourism; it's too harsh a statement; once you mention politics or religion that suggests bias, negativity . . . [political tourism] might be under this cultural thing, but I wouldn't brand it as political tourism" (Northern Ireland Tourist Board, personal communication, June 10, 2008). Another informant voiced a similar view:

> Political tourism is not a word that I would use, I would use cultural tourism and we very much want to be part of cultural tourism. I am not sure about political tourism. That word doesn't fit what we are trying to achieve. We are trying to achieve a better understanding of our history, of our traditions, and obviously of a culture that we all share. I would refer to it as cultural tourism rather than political tourism. (W. Moore, personal communication, June 27, 2008)

The Potential to Promote Politico-Religious Tourism

Although all interviewees agreed that both political and religious tourism contribute to attract visitors to the province, there were mixed views with regard to linking religious and political tourism and promoting them together. Half of the interviewees stated that religious and political tourism should not be promoted together. Of these a small group of respondents claimed that political and religious tourism are not intertwined because religion and politics are not interlinked in Northern Ireland. They believed that the conflict was never a religious conflict, but was portrayed as such by the British media for convenience. One interviewee stated:

> I believe that religion should be kept out of politics. I don't think the conflict in Northern Ireland was necessarily Protestant faith against Catholic faith . . . A lot of us grew up in areas that were mixed and we didn't care . . . The conflict was a political conflict . . . It was a very crafty manipulation by the government to portray it as a religious conflict. (R. Small, personal communication, May 20, 2008)

Another small group believed that although religion and politics are somehow interlinked in the Province, a joint promotion of political and religious tourism would only exacerbate certain sensitivities and polarize situations even more. One interviewee also stated that promoting religious and political tourism together could be off-putting for visitors:

> You need to be very careful as to what your consumer is looking for and you could end up upsetting those who are looking for some sort of pilgrimage/spiritual/cultural heritage experience. By linking these together I think it is a specialized niche. (Northern Ireland Tourist Board, personal communication, June 29, 2008)

In contrast, the remaining half of the participants believed that because religion and politics are so closely interlinked in Northern Ireland, in order to explain the Province historically and culturally to visitors, it is important that religious and political tourism are not separated. One participant even affirmed that it is actually impossible to separate them:

> Initially people come to Armagh with a curiosity to visit the cathedrals and obviously they are either one denomination or the other . . . So it turns indirectly into a political tour as well because you can't explain the history of the church without going into [politics]. (B. Ferguson, personal communication, June 18, 2008)

This group also indicated that political and religious tourism should be packaged together and promoted as cultural tourism. One interviewee summed this up in the following manner:

> We aren't promoting the Museum of Free Derry to the detriment of the Apprentice Boys Museum because we see each of those communities have their story to tell within the history of the city . . . What we want to do is to give each the space to tell their own story and when we bring all those stories together, then only then we have the story of the whole city . . . We are not packaging it as political tourism or religious tourism; it's cultural tourism and it's part of the city's culture and these are the influences that have made the people what we are now and the city what it is now. (D. Harrigan, personal communication, June 19, 2008)

Tourist Organizations' Willingness to Collaborate with the Public and Private Sectors

As regards cooperation in order to assist opportunities associated with political and religious sites and attractions, most interviewees stated that they already collaborate with both public and private sector organizations. Nonetheless, the general view among private sector organizations was that the statutory bodies are too bureaucratic, slow, and fragmented. For example, one private sector organization stated:

> It seems to us that any time we work with the government agencies we are dealing with civil servants, who have no real awareness of the commercial realities and no real awareness of the day-to-day tourism issues . . . The problem with Northern Ireland civil service is [that there are] five or six departments and they all have a wee bit of responsibility, so you are dealing with different people who don't talk to each other . . . Certainly [cooperation] is possible, we would always be happy to work with anybody, but sometimes it's just unfeasible. (A. McCormack, May 12, 2008)

Some private tourist organizations also stated that while they would be happy and willing to collaborate with public tourist bodies, at the same time they would not be prepared to loose their identity or to provide watered down versions of their story in the name of compromise. From the point of view of private sector organizations collaborating with each other, some indicated competition as one of the main difficulties. On the other hand, most public sector bodies stated that private sector organizations should be less reliant on the statutory bodies and should contribute more financially. This point was illustrated by one public sector organization:

> Obviously we would love to be in a position where the private sector makes a bigger contribution to assist us, but the private sector is not a vibrant private sector yet. Unlike other countries in the world that have had good tourism, we are coming out after many years of struggling . . . People are now starting to do well, but they still have the perception that it is up to [the public sector] to promote them . . . That's one of the difficulties. (A. Gilchrist, personal communication, June 26, 2008)

Tourist Organizations' Willingness to Collaborate with Political and Religious Institutions

When asked if they would collaborate with political and religious institutions, all public sector bodies agreed that it is essential to collaborate with organizations of this kind in order to provide authentic experiences, which are also acceptable to the local communities. Most public sector bodies stated that the way they collaborate with these organizations is by means of providing training and organizing workshops to facilitate networking opportunities and exposure to the international media. Some public sector organizations, however, also stated that there was a need for leadership to be provided by the government on how to liaise with organizations of this type. For example, one informant stated:

> These are all the bodies involved in telling the story . . . We need some direction from DETI [Department of Enterprise, Trade and Investment] and they are currently writing a policy paper on how the last 30 years . . . Really the barriers and boundaries to it . . . Once policy has been established and there is agreement about how the story is told, then absolutely [we would collaborate]. (Northern Ireland Tourist Board, personal communication, July 8, 2008)

As for private sector organizations, all participants but one indicated that they already collaborate with other organizations, which promote the same type of tourism or they would if opportunities arose, for example, if money was made available. One informant even stated: "If this had been done years ago, then possibly we wouldn't have had 3,500 deaths in our country. There would have been a better understanding of each other's communities and each other's traditions" (W. Moore, personal communication, June 27, 2008). The only interviewee, who stated that collaboration was not an option, made this point:

> At this point in time, at this juncture in the history of our organization, we would have nothing to do with ex-prisoners organizations. We did not support paramilitaries on the unionist side and certainly we will not be supporting anything to do with republican ex-prisoners. We are conscious that not only did they murder thousands of people here both Roman Catholics and Protestants, but they murdered over 300 Orangemen mostly off duty in the Orange Halls and in their churches in foul and despicable ways . . . So the answer to that one is a resounding no. (Orange Order, personal communication, June 9, 2008)

The Role of Public and Private Tourist Organizations in the Development and Promotion of Religious and Political Tourism

With regard to their role in the development and promotion of religious and/or political tourism, there was a conflict of views between public and private sector interviewees. In fact, although all public sector institutions believed that the private sector should lead, they admitted that in fact the statutory authorities were leading because the private sector was not mature enough yet. However, private sector organizations too believed that they played a major role as in most cases they developed the tourism product on the ground, engaged the communities, and promoted themselves. For example, an interviewee argued:

> Whenever we started the company there was no tourism product at all . . . We more or less had to develop a whole tourism product our own, design our route and whole infrastructure of the business, especially in those areas that never had a tourism product before. There was a lot of community engagement; communities were a wee bit cautious; people thought it's not fair to come and stare at us from a bus . . . It's now regarded to be completely normal. (A. McCormack, personal communication, May 12, 2008)

DISCUSSIONS

The findings revealed that all organizations both from the public and private sector recognize the importance of religious tourism and political tourism in terms of attracting visitors to Northern Ireland. This is in line with Timothy and Olsen's (2006) view that religious tourism is one of the most significant types of tourism in the world today and that visitors are increasingly being attracted by sites of death and disaster (Foley & Lennon, 1996; Lennon & Foley, 2000). However, it emerged that while all organizations are happy to debate and support religious tourism as connected to St. Patrick and the Christian heritage, there are still sensitivities surrounding the terms political tourism and religious tourism as they are connected to the Troubles. Because of this, many avoid using the term political tourism and refer to it as cultural tourism. Accordingly, the need to handle political tourism sensitively and in a balanced way was stressed.

Second, and in contrast with current research which highlights the existence of links between religion and politics (Green, 2003), the study revealed that there was no consensus around the intertwinement of religion and politics in Northern Ireland. In fact, while some believed that the two are inexorably interlinked, others believed that the interconnection was an artificial creation of the British media and that while the two communities involved in the conflict happened to be Protestant and Catholic, the nature of the conflict was not religious but political. As a consequence, there were mixed views with regard to linking political and religious tourism and promoting them together as politico-religious tourism. In fact, even those who believed that religion and politics are connected in Northern Ireland feared that the promotion of politico-religious tourism could be perceived negatively and had the potential to polarize the sensitivities mentioned above. As a result, the Northern Ireland Tourist Board and other statutory bodies prefer to promote political tourism and religious tourism as connected to the Troubles under the cultural tourism umbrella.

Third, the research indicated that cooperation is welcomed by both the public and private sectors. However, the private sector complained that dealing with the statutory authorities was a difficult and frustrating process due to the bureaucracy involved and because of the existence of numerous government departments with overlapping responsibilities. In addition, private sector organizations stated that they were not prepared to provide sanitized accounts of the conflict and the history of Northern Ireland to please public sector institutions. They also suggested that sometimes it was difficult to collaborate with other private tourist organizations because of the competitive nature of the tourism industry. On the other hand, public sector organizations suggested that the private sector is not as proactive and financially independent as it should be. The findings also indicated that most organizations would collaborate with political and religious institutions, although some found dealing with ex-prisoners organizations too much of a challenge. Moreover, some public tourist organizations believed that the government should provide clear leadership as to how to deal with organizations involved with politics and religion. It follows that the relationship between public and some private sector organizations is an uneasy one and that there are some barriers that need to be overcome before trust is instilled and cooperation can take place. Perhaps private and public sector organizations are simply not used to work in partnership because during the Troubles there would have not been many private organizations involved in the business of tourism. In addition, the lack of trust could be rooted in the political history of the Province as a certain number of private organizations are community and ex-prisoners' organizations while the public tourist sector tends to be associated with the statutory authorities.

Fourth, the findings revealed that there were conflicting views between the private and public tourism sectors in relation to the role they played in the development and promotion of religious and political tourism, and with regard to their respective responsibilities. In fact, both sectors believed that they played a major role and each sector believed that their counterpart should contribute more. In addition, it emerged that public and private sector had differing interests and priorities. For example, while the Northern Ireland Tourist Board is prioritizing the development and promotion of Christian Heritage and its link with St. Patrick, and believes that markets are not motivated to visit Northern Ireland by political tourism, private tourism organizations maintain that political tourism is a key driver at the moment. It is essential that the confusion regarding public and private sector's roles and responsibilities is overcome and that cooperation is embraced for religious and political tourism to develop successfully. Private sector organizations, in fact, possess invaluable knowledge of the attractions and sites forming the religious and political tourism products on the ground in their area, while public sector tourist bodies and political institutions possess the resources, networks, expertise, and lobbying power much needed by the private sector organizations.

Finally, it emerged that the viewpoint held by many in the private sector is incorrect when it comes to the role played by the National Tourism Organization, as this latter body recognizes that political tourism is an emergent attraction for many visitors. Although political tourism is not mentioned in any of the tourism information produced by the Northern Ireland Tourist Board, it is promoted under the wider cultural tourism umbrella, encouraging visitors to "experience our awakening" and "uncover our stories" (NITB, 2008a).

CONCLUSIONS, LIMITATIONS, AND FUTURE RESEARCH

This research set out to investigate the interconnections of religious tourism and political tourism using Northern Ireland as a case study. Through an exploratory investigation, the article sought to ascertain the extent to which public and private tourism sector organizations supported the promotion of politico-religious tourism in the Province and whether willingness existed, among the different players, to collaborate in order to assist opportunities associated with political and religious sites and attractions and promote this specialized form of tourism.

Based on the findings of this research, the authors argue for caution in linking religious and political tourism at this time; instead there is stronger support across industry sectors to embrace religious and political tourism as separate entities and to present these to visitors under less emotive terms such as cultural tourism. The research findings also suggest that while different viewpoints are held across public and private sector tourist organizations with regard to their roles and responsibilities in the development and promotion of religious and political tourism, there is equally scope to have strong effective management to create partnerships to develop these niche tourism products.

However, the present investigation has a number of limitations. First of all it is at the stage of a single case study and, therefore, it does not allow for the generalization of results. More comprehensive research that embraces comparative investigations is required to uncover similarities and differences. Second, the interpretivistic nature of the research approach adopted has implications in terms of research validity and researcher bias. Future research should consider different research designs perhaps of a more quantitative nature. Moreover, the interconnections between religious and political tourism based on the similarities between the motivations of religious and political tourists and their use of similar cultural heritage attractions are not investigated in this article through the perspective of visitors, but only through those industry sectors that are responsible for the planning and development of these niche tourist products.

In order to establish if political and religious tourism can be connected, a detailed survey of visitor expectation is needed. This is however beyond the scope of this study, but nonetheless important in order to understand if the boundaries between politics, religion, and tourism by visitors are seen as linked, fuzzy, or separate. Such research is currently underway by the authors. A decade after a peace settlement being put in place for Northern Ireland, its tourism industry is coming of age in how it promotes the destination and communicates its past to visitors. Political tourism must become part of the story that is told to visitors; it, however, must remain only part of the offering as the destination has more to offer in terms of culture and heritage.

REFERENCES

Alderman, D. H. (2002). Writing on the Graceland wall: On the importance of authorship in pilgrimage landscapes. *Tourism Recreation Research*, *27*(2), 27–33.

Altinay, L., & Bowen, D. (2006). Politics and tourism interface: The case of Cyprus. *Annals of Tourism Research*, *33*, 939–956.

Baum, G. (2000). Solidarity with the poor. In S. M. P. Harper (Ed.), *The lab, the temple, and the market* (pp. 123–135). Ottawa, Ontario, Canada: International Development Research Centre.

Belfast City Council. (2006). *Cultural tourism strategy*. Belfast, Ireland: Author.

Blasi, A. J. (2002). Visitation to disaster sites. In W. H. Swatos & L. Tomasi (Eds.), *From medieval pilgrimage to religious tourism* (pp. 139–155). Westport, CT: Praeger.

Boyd, S. W. (2000). "Heritage" tourism in Northern Ireland: Opportunity under peace. *Current Issues in Tourism, 3*, 150–174.

Brin, E. (2006). Politically-oriented tourism in Jerusalem. *Tourist Studies, 6*, 215–243.

Burnhill, E. (2007). Weeds and wild flowers: Political tourism in West Belfast. Retrieved from http://www.eurozine.com

Card, J. A., & Kestel, C. (1988). Motivational factors and demographic characteristics of travelers to and from Germany. *Society and Leisure, 11*(1), 49–58.

Casson, L. (1974). *Travel in the ancient world*. London, England: Allen and Unwin.

Causevic, S., & Lynch, P. (2007, April). *The significance of dark tourism in the process of tourism development after a long-term political conflict: An issue of Northern Ireland*. Paper Presented at the ASA Conference 2007, Thinking Through Tourism, London Metropolitan University, London.

Clarke, R. (2000). Self-presentation in a contested city: Palestinian and Israeli political tourism in Hebron. *Anthropology Today, 16*(5), 12–18.

Collins-Kreiner, N., & Gatrell, J. D. (2006). Tourism, heritage and pilgrimage: The case of Haifa's Baháʾí Gardens. *Journal of Heritage Tourism, 1*(1), 32–50.

Conran, T. (2002). Solemn witness: A pilgrimage to Ground Zero at the World Trade Centre. *Journal of Systemic Therapies, 21*(3), 39–47.

Crompton, J. L. (1979). Motivations for pleasure vacation. *Annals of Tourism Research, 6*, 408–424.

Crooke, E. (2005). Dealing with the past: Museums and heritage in Northern Ireland and Cape Town, South Africa. *International Journal of Heritage Studies, 11*(2), 131–142.

Devine, A., & Connor, R. (2005, June). *Cultural tourism—promoting diversity in the aftermath of conflict*. Paper Presented at the Tourism and Hospitality Research in Ireland: Exploring the Issues Conference, University of Ulster, Portrush.

Digance, J. (2003). Pilgrimage at contested sites. *Annals of Tourism Research, 30*(1), 143–159.

Foley, M., & Lennon, J. (1996). JFK and dark tourism: A fascination with assassination. *International Journal of Heritage Studies, 2*, 198–212.

Gammon, S. (2004). Secular pilgrimage and sport tourism. In B. W. Ritchie & D. Adair (Eds.), *Sport tourism: Interrelationships, impacts and issues* (pp. 57–70). Clevedon, England: Channel View.

Graham, B. J. (1994). Heritage conservation and revisionist nationalism in Ireland. In G. J. Ashworth & P. Larkham (Eds.), *Building a new heritage: Tourism, culture and identity in the new Europe* (pp. 135–158). London, England: Routledge.

Green, W. S. (2003). Religion and politics—a volatile mix. In J. Neusner (Ed.), *God's rule: The politics of world religions* (pp. 1–9). Washington, DC: Georgetown University Press.

Guth, K. (1995). Pilgrimages in contemporary Europe: Signs of national and universal culture. *History of European Ideas*, *20*(4–6), 821–835.

Hall, C. M. (1994). *Tourism and politics: Policy, power and place*. Chichester, England: Wiley.

Hall, C. M. (2002). ANZAC Day and secular pilgrimage. *Tourism Recreation Research*, *27*(2), 87–91.

Hall, C. M. (2006). Travel and journeying on the sea of faith: Perspectives from religious humanism. In D. J. Timothy & D. H. Olsen (Eds.), *Tourism, Religion & Spiritual Journeys* (pp. 64–77). Oxford, England: Routledge.

Hall, C. M., & O'Sullivan, V. (1996). Tourism, political stability and violence. In A. Pizam & Y. Mansfeld, (Eds.), *Tourism, crime and international security issues* (pp. 105–121). New York, NY: Wiley.

Hall, C. M., & Weiler, B. (1992). Introduction: What's special about special interest tourism? In B. Weiler & C. M. Hall (Eds.), *Special interest tourism* (pp. 1–14). London, England: Belhaven Press.

Heelas, P. (1998). Introduction: On differentiation and dedifferentiation. In P. Heelas (Ed.), *Religion, modernity and postmodernity* (pp. 1–17). Oxford, England: Blackwell.

Hemmington, N. (1999). Sampling. In B. Brotherton (Ed.), *The contemporary hospitality management research* (pp. 235–244). New York, NY: Wiley.

Henderson, J. C. (2007). Communism, heritage and tourism in East Asia. *International Journal of Heritage Studies*, *13*, 240–254.

Herbert, D. (2001). Literary places, tourism and the heritage experience. *Annals of Tourism Research*, *28*, 312–333.

Johnstone, I. M. (1994). A visit to the Western front: A pilgrimage tour of World War I cemeteries and memorials in Northern France and Belgium, August–September 1993. *Australian Folklore*, *9*, 60–76.

Kaelber, L. (2006). Paradigms of travel: From medieval pilgrimage to the postmodern virtual tour. In D. J. Timothy & D. H. Olsen (Eds.), *Tourism, religion & spiritual journeys* (pp. 49–63). Oxford, England: Routledge.

Kneafsey, M. (1994). The cultural tourist: Patron saint of Ireland. In U. Kockel (Ed.), *Culture, tourism and development—the case of Ireland* (pp. 104–117). Liverpool, England: University Press.

Knight, C. K. (1999). Mickey, Minnie, and Mecca: Destination Disney World. Pilgrimage in the twentieth century. In D. Perlmutter & D. Koppman (Eds.), *Reclaiming the spiritual in art* (pp. 36–48). Albany, NY: State University of New York Press.

Kozak, M. (2002). Comparative analysis of tourist motivations by nationality and destinations. *Tourism Management*, *23*, 221–232.

Lennon, J., & Foley, M. (2000). *Dark tourism: The attractions of death and disaster*. London, England: Continuum.

Lloyd, D. W. (1998). *Battlefield tourism*. New York, NY: Berg.

McCormick, J., & Jarman, N. (2005). Death of a mural. *Journal of Material Culture*, *10*(1), 49–71.

McDowell, S. (2008). Selling conflict heritage through tourism in peacetime Northern Ireland: Transforming conflict or exacerbating difference? *International Journal of Heritage Studies*, *14*, 405–421.

Morinis, E. A. (1992). Introduction: The territory of the anthropology of pilgrimage. In E. A. Morinis (Ed.), *Sacred journeys: The anthropology of pilgrimage* (pp. 1–14). Westport, CT: Greenwood.

Nic Craith, M. (2003). *Culture and identity politics in Northern Ireland*. Hampshire, England: Palgrave Macmillan.

Northern Ireland Assembly. (2009). Retrieved http://www.niassembly.gov.uk/the-work.htm

Northern Ireland Assembly Official Report. (2008, February 19). Northern Ireland Assembly. *Hansard,* 27. Retrieved from http://www.niassembly.gov.uk/record/reports2007/080219.htm

Northern Ireland Tourist Board. (2000). *Building the proposition: Foundations of future tourism in Northern Ireland*. Belfast, Ireland: Author.

Northern Ireland Tourist Board. (2003). *Visits to NI and revenue generated (1959–2003)*. Belfast, Ireland: Author.

Northern Ireland Tourist Board. (2005). *Tourism facts 2004*. Belfast, Ireland: Author.

Northern Ireland Tourist Board. (2006a). *Culture and Heritage Tourism Action Plan 2005*. Belfast, Ireland: Author.

Northern Ireland Tourist Board. (2006b). *Tourism facts 2005*. Belfast, Ireland: Author.

Northern Ireland Tourist Board. (2007). *Tourism facts 2006*. Belfast, Ireland: Author.

Northern Ireland Tourist Board. (2008a). *Planning our route to success. Northern Ireland tourist board corporate plan 2008–2011*. Belfast, Ireland: Author.

Northern Ireland Tourist Board. (2008b). *Tourism facts 2007*. Belfast, Ireland: Author.

Olsen, D. H. (2006). Management issues for religious heritage attractions. In D. J. Timothy & D. H. Olsen (Eds.), *Tourism, religion & spiritual journeys* (pp. 104–118). Oxford, England: Routledge.

Olsen, D. H., & Timothy, D. J. (2006). Tourism and religious journeys. In D. J. Timothy & D. H. Olsen (Eds.), *Tourism, religion & spiritual journeys* (pp. 1–21). Oxford, England: Routledge.

Pahl, J. (2003). Pilgrimage to the Mall of America. *Word and World, 23*, 263–271.

Patton, M. Q. (2002). *Qualitative evaluation and research methods* (3rd ed.). Thousand Oaks, CA: Sage.

Peace Line Tours. (2006). *Northern Ireland murals, pictures of Belfast murals*. Retrieved from http://peacelinetours.g2gm.com

Poria, Y., Butler, R., & Airey, D. (2003). Tourism, religion and religiosity: A holy mess. *Current Issues in Tourism, 6*, 340–363.

Richter, L. K. (1983). Tourism politics and political science: A case of not so benign neglect. *Annals of Tourism Research, 10*, 313–315.

Rinschede, G. (1992). Forms of religious tourism. *Annals of Tourism Research, 19*(1), 51–67.

Robinson, M., & Novelli, M. (2005). Niche tourism: An introduction. In M. Novelli (Ed.), *Niche tourism: Contemporary issues, trends and cases* (pp. 1–14). Oxford, England: Elsevier Butterworth-Heinemann.

Rountree, K. (2002). Goddess pilgrims as tourists: Inscribing their body through sacred travel. *Sociology of Religion, 63*, 475–496.

Ryan, C., & Glendon, I. (1998). Application of leisure motivation scale to tourism. *Annals of Tourism Research, 25*(1), 169–184.

Santos, X. M. (2002). Pilgrimage and tourism at Santiago de Compostela. *Tourism Recreation Research, 27*(2), 41–50.

Saunders, M., Lewis, P., & Thornhill, A. (2007). *Research methods for business students* (4th ed.). Harlow, England: Prentice Hall.

Seaton, A. V. (2002). Thanatourism's final frontiers? Visits to cemeteries, churchyards and funerary sites as sacred and secular pilgrimage. *Tourism Recreation Research, 27*(2), 73–82.

Shackley, M. (2001a). *Managing sacred sites: Service provision and visitor experience.* London, England: Thomson.

Shackley, M. (2001b). Potential futures for Robben Island: Shrine, museum or theme park? *International Journal of Heritage Studies, 7*, 355–363.

Shackley, M. (2002). Space, sanctity and service: The English cathedral as heterotopia. *International Journal of Tourism Research, 4*, 345–352.

Sharpley, R., & Sundaram, P. (2005). Tourism: A sacred journey? The case of ashram tourism, India. *International Journal of Tourism Research, 7*(1), 161–171.

Sigaux, J. (1996). *History of tourism.* London, England: Leisure Arts.

Simone-Charteris, M. T., & Boyd, S. W. (2008, November). *The potential for Northern Ireland to promote politico-religious tourism.* Paper Presented at the International Tourism Conference 2008: Cultural and Event Tourism: Issues & Debates, Akdeniz University, Alanya, Turkey.

Smith, M. K. (2003). *Issues in cultural tourism studies.* London, England: Routledge.

Smith, V. L. (1992). Introduction: The quest in guest. *Annals of Tourism Research, 19*(1), 1–17.

Smith, V. L. (1996). War and its tourist attractions. In A. Pizam & Y. Mansfeld (Eds.), *Tourism, crime and international security issues* (pp. 247–264). New York, NY: Wiley.

Solidarity Boosts P. A. Tourism, But Not Enough. (2006). Retrieved from http://www.themedialine.org

Stemler, S. (2001). An overview of content analysis. *Practical Assessment, Research & Evaluation, 7*(17). Retrieved from http://pareonline.net/getvn.asp?v=7&n=17

Timothy, D. J. (2001). *Tourism and political boundaries.* London, England: Routledge.

Timothy, D. J., & Boyd, S. W. (2003). *Heritage tourism.* Harlow, England: Prentice Hall.

Timothy, D. J., & Boyd, S. W. (2006). Heritage tourism in the 21st century: Valued traditions and new perspectives. *Journal of Heritage Tourism, 1*(1), 1–16.

Timothy, D. J., & Olsen, D. H. (2006). Conclusion: Whither religious tourism? In D. J. Timothy & D. H. Olsen (Eds.), *Tourism, religion & spiritual journeys* (pp. 271–278). Oxford, England: Routledge.

Tomasi, L. (2002). Homo viator: From pilgrimage to religious tourism via the journey. In W. H. Swatos Jr. & L. Tomasi (Eds.), *From medieval pilgrimage to religious tourism: The social and cultural economics of piety* (pp. 70–91). Westport, CT: Praeger.

Vukonić, B. (1996). *Tourism and religion.* Oxford, England: Pergamon.

Vukonić, B. (2002). Religion, tourism and economics: A convenient symbiosis. *Tourism Recreation Research*, 27(2), 59–64.

Wall, G. (1996). Terrorism and tourism: An overview and an Irish example. In A. Pizam & Y. Mansfeld (Eds.), *Tourism, crime and international security issues* (pp. 143–156). Chichester, England: John Wiley & Sons.

Weiler, B., & Hall, C. M. (1992). Conclusion. Special interest tourism: In search of an alternative. In B. Weiler & C. M. Hall (Eds.), *Special interest tourism* (pp. 199–204). London, England: Belhaven Press.

Westwood, J. (1997). *Sacred journeys: An illustrated guide to pilgrimages around the world*. New York, NY: Harry Holt.

Wilson, D. (1993). Tourism, public policy and the image of Northern Ireland since the troubles. In B. O'Connor & M. Cronin (Eds.), *Tourism in Ireland: A critical analysis* (pp. 138–161). Cork, Ireland: Cork University Press.

Yavuz, N., Baloglu, S., & Uysal, M. (1998). Market segmentation of European and Turkish travelers to North Cyprus. *Anatolia*, 9(1), 4–18.

Zelinsky, W. (1990). Nationalistic pilgrimages in the United States. In G. Rinschede & S. M. Bhardwaj (Eds.), *Pilgrimage in the United States* (pp. 105–120). Berlin, Germany: Dietrich Reimer Verlag.

The Potential of Small Tourism Operators in the Promotion of Pro-Poor Tourism

JENNIFER BRIEDENHANN

Department of Travel and Aviation, Bucks New University,
High Wycombe Campus, Buckinghamshire, United Kingdom

South Africa, like many developing countries, views tourism as a panacea to the evils of poverty that bedevil the country's rural African communities. Whilst there has been substantial growth in the tourism sector since 1994, the anticipated benefits have not materialized for those most in need of an improved quality of life. Work undertaken in the field of pro-poor tourism focuses predominantly on the large tourism actors and their potential role in the alleviation of poverty through the development of sustainable supply chains and joint venture arrangements. The role that could be played by the myriad small operators, who collectively comprise the bulk of the South African tourism industry, has largely been ignored. This article argues that greater attention should be paid to the cumulative potential of small tourism operators to play a significant role in the alleviation of poverty through tourism to the mutual benefit of both operators and local communities.

INTRODUCTION

Over the past decade, attention has increasingly focused on the concept of pro-poor tourism (Hall, 2007) as the engine of development which unlocks opportunities for the poor through the enhancement of tourism's positive, and concurrent reduction of its negative, impacts (Ashley, Bennett, & Roe, 1999, p. iii). In postapartheid South Africa, emphasis has been placed on the role of tourism as a means of mitigating poverty (Nel & Binns, 2001). In particular tourism is propounded as a panacea to the evils of poverty and underdevelopment that bedevil the country's rural African communities. In Dann's (2002, p. 236) terms, tourism has come to be regarded as a "passport to development." The Tourism White Paper (Government of South Africa, 1996, p. 19) promotes the development of "a new tourism . . . that would boost other sectors of the economy and create entrepreneurial opportunities for the previously neglected groups." It further describes this "new tourism" as being responsible, sensitive to host cultures, involving local communities in planning and decision-making, and ensuring their involvement in and benefit from tourism. Furthermore, the Tourism White Paper places an onus on local communities to become actively involved in the tourism industry, to practice sustainable development and to ensure the safety and security of visitors. The definition of pro-poor tourism as:

> Tourism that results in increased net benefits for poor people . . . an approach to tourism development and management. It enhances the linkages between tourism businesses and poor people, so that tourism's contribution to poverty reduction is increased and poor people are able to participate more effectively in product development (Ashley, 2002, p. 18)

is thus well aligned to the precepts of the type of tourism development envisaged in the South African Tourism White Paper. Furthermore, the concept of pro-poor tourism does not imply the restriction of benefits solely to the poor "non-poor people may also benefit as much or more from pro-poor tourism development" (Ashley et al., 1999, p. 6). This article focuses on a case study of a cultural village, which, although neither developed nor recognized as a pro-poor tourism project, has proved that a small rural enterprise can have significant impact on the lives of local people and the sustainability of the project itself.

CONCEPTUALIZING PRO-POOR TOURISM

There is evidence of confusion in relation to the interpretation of pro-poor tourism. In their study on sustainable development and poverty alleviation, Ashley et al. (1999, p. 14) specifically differentiated between sustainable tourism, in which benefits to local people are perceived as a means of achieving sustainability; community-based tourism, in which the aim is the expansion of enterprises run by local communities; and pro-poor tourism, which places net benefits to the poor as the underlying goal. Goodwin (2005) highlights three categories of benefits to be derived from pro-poor tourism: economic benefits; livelihood benefits which may include improved living conditions, such as a clean water supply; and the empowerment of the poor. Pro-poor tourism includes the aims and benefits of sustainable and community-based tourism but additionally accentuates the maximization of local employment and services, the expansion of local linkages, and the development of infrastructure that benefits the poor. Furthermore, tourism fits well with the concept of pro-poor growth due to its labor intensive and inclusive nature and its ability to build on the natural and cultural assets of poor rural communities with few other growth options (Scheyvens, 2007). However, despite the assertion that pro-poor tourism is neither a specific product nor a niche sector but an approach to tourism development and management, Harrison (2008) argues for a change from the narrow focus on pro-poor tourism to one in which the potential of mass tourism, as an agent of poverty alleviation and catalyst of development, receives increased attention.

It can be argued that the work undertaken in the field of pro-poor tourism, particularly in the South African context, has focused predominantly on the large tourism actors (hotels, wine estates, game lodges) and their potential role in the alleviation of poverty through the development of sustainable supply chains, joint ventures and linkages with local communities and entrepreneurs. Much of the work undertaken has been government funded (for example the SDI program at Makulele and Manyeleti and the St. Lucia Heritage Tourism Program; Ashley, 2005). In addition, under new Local Economic Development (LED) initiatives, local authorities have formulated strategies aimed at the promotion of indigenous arts and crafts, visits to South Africa's black townships and the development of cultural tourism enterprises and activities (Binns & Nel, 2002). The role that could be played by small, private sector tourism operators, who collectively comprise the bulk of the South African tourism industry, has to date largely been ignored. This is, however, not untoward. "Small businesses make up about 97% of the total tourism industry and can cumulatively have a significant impact but they are generally excluded from certification schemes" (Roe, Harris, & de Andrade, 2003, p. 18).

The South African National Tourism White Paper placed emphasis on the role of tourism as a catalyst for the development of rural areas listing the use of "tourism to aid the development of rural communities" as a key economic objective (Government of South Africa, 1996, p. 25). Furthermore, Matlou (2001), a senior official in the Department of Environmental Affairs and Tourism, propounded that tourism growth should be integrated with environmental management, job creation, rural development, and poverty alleviation in a manner which would ensure its contribution to the improvement of the quality of life of all South Africans. Whilst Sharpley (2002) acknowledged that tourism has long been perceived as an effective tool of rural economic development, he questions the tendency to regard tourism as the universal remedy to the ills of rural areas. Others (e.g., Roberts & Hall, 2001) cautioned that the benefits of rural tourism are seldom widely spread since rural tourism operators generally focus solely on their own businesses rather than considering how they might actively contribute to wider development goals, a factor which diminishes their contribution to the rural economy and the host community. Goodwin (2005) purported that the benefits of pro-poor tourism include diversification of the local tourism product and the enrichment of the tourism experience through addition of complementary products that benefit new entrants and established stakeholders. Previous research in South Africa found evidence that, whilst champions of projects with a pro-poor tourism focus emphasize the importance and the difficulties of networking, operators failed to see the contribution of collaboration and community linkages to the wider development goals of the area or the benefits that could be leveraged from addition to the diversity of product and the resultant potential for longer stays in the area (Briedenhann, 2004). Access to markets is said to require pushing, pulling, and punting at all levels but particularly mainstream tourism business. "The trick was not to take away their business but to add value to the product and to convince them of this" (Rossouw, 1999, p. 8). The obdurate attitude, evinced by the mainstream tourism industry, runs contrary to Greffe's (1994) contention that the establishment of networks of different service providers presents a unique opportunity for rural operators to manage in terms of economies of scope, something which individually they are not able to accomplish. Furthermore, the development of such networks offers the opportunity for the inclusion of small entrepreneurial ventures managed by the local community.

PRO-POOR TOURISM STRATEGIES

Proponents emphasize that the strength of the concept is the fact that it integrates a wide range of interlinked strategies all of which should be considered, as opposed to concentrating only on one issue such as employment (Meyer, 2003). However, in a study undertaken to assess the impacts and costs of pro-poor tourism strategies in South Africa, researchers found that the impact of most significance to the poor arose from employment and wages earned (Spenceley & Seif, 2003). The importance of this issue is exemplified by the snowball effect of tourism employment in rural communities. In one instance, 20 employees in a small rural hotel were found to be supporting 140 local community residents. It was alleged "jobs are valued far more than actual ownership of tourism product—jobs are everything" (Briedenhann, 2004, p. 206). Operator benefits in this regard are encapsulated in the argument that local people stay in employment longer since they are within their own social network.

The establishment of business linkages is instrumental in implementing a pro-poor tourism approach. A business unit that supports linkages between business and communities has been established in South Africa to offer guidance and facilitation in extending the scope and scale of linkages with a pro-poor tourism emphasis. There are two issues of particular interest in the project, which spawned this unit. Firstly, the project was run in collaboration with so-termed "leading industry partners" (Wilderness Safaris; Southern Sun; Sun City; Spier and Ker and Downey, Tanzania). Secondly, the project was scarcely cost effective with only 24 linkages, creating fewer than 8 jobs each, resulting from a grant of £225,000. The point is, however, made that the linkages created were with new suppliers and partners rather than pre-existing businesses (see Ashley, 2006). Since rural tourism operators are generally widely dispersed, in areas adjacent to poor communities, this begs the question as to whether linkages could not be more cost-effectively established by these enterprises creating employment, and the opportunity for the community to supply the establishment with produce and sell locally produced artifacts to its tourists. If all small operators in a particular area worked collaboratively in establishing such linkages the cumulative impact could be substantial.

Throughout the literature emphasis is placed on "empowerment." There are, however, many different interpretations of this concept. The Pro-Poor Tourism Partnership (2004) asserts "empowerment occurs when people take greater control over the social and institutional context that affects their livelihood." Taylor (2000, p. 4) concurs that empowerment processes are those "which result in people exercising more control over the decisions and resources that directly affect the quality of their lives." Others underscore the importance of enhancing human capacity, what Sen (1984, p. 510) termed as a focus "on what people can do or can be." Fetterman (2001, p. 3) concurred, emphasizing that nobody can empower somebody else "people empower themselves, often with assistance and coaching." Fetterman further argued that processes aimed at empowerment are those that help people to develop the skills needed to solve their own problems and take their own decisions.

Researchers (e.g., Timothy & Tosun, 2003) emphasize that for tourism development to bring benefits to poor communities a "people-centric" approach must be adopted, in which voices of local communities are heard and decisions relating to the type, scale and rate of tourism development informed by their input. The imperative of enhancing human capacity in poor communities is thus underscored both by the literature and by the pro-poor principle of involving local communities in decision-making in relation to tourism development and the utilization of assets and resources. In South Africa historic lack of access to tourism either as entrepreneurs or tourists has engendered limited understanding of tourism, its impacts or its potential benefits amongst its marginalized rural communities. As a result of this many communities do not realize their own potential, or the value of their resources, as tourist attractions (Briedenhann & Wickens, 2004). Furthermore, those initiating discussion with communities frequently have little understanding of the state of readiness of communities to engage in development planning or decision-making. Engagement thus becomes a slow, ongoing process in which people need time to absorb and unravel concepts that hitherto have been foreign to them (Fowkes & Jonsson, 1994). The ability to take decisions based on an understanding of the consequences and implications of those decisions is crucial lest poor rural communities, desperate for alleviation of their economic hardship, accept any proposal that portends to offer economic growth, with little or no consideration of future detrimental impacts (Kinsley, 2000, p. 1). Although Timothy (2000) places the onus for development of tourism awareness on government, he fails to take into account that in less developed countries, such as South Africa, many tourism officials are ill equipped to understand the complexities of tourism and are frequently the origin of the unrealistic expectations that are fostered amongst communities (Briedenhann, 2008).

The disparate outcomes of two tourism-led development projects in South Africa portray the importance of self-reliance. What is notable in the first (for a full exposé of the Melkhoutfontein project see Binns & Nel, 2002) is that from the outset the community were led to independence and taking ownership of the project themselves. To this end the project adopted a focused approach to fostering self-reliance. An in-depth program was launched in which community members were trained with a specific purpose. A secondary project involved fundraising for a botanic garden, which now forms the township's primary tourist attraction. A large proportion of the funds required were raised by the community by means of simple endeavors such as cake sales. In stark contrast is a project initiated by a local tourism operator in an impoverished rural community in Mpumalanga. The project involved a "cultural tourism experience" that included a visit to the local chief's village, an experience that visitors hailed as the "highlight" of their travels. That the community held their champion in high esteem, were extremely grateful for the opportunity they had been given and benefited financially is indisputable. However, after 8 years it became unsustainable for the operator to continue her support and the project, which had remained totally reliant on the largesse of their champion, ceased to operate (see Briedenhann & Wickens, 2003a). As the champion of the Melkhoutfontein project points out, self-reliance does not happen overnight. Ultimately, however, "you must be able to make a difference where it really counts and then stand back and allow the project and the community to walk forward to freedom" (Rossouw, 1999, p. 12). This, it can be argued, represents true empowerment.

As is the case with all tourism projects, commercial sustainability and market access is critical. Whilst philanthropic motives in developing pro-poor tourism products are commendable, there is a limited market in appealing to people's conscience. Few people will visit a project from altruistic values if it does not interest them. Similarly, as Goodwin (2005, p. 4) points out "very few people will purchase a product just because it is pro-poor." An inherent danger in many tourism projects, initiated as mechanisms of poverty alleviation, is the fact that they tend to be ad hoc and supply led rather than demand driven. The aforementioned projects emphasized both the necessity and difficulty of securing tour operator support and achieving integration into mainstream tourism itineraries. In Melkhoutfontein networking with tour operators was described as a huge, uphill battle (Rossouw, 1999). In Mpumalanga, an effort to interest tour operators in including the project in their itineraries was met with negativity and derision: the community could not offer the standards tourists demanded; the tour would not be value for money; and the project was situated too far off the main routes for tour operators to divert their vehicles (Briedenhann & Wickens, 2003a; 2003b). Unless consideration is given to tour operator linkages at the planning stage of a project its success is likely to be doomed from the outset.

Goodwin (1998, p. 3) advocated that tourism development projects should be evaluated "for their contribution to local economic development not just for their national revenue generation." Whilst this suggestion appears sensible it raises several questions. To what purpose would such evaluation be undertaken? Would it be to block the development of projects which were not perceived to contain significant pro-poor tourism elements or would it follow Patton's (1997) tenet of utilization-focused evaluation in which findings assist in identifying the strengths and weaknesses of a project and generating the understanding required for its improvement? Who would decide on the criteria to be used? Who would implement such an evaluation—the public sector using a bureaucratic approach that might kill off worthy projects before they started? Alternatively, might the criteria be project specific, decided on by mutual agreement between the prospective operator, the public sector authority and the community who stand to enjoy the benefits or suffer the negative impacts of the development? In the interest of maximizing the benefits of pro-poor tourism to local communities, and further convincing the mainstream private sector of the opportunities that such an approach lends to their own businesses, these are questions that need an answer lest such evaluation is negatively perceived and rejected.

This article focuses on a study of the Shangana Cultural Village, situated near the small town of Hazyview in Mpumalanga Province. The area is one of South Africa's premier tourist destinations, boasting the world famous Kruger National Park and luxurious private game reserves such as the Sabie Sand. The tourism prosperity of the area, however, masks a situation in which 86% of the local population (predominantly Shangaan people) between the ages of 15 and 65 are either unemployed or economically inactive (Newmarch, 2008).

METHODOLOGY

The interpretive paradigm adopts an insider-centered approach to research (Punch, 1998), relies on respondents to explain, in their own terms, their situation or behavior (Veal, 1997) and is concerned with understanding the meanings that events have for the people being studied (Patton, 1990). The paradigm is thus concerned with an examination of the phenomenon being studied from the perspective of those experiencing it. Over a continuous 5-year period the researcher visited the project both as a tourist and as CEO of the Provincial Tourism Board accompanied on various occasions by international media such as ABC television; international tour operators undertaking familiarization tours of South Africa; colleagues from the Provincial Tourism Board; and members of the Provincial Tourism Department. The use of qualitative methods of data collection during these visits allowed for an enriched collection of data and a more profound understanding of respondent perspectives (Bryman, 2001; Maykut & Morehouse, 1994) than could have been provided by quantitative data collection methods. A case study approach was adopted for the study. Within this framework, qualitative data collection methods, specifically participant observation and face-to-face, semistructured interviews were utilized.

Jorgensen (1989) argued that participant observation is a suitable data collection tool when the researcher is able to gain access to the appropriate setting and the research question can be addressed by qualitative data gathered through direct observation. The fact that the researcher was able to move freely as a tourist, frequently accompanied by other tourists, allowed for the establishment of common ground and for unobtrusive observation of both participants in and visitors to the cultural village which comprised the case study. Visits to Shangana provided abundant opportunities to listen to conversations between tourists visiting the project; between members of staff at the project; between members of staff and visitors; and to observe the engagement of members of the cultural group with the programs in which they participated. Field notes, which included descriptive observations in relation to "the physical setting, the key participants and their activities, particular events and their sequence and the attendant processes and emotions involved" (Saunders, Lewis, & Thornhill, 2007, p. 290) were recorded as soon as possible after each visit.

The face-to-face interview, which seeks to see through the eyes of the respondent, is probably the most widely used data collection method in qualitative research. In all, 30 interviews, in the form of semistructured conversations, were conducted over a period of 5 years. Whilst the interview guide used in the semistructured interviews had predetermined questions a significant degree of flexibility was permitted, affording interviewees the freedom to introduce new issues, determine the content of the discussion and provide information they thought important to engendering a deeper understanding of the way in which they perceived the project (Bernard, 1988; Patton, 1990). Purposively selected interviewees included the owners and operators of the cultural village; senior management at the venue; members of the cultural group which participated in the program; visiting media representatives; members of the local tourism industry; officials of the Provincial Tourism Department and members of the author's own staff. Approaches, with a request for interview, made to tourists at the village were opportunistic (Honigmann, 1987). Sekaran (1992, p. 237) argued that although purposive sampling diminishes the potential of generalizing research findings it is sometimes the "only meaningful way to investigate" in that it allows for the selection of "information rich" respondents who are of central importance to the research (Patton, 1990). Both the purposive and opportunistic sampling methods adopted in selecting respondents for the semi-structured interviews were based on the assumption that the perspectives of these respondents would be significant, useful and comprehensible and would produce rich detailed data for analysis (Frechtling & Sharp, 1997; Patton, 1990).

The data analysis followed Miles and Huberman (1994, p. 433) cyclical interaction through which data is summarized; themes, patterns, and relationships identified and plotted; and explanations developed. A manual system of color-coding was adopted in condensing and sorting the data. Observational field notes and transcripts were summarized to reduce the data into a more manageable format. At the first level of analysis key words and phrases in both data sets were coded. Where new codes were suggested by the data these were developed as the analysis progressed. At the second level of analysis themes and patterns in the data were identified and integrated whilst at the third level links between themes running throughout the data were traced.

FINDINGS OF THE STUDY

Although the project was initiated by private investors as a commercial opportunity, the developers nonetheless claim to have placed socio-cultural, socio-economic and socio-environmental responsibility at the heart of their venture. This assertion is substantiated by the fact that in 2001 the Shangana Cultural Village received a highly commended award for the built environment from British Airways in their Tourism for Tomorrow campaign. This achievement was repeated in 2002 when the project was a finalist in the Imvelo Awards in the category Best Community Involvement Programme and winner in the same year of the Best Practice category. The Imvelo Responsible Tourism awards, initiated to coincide with the World Summit on Sustainable Development held in South Africa in 2002, recognize tourism and hospitality businesses that make a real, measurable and sustained contribution to responsible tourism. The Best Practice category is based on local purchasing, employment equity, Black Economic Empowerment, employee training and development and adherence to general and industry legislation while the Best Community Involvement Program includes community investment, local outsourcing, community health, welfare and education participation, promotion of local SMME enterprises as well as local HIV/Aids programs (www.imvaloawards.co.za). Additionally, in 2005 the village secured second place in the Conde Nast Traveller magazine's Green List," which recognizes the best in ecotourism around the world. Conde Nast Traveler looks for operations that 'demonstrate how they preserve natural surroundings, contribute to local cultures, and provide a rich guest experience'. The village scored 68% for nature preservation, 82% for guest experience and 88% for local contribution (Courtenay, 2005).

The village comprises a cluster of traditional homesteads set in the shade of ancient indigenous trees. An African market forms the central area from which guests leave on the various tours on offer. A large amphitheatre hosts a spectacular evening performance that depicts the history of the Shangaan people. Three different programs are on offer at the village. During the day tours are led by guides through the bush and fields, where crops are grown, to a living village where they meet the resident Shangaan family. The guide explains different facets of the way of life and guests are encouraged to participate, whilst simultaneously safeguarding the privacy of the family. The lunchtime tour follows a similar pattern but guests are invited to join the family in a traditional meal. Information imparted by the guide includes history and customs, including initiation and the practice of polygamy, the construction of homes, making of beadwork clothing and food preparation. A visit to the *sangoma*, a traditional healer, is also included. During the evening a traditional meal is complemented by a spectacular performance in which choirs, actors and dancers re-enact the story of the Shangaan people. A visitor review comments:

> Originally, we weren't sure whether or not to stop at Shangana Village and were so glad that we did. It's a fantastic learning opportunity and was surprisingly less touristy than I had imagined . . . this was not a cheap activity; minute for minute it was one of the most expensive things we did in South Africa. That said, it was really interesting, surprisingly authentic, and a great experience for any visitor to the area (Davies, 2008).

From the onset the project developers argued that they were fulfilling the principles of pro-poor tourism. A policy of local consultation and decision-making was adopted in relation to the type, scale and nature of the project, which was developed by building on and enhancing pride in the skills and knowledge inherent in the local community (Ashley & Roe, 2002). The developers thus followed a "people-centric" approach in which local communities were afforded the opportunity of expressing views and influencing decision-making in relation both to the physical development of the project and to the presentation of their culture.

The Shangaan vernacular architecture, found only in scattered rural communities, is steadily being replaced by western construction with concurrent erosion of traditional building skills. In an approach congruent with the contention that prominence should be afforded to traditional architecture and physical design in the context of locally approved norms, and to the incorporation of local ethnic designs and artifacts into buildings (Page & Getz, 1997; Briedenhann, 2004), the developers employed rural Shangaan craftsmen to design and build the village using natural materials and traditional skills, regenerating interest in the value of traditional architecture in surrounding communities. These villages became home to the workforce and their families. Tourists to the project described the architecture as "beautiful"; "the architecture gives you a real feel for the culture and the people"; "the homesteads look warm and friendly." Development of the tourism product followed a similar ethos. A locally commissioned musician and playwright choreographed the cultural presentation on a consultative basis between himself, the community and the project developers. Interviews, in which members of the cultural group expressed pride in and enthusiasm for the presentation of their culture were confirmed by observation of the genuine enjoyment of participants in the various programs, factors which visitors claimed had engendered their respect for the Shangaan culture and people. These findings underpin Mearns (2006), study in which visitors to Shangana expressed the belief that, as opposed to exploiting the local culture, the cultural village contributed to its conservation. As Marais (n.d., p. 2) posited, "you can get it horribly wrong with a cultural village . . . but at Shangana things are different. The atmosphere is more genuine, friendlier and far more interesting than at your bog-standard so-called cultural village."

From the outset an "employ local" policy was adopted. Whilst two White managers were initially employed, empowerment of employees through the building of local capacity was a priority. The opportunities for advancement were eagerly received and three years into the project key positions were held by members of previously disadvantaged local communities. A consultative decision-making process was adopted with staff members encouraged to voice their ideas and concerns. Mearns (2006, p. 125) study found evidence of a positive attitude amongst employees at Shangana Cultural Village and, congruent with the opinion expressed by tourists to the village, "a strong belief among the Shangana employees that what they do at the cultural village contributes to a large extent to the conservation of their culture." Similarly employees were of the opinion that there was no commercial exploitation of their culture and that "their culture benefits to a large extent from being used to generate money" (Mearns, 2006, p. 126). These findings support the contention of the developers who claimed that the culture of ownership instilled a strong sense of pride in delivering a quality tourism experience since employees felt valued in terms of joint decision-making, active participation in project operation, and the ability to influence future direction.

Whilst the economic benefits to the surrounding communities were miniscule when measured against the debilitating poverty permeating the area, they were nonetheless significant. In 2004, 34 permanent and 100 part-time jobs had been created. Fifty-four percent of the total labor force and 60% of management were female. Twenty local entrepreneurs from disadvantaged communities supplied products and services to the village creating employment for 100 additional people. In total 63% of the project's monthly expenditure flowed to businesses owned wholly or partly by members of previously disadvantaged communities. The Marula craft market, which provided access to fifteen local crafters and curio makers, is described on the Shangana Web site (www.shangana.co.za) as:

> A gathering place for craftspeople from all over the region ... many of the artists work at their homes in nearby villages, and they leave their work at the market to be sold. The Marula Market has been an important catalyst for enabling local crafters to make a living and create small businesses for themselves.

This claim is, however, contradicted by Mearns' (2006) who found a large range of non-Shangaan craft for sale at the market leading visitors to recommend a greater emphasis on the sale of craft specific to the Shangaan culture.

Capacity building activities continued through the provision of information, advice, planning assistance, and training to local people planning to start community-based projects. Donations of time and money secured from overseas visitors benefited 400 members of local youth groups, schools, churches and orphanages. Project responsibility thus extended to taking into account the greater "well-being" of local communities. One of the most important activities related to health issues (tuberculosis and HIV/AIDS). A mobile clinic supplied condoms, vaccines and medical advice and counseling. Environmental management was practiced with biodegradable waste (45% of the total) converted to compost and supplied to the village where it was used to farm vegetables. A further 32% of waste was recycled. Alien trees were removed from the property and 100 indigenous trees reintroduced.

The developers claim to have struggled to gain support from members of the local hospitality industry and the public sector. Interviews provided evidence that accommodation providers and restaurants in initially viewed the project as a competitor in the provision of evening meals. These attitudes progressively changed as realization dawned that additional tourists were being drawn to overnight locally in order to attend the evening performance at the cultural village. In interviews members of the public sector and

Provincial Tourism Board were dismissive of the project in view of its white ownership and claimed that the Shangana people and culture were being exploited. These arguments were also expressed in conversations between members of the public sector (of which the Provincial Tourism Board was part) on visits to the village. Despite this resistance, by 2004 the project drew 22,000 visitors annually, had been the recipient of numerous awards and was a favorite destination of tour operators and tourists alike. A management-staff shareholding scheme was in place and the property had been offered through the Lands Claim Commission to the local community. The subsequent restoration of the land and villages to the Mapulana community led to the formation of a separate operating company, which leased the land from the community. Shareholders of the new company included the founding investors, the Mapulana community and the project's employees. Shangana Cultural Village has since been transferred to full community ownership. A management agreement has ceded the marketing and development of the project to Thokozela Leisure Management. A partnership has been entered into with Dreamworld Investments to build accommodation facilities for 50 guests in comfortable traditional huts thus further enhancing the village's potential to offer additional services to its visitors and grow its tourist numbers ensuring increased benefits to the community (Mearns, 2006).

CONCLUSIONS

Arguments that the project was a successful example of the principles of pro-poor tourism are based on several factors. Firstly, it can be argued that the project, which built upon the natural and cultural assets of a poor rural community with limited growth options (Scheyvens, 2007), made significant contributions in terms of both economic and livelihood benefits and the empowerment of its employees. Secondly, in the sphere of economic benefits local employment, the most significant benefit to the poor (Spenceley & Seif, 2003; Briedenhann, 2004), was maximized. Thirdly, linkages for the supply of goods and services were forged with entrepreneurs and craftspeople from the local community providing access to economic opportunity of which they could take advantage (Zhao & Ritchie, 2007). Fourthly, improved access to advice and facilities contributed to community ability to deal with ailments such as tuberculosis and AIDS thus assisting in reducing vulnerability to the risks of chronic ill health (Zhao & Ritchie, 2007). Finally, and most importantly, participants in the project were afforded the opportunity of self-empowerment (Fetterman, 2001) through processes of participation, decision-making, and the opportunity to influence the direction of the project. The capacity of local employees was further developed through ongoing training and skills development and the appointment of local people to senior management positions, an approach which assisted in ensuring project sustainability and pride in the delivery of a first class tourism product. This contributed to the hard-earned recognition from tour operators and other local tourism suppliers who came to acknowledge the project's importance in diversifying the local tourism offer and enriching the tourist experience (Goodwin, 2005).

The project was to a significant degree both physically and conceptually created by the local Shangaan people building on and enhancing pride in the skills and knowledge residing in the local community (Ashley & Roe, 2002) and in the Shangaan culture. Not all small tourism enterprises offer the same opportunity for participation by members of poor communities and indisputably not all small privately initiated tourism enterprises will eventually pass into community ownership. However, discounting this later development, the Shangana Cultural Village project can claim to have supported the principles of pro-poor tourism and to have conferred benefits on the local community in an area of crippling poverty. Furthermore, the project can claim to have fulfilled the precepts of the "new tourism" envisaged by the Tourism White Paper in terms of responsibility, sensitivity to host cultures, and involvement of local communities in planning, decision-making and participation in and benefit from tourism (Government of South Africa, 1996) whilst simultaneously conferring benefits on the investors and developers of the project (Ashley et al., 1999).

It can be argued that to a greater or lesser degree "it is possible for almost any tourism attraction or product to meet pro-poor tourism objectives" (UNESCAP, 2003, p. 4) through the maximization of local labor, goods and services and the expansion of local linkages creating opportunities for small-scale entrepreneurs (Ashley et al, 1999). On a project-by-project basis the contribution to poverty alleviation may be small. Cumulatively, however, the contribution by the myriad small tourism enterprises, which comprise the bulk of the tourism industry in a country such as South Africa, would be significant. In countries ravaged by poverty, particularly in rural areas, the potential of both mass (Harrison, 2008) and small-scale tourism to contribute to poverty alleviation should be harnessed and exploited to the full. This article thus strongly argues that greater attention should be paid to the cumulative potential of small tourism operators to play a significant role in the alleviation of poverty to the mutual benefit of both operators and poor members of their local communities.

REFERENCES

Ashley, C. (2002). *Methodology for pro-poor tourism case studies*. London, England: Overseas Development Institute.

Ashley, C. (2005). *Facilitating pro-poor tourism with the private sector. Lessons learned from pro-poor tourism pilots in Southern Africa*. London, England: Overseas Development Institute.

Ashley, C., Bennett, O., & Roe, D. (1999). *Sustainable tourism and poverty elimination study*. London, England: Deloitte and Touche, International Institute for Environment and Development and Overseas Development Institute London.

Ashley, C., & Roe, D. (2002). Making tourism work for the poor: Strategies and challenges in Southern Africa. *Development Southern Africa, 19*(1), 61–82.

Bernard, H. R. (1988). *Research methods in cultural anthropology*, Newbury Park, CA: Sage.

Binns, T., & Nel, E. (2002). Tourism as a local development strategy in South Africa. *The Geographical Journal, 168*, 235–247.

Briedenhann, J. (2004). *An evaluation framework for rural tourism projects: A respondent perspective*, Unpublished PhD thesis, Brunel University.

Briedenhann, J. (2008). The role of the public sector in rural tourism: A respondent perspective. *Current Issues in Tourism, 10*, 584–607.

Briedenhann, J., & Wickens, E. (2003a). Community involvement in tourism development white elephant or empowerment? In S. Weber & R. Tomljenović (Eds.), *Reinventing a tourism destination* (pp. 167–179). Zagreb, Croatia: Scientific Edition Institute for Tourism.

Briedenhann, J., & Wickens, E. (2003b, Spring). Rural tourism: Meeting the challenges of the new South Africa. *International Journal of Tourism Research, 6*, 189–203.

Briedenhann, J., & Wickens, E. (2004). Tourism routes as a tool for the economic development of rural areas—vibrant hope or impossible dream? *Tourism Management, 25*, 71–79.

Bryman, A. (2001). *Social research methods*. Oxford, England: Oxford University Press.

Courtenay, E. (2005). *Conde Nast green list 2005*. Retrieved from http://www.treehugger.com/files/2005/09/via_shoppingblo.php

Dann, G. (2002). Tourism and development. In V. Desai & R. Potter (Eds.), *The companion to development studies* (pp. 236–240). London, England: Arnold.

Davies, C. (2008). Shangana Cultural Village: Traveler reviews. Retrieved from www.tripadvisor.com.

Fetterman, D. M. (2001). *Foundations of empowerment evaluation*, Thousand Oaks, CA: Sage.

Fowkes, J., & Jonsson, P. (1994, October). *Lessons learned during a pilot project to introduce a tourism development programme to rural communities in Kwazulu, South Africa*, Unpublished paper.

Frechtling, J., & Sharp, L. (1997). *User-friendly handbook for mixed method evaluations*. Washington, DC: The National Science Foundation.

Goodwin, H. (1998, October, 13). *Sustainable tourism and poverty elimination*. DFID/DETR Workshop on Sustainable Tourism and Poverty, London, England.

Goodwin, H. (2005, May). *Pro-poor tourism: Principles, methodologies and mainstreaming*. International Conference on Pro-poor Tourism Mechanisms and Mainstreaming, University Technology Malaysia, Johor, Malaysia.

Government of South Africa. (1996). *The development and promotion of tourism in South Africa*. Pretoria, South Africa: Government Printer.

Greffe, X. (1994). Is rural tourism a lever for economic and social development? *Journal of Sustainable Tourism, 2*, 23–40.

Hall, C. M. (2007). *Pro-poor tourism: Perspectives on tourism and poverty reduction.* Bristol, England: Channel View Publications.

Harrison, D. (2008). Pro-poor tourism: A critique. *Third World Quarterly, 29,* 851–868.

Honigmann, J. (1987). Sampling in ethnographic fieldwork. In R. Burgess (Ed.), *Field research: A sourcebook and field manual.* London, England: Allen and Unwin.

Jorgensen, D. L. (1989). *Participant observation: Methodology for human studies.* Newbury, CA: Sage.

Kinsley, M. (2000). *Economic renewal guide: A collaborative process for sustainable community development.* Snowmass, CO: Rocky Mountain Institute.

Marais, C. (n.d.). *Responsible travel in South Africa.* Retrieved from http://www.cogta.gov.za/isrdp/index.php?option=com_content&task=view&id=82&Itemid=2

Matlou, P. (2001, March). *The potential of ecotourism development and its partnership with spatial development initiatives.* Seminar on Planning, Development and Management of Ecotourism in Africa, Regional Preparatory Meeting for the International Year of Ecotourism, Maputo, Mozambique.

Maykut, P., & Morehouse, R. (1994). *Beginning qualitative research: A philosophic and practical guide.* London, England: The Falmer Press.

Mearns, M. A. (2006). *Conservation of indigenous knowledge* (Unpublished doctoral dissertation). University of Johannesburg, Johannesburg.s

Meyer, D. (2003). *Review of the impacts of previous pro-poor tourism research* (PPT Working Paper No 9). London, England: Overseas Development Institute.

Miles, M. B., & Huberman, A. M. (1994). *Qualitative data analysis* (2nd ed.). Thousand Oaks, CA: Sage.

Nel, E., & Binns, T. (2001). Initiating developmental local government in South Africa: Evolving local economic development policy. *Regional Studies, 35,* 355–362.

Newmarch, J. (2008). *Land alone can't feed families.* Department of Provincial and Local Government South Africa. Retrieved from www.thedplg.gov.za/isrdp

Page, S. J., & Getz, D. (1997). The business of rural tourism: International perspectives. In S. J. Page & D. Getz (Eds.), *The Business of Rural Tourism: International Perspectives* (pp. 3–37). New York, NY: International Thomson Business Press.

Patton, M. Q. (1997). *Utilisation – focused evaluation: The new century text* (3rd ed.). Newbury Park, CA: Sage.

Pro-Poor Tourism Partnership. (2004). *Pro-poor tourism info sheet no. 11: Key terms.* London, England: Author.

Punch, K. F. (1998). *Introduction to social research: Quantitative and qualitative approaches.* London: Sage Publications.

Roberts, L., & Hall, D. (2001). *Rural tourism and recreation: Principles to practice.* Cambridge: CABI Publishing.

Roe, D., Harris, C., & de Andrade, J. (2003). *Addressing poverty issues in tourism: Standards, a review of experiences. PPT working paper no. 14.* London: Overseas Development Institute.

Rossouw, A. (1999). *Dreamcatcher: The inside story to making Mandela's dream work for tourism in South African communities.* Cape Town, South Africa: Flamingo Print.

Saunders, M., Lewis, P., & Thornhill, A. (2007). *Research methods for business students* (4th ed.). Harlow, England: Pearson Education Limited.

Scheyvens, R. (2007). Exploring the tourism-poverty nexus. In C. M. Hall (Ed.), *Pro-poor tourism: Perspectives on tourism and poverty reduction* (pp. 121–144). Bristol, England: Channel View Publications.

Sekaran, U. (1992). *Research methods for business*. Chichester, England: John Wiley and Sons.

Sen, A. (1984). *Resources, values and development*. Oxford, England: Blackwell.

Sharpley, R. (2002). Rural tourism and the challenge of tourism diversification: The case of Cyprus. *Tourism Management, 23*, 233–244.

Spenceley, A., & Seif, J. (2003). *Strategies, impacts and costs of pro-poor tourism approaches in South Africa* (PPT Working Paper No. 11). London, England: Overseas Development Institute.

Taylor, J. (2000). *So now they are going to measure empowerment*. Woodstock, NY: The Community Development Resource Association.

Timothy, D. J. (2000). Building community awareness of tourism in a developing country destination. *Tourism Recreation Research, 25*(2), 111–116.

Timothy, D. J., & Tosun, C. (2003). Appropriate planning for tourism in destination communities: Participation, incremental growth and collaboration. In S. Singh, D. J. Timothy, & R. K. Dowling (Eds.), *Tourism in destination communities* (pp. 181–204). Wallingford, England: CABI.

United Nations Economic and Social Commission for Asia and the Pacific. (2003). *Poverty alleviation through sustainable development*. Retrieved from http://www.unescap.org/publications/detail.asp?id=1020

Veal, A. J. (1997). *Research methods for leisure and tourism: A practical guide* (2nd ed.). London, England: Pearson Professional.

Zhao, W., & Ritchie, J. (2007). Tourism and poverty alleviation: An integrative research framework. In C. H. Hall (Ed.), *Pro-poor tourism: Perspectives on tourism and poverty reduction* (pp. 9–33). Bristol, England: Channel View Publications.

Index

Page numbers in *Italics* represent tables.
Page numbers in **Bold** represent figures.